Roland Barthes
The Proust Variations

Contemporary French and Francophone Cultures, 62

Contemporary French and Francophone Cultures

Series Editor

CHARLES FORSDICK
University of Liverpool

Editorial Board

TOM CONLEY
Harvard University

JACQUELINE DUTTON
University of Melbourne

LYNN A. HIGGINS
Dartmouth College

MIREILLE ROSELLO
University of Amsterdam

DEREK SCHILLING
Johns Hopkins University

This series aims to provide a forum for new research on modern and contemporary French and francophone cultures and writing. The books published in *Contemporary French and Francophone Cultures* reflect a wide variety of critical practices and theoretical approaches, in harmony with the intellectual, cultural and social developments which have taken place over the past few decades. All manifestations of contemporary French and francophone culture and expression are considered, including literature, cinema, popular culture, theory. The volumes in the series will participate in the wider debate on key aspects of contemporary culture.

Recent titles in the series:

THOMAS BALDWIN

Roland Barthes

The Proust Variations

LIVERPOOL UNIVERSITY PRESS

First published 2019 by
Liverpool University Press
4 Cambridge Street
Liverpool
L69 7ZU

This paperback edition published 2022

British Library Cataloguing-in-Publication data
A British Library CIP record is available

ISBN 978-1-78962-001-6 cased
ISBN 978-1-80207-738-4 paperback

Typeset by Carnegie Book Production, Lancaster
Printed and bound by CPI Group (UK) Ltd, Croydon CR0 4YY

Contents

Acknowledgements

Chapters One, Two and Three contain revised and extended versions of material that has appeared in the following journal articles: 'On Barthes on Proust', *Forum for Modern Language Studies*, 48/3 (June 2012), pp. 274–87; 'Charlus/z', *Writing, Reading, Grieving: Essays in Memory of Suzanne Dow*, ed. Ruth Cruickshank and Adam Watt, *Nottingham French Studies* (Special Issue), 53/1 (Spring 2014), pp. 90–101; 'Rewriting Proust', *What's So Great About Roland Barthes?*, ed. Thomas Baldwin, Katja Haustein and Lucy O'Meara, *L'Esprit Créateur* (Special Issue), 55/4 (Winter 2015), pp. 70–85. I should like to thank all the publishers concerned for permission to reuse material that originally appeared in their pages.

I am indebted in many ways to the following people: Synne Ytre Arne, Fabien Arribert-Narce, Jim Baldwin, Lynn Baldwin, Michael Baldwin, Susannah Baldwin, Dan Brewer, Mária Minich Brewer, Kate Briggs, John Chisholm, Claude Coste, Larry Duffy, Patrick ffrench, Alison Finch, Charles Forsdick, Gonzalo Ceron Garcia, Marie-Odile Germain, Suzanne Guerlac, Katja Haustein, Abi Heller, Cathy Hills, Lawrie Hills, Richard Hills, Ben Hutchinson, Jon Kear, Diana Knight, Roland-François Lack, Jo Malt, Éric Marty, Tim Matthews, Lucy O'Meara, Mathilde Poizat-Amar, Nigel Saint, Cecilia Sayad, Samuel Smith, Andy Stafford, Adam Watt and Shane Weller.

Susannah, this book is for you.

Note on the Text

Unless indicated otherwise, all references to Barthes's works are to the five-volume edition of the *Œuvres complètes*, edited by Éric Marty (Paris: Seuil, 2002). They take the form (I, 234), that is, volume number, followed by page reference. References to *À la recherche du temps perdu* are to the four-volume 'Pléiade' edition, produced under the general editorship of Jean-Yves Tadié (Paris: Gallimard, Bibliothèque de la Pléiade, 1987–89), and are given in the form (*ALR*, IV, 321). Where I have used a published English translation of Barthes's work, this is indicated in a note. Translations of Proust's novel are taken from the six-volume Vintage Classics edition of *In Search of Lost Time*, translated by C. K. Scott Moncrieff (except for *Time Regained*, translated by Andreas Mayor and Terence Kilmartin), revised by Terence Kilmartin and D. J. Enright (London: Vintage, 2000–02). I have occasionally tweaked passages quoted from the latter. All other translations of French texts are my own.

Introduction

By excavating and describing the multiple variations in Roland Barthes's encounters with Marcel Proust's monumental masterpiece À *la recherche du temps perdu* (1913–27), this book seeks out new creative tensions between literary texts and critical approaches to them. 'Proust' is one of the most powerful names in twentieth-century French literature and indeed in modern European literature more widely. 'Proustian', in current usage, designates an ill-defined variety of experiences, cultural and historical points of reference, styles of living and of writing, aspects of sexuality, love, hermeticism, aestheticism, a sense of déjà vu, recovered memory, long sentences and the dominance of art over life. A vague sense of his biography and an awareness of the remarkable scale and difficult syntax of his novel also serve to single Proust out as the ultimate example of a life lived in the name of art, and of literariness as such. Furthermore, as several commentators have noted, objects and artefacts that bear the name – or are conjoined with it – circulate in an economy of Proustian objects, a species of 'Proustiana', which includes not only items of clothing and a variety of trinkets,[1] but also cookbooks, self-help guides and works of popular science.[2] Moreover, as André Benhaïm observes, '"Proust" (the work, the man, their joint image) has been so much read (that is, been so well assimilated), that it has transcended the canonical library and has been adopted into the culture at large'.[3] The currency of Proust is thus distributed in the streams of cultural production and reproduction: the Proust brand sells.

At the same time, Proust has a currency of a different nature. His novel has been a privileged object of study for literary critics, theorists and philosophers in the twentieth and twenty-first centuries. Roland Barthes figures prominently and distinctively among them.[4] For him, as Malcolm Bowie puts it, À *la recherche* is the 'crucial empowerment': it is no less than an 'emblematic distillation of literature itself in its triumphant mode'.[5] Barthes, too, is exemplary: he is among the major critics and creative writers of the age (of the post-war era to the present); his career both encompasses French structuralism and post-structuralism and contributes significantly to making them what they are; and he, like Proust, is emblematic of a certain ethics of literature in which plurality, ambivalence and nuance are affirmed over and above stable and secure meanings and interpretations.[6]

It is widely recognized that Barthes could not do without Proust, especially in the last decade of his life.[7] What has not been recognized, though, is the relationship between Proust's contradictory but persistent circulation throughout Barthes's oeuvre (to which we shall return in a moment) and the vast array of metaphors Barthes uses to describe the mobile and inconsistent texture of *À la recherche*. In January 1972, for example, two years after the publication of *S/Z* (1970) and only one year before the appearance of *Le Plaisir du texte*, Barthes began a round-table discussion at the École normale supérieure in Paris by observing that the 'particles' of *À la recherche* are mobile and transposable ('les particules en changent de place et permutent entre elles').[8] As such, he says, they constitute an infinitely explorable 'galaxie'[9] and bear significantly upon our attempts to respond to Proust's work critically:

> In my view, *À la recherche du temps perdu* [...] can only elicit ideas of research and not research itself. In this sense, Proust's text is excellent material for critical desire. It is a true object of desire for the critic, since everything is spent in the fantasy of research, in the idea of searching for something in Proust, thereby making the idea of an end of that research seem illusory. Proust is unique to the extent that all he leaves us to do is *rewrite him*, which is the exact contrary of exhausting him.[10]

There is plenty that critics – literary or otherwise – might learn from Barthes's brief opening address. It contains clear echoes of *S/Z*: Proust's novel is described as the embodiment of a writerly – and rewritable – ideal about which, Barthes suggests (in *S/Z*), there may be nothing to say.[11] Furthermore, as he kicks off the round-table discussion in 1972, Barthes's emphasis is on research as a productive activity that must remain incomplete: it is driven, ultimately, by the quotient of pleasure to be gained from it. (This rather deflates the idea of research as a positive contribution to knowledge, or as an activity that makes the kind of impact often imagined by academic authorities.) *À la recherche*, he says, is an ideal space in which the *fantasme* of research can be played out.

This is a fantasy in which the search itself – rather than the object or the evidence to be found – gives pleasure. According to Barthes, Proust's novel is ideal as an object of critical desire, and for endless seeking, because it is possessed of a permutability that makes its particles move around unpredictably. Its 'illusory' landscape ('paysage illusoire'),[12] he observes, is illuminated 'by a succession of lights governed by a sort of variable rheostat that makes the décor pass gradually, and tirelessly, through different volumes, different levels of perception, and different degrees of intelligibility'.[13] For Barthes, then, the singular mobility of the novel is powered by a generator of difference, imagined as something akin to the variable current of a resistor, that makes the text (its light) appear to change every time we read it: it is as much productive as it is infinitely seductive.

Later, in response to Gérard Genette's lengthy contribution to the same round table concerning an effect of variation ('effet de variation')[14] at work in Proust's novel, Barthes uses a musical metaphor, from which the present study takes its title, not only to invoke the plurality of *À la recherche*, but also to redescribe and redefine the role of the critic. He suggests that, like Beethoven (Barthes refers to, and lifts material from, André Boucourechliev's work on the composer),[15] Proust does not supply a conventional form of theme and variation in which 'the theme is given first and then there are ten, twelve, or fifteen variations' that follow ('il y a un thème qui est donné d'abord, et ensuite il y a dix, douze ou quinze variations').[16] Instead, both the composer – in his *Diabelli Variations* – and the novelist produce 'variations sans thème' in which the theme is fully 'diffracted' in the variations.[17] Barthes also rejects Genette's notion that the role of the critic is to interpret variations. For Barthes, the critic is neither interpreter, executor, nor performer of the variations that subsist in Proust's text, but the *operator*, one might also say the author, of his or her own variations upon them.[18] In this role, the critic is no longer held entirely within a 'hermeneutic': he or she does not follow a 'vertical climb to a central object' ('une voie de remontée verticale vers un objet central'),[19] but rather brings about a 'déstructuration' of the Proustian text by working to undermine a form of rhetorical schematization (a 'plan' or 'structuration rhétorique') which, according to Barthes, is prevalent in critical studies of Proust's work that capture and domesticate its recurrent imagery and dominant motifs.[20] The critic as a writer who operates is thus required to engage with the novel heterogeneously and intensively. The aspiration of reading and of criticism is not to exhaust the work through the postulation of an ultimate, transcendent meaning (a theme) or to add to the pile of efforts to that end, but to rewrite and to de-structure. This is a mode of critical engagement that does not arise solely as an exogenous purpose of the critic, but also as something that the digressive, perforated and deconstructed discourse of Proust's work demands.[21]

In view of Barthes's ideas about the Beethoven-like variations in Proust's novel and the kind of critical work to which they should give rise, my aim in what follows is to answer the following questions, which focus on how Proust's work is put together, on the mode (or rhythm) of Barthes's critical engagement with *À la recherche*, and on the broader significance of that engagement: 1) Are the variations in Proust's novel indeed theme-less, or such that a theme is entirely diffracted in them? (It is difficult to tell what Barthes is getting at here: his assertions are not backed up with examples. Can his other writing on *À la recherche*, or on other things, help us to shed light on the significance of these metaphors?); 2) What is it, precisely, that makes Proust's writing, for Barthes or generally, both endlessly seductive, productive and unamenable to more conventional, hermeneutical forms of criticism? 3) What does Barthes do with *À la recherche*? (Beyond an identification with Proust – or rather with 'Marcel' – that informs several of his later texts and on which a large number of critics have focused,[22] how does Barthes rewrite or operate variations upon Proust's novel in – or across – his own work? Moreover, in what sense can his writing on Proust be said to do justice to, or even to reproduce, the mobile and uncertain topography of *À la recherche*'s 'illusory' landscape?) 4) Why does any of this matter? (How, in his approach, is Barthes different from other critics who have written about Proust, and what possibilities do Barthes's Proust variations open up for the future of criticism more generally?)

An answer to the third and fourth questions is provided by Malcolm Bowie. In his 2001 article 'Barthes on Proust', Bowie says that Barthes often 'seems to warn against an excess of seriousness. Good readings, of this author at least, [Barthes] suggests, are light, partial and tangential'.[23] *À la recherche* mattered to Barthes, he argues, 'more in its generalized "loomings" than in the copious and artful individual sentences by which other critics have been so readily seduced'.[24] For Bowie, the relative *légèreté* of Barthes's writing on *À la recherche* reproduces in a special sense what, in an interview for *Le Monde-dimanche* in 1979, Barthes describes as Proust's 'idleness' ('paresse'): in Bowie's view, Barthes presents Proust's 'entire undertaking' as an exercise in idling, and it would not, he argues, 'be in keeping [for Barthes] with the book's delicious associative textures to read it in an other than idly pleasure-seeking frame of mind'.[25] Consequently, according to Bowie, Barthes co-opts Proust's work 'in the form of an eloquent excerpt, to underwrite an argument or to reinforce an assertion'.[26] In contrast to the obsessive and fetishizing habits of Proust specialists, then, the novelist is frequently made to inhabit Barthes's oeuvre not as part of an instrumentalizing, 'studious elaboration',[27] but as a series of *punctum*-like intensities.

Some of Bowie's comments are echoed by Éric Marty in his 'Marcel Proust dans "la chambre claire"' (2006). Marty suggests that the 'omniprésence' of Proust in Barthes's work is of a special kind ('bien particulière'), and he characterizes Barthes's critical writings on the author as timid and slight ('très timides').[28] He argues further, however, that Proust is nowhere in Barthes's oeuvre precisely because he is everywhere ('partout'),[29] and he cites Barthes's claim that it is by reading the likes of Proust, Antonin Artaud, Maurice Blanchot and Franz Kafka that he is empowered *to write* – rather than to write on, or even 'like', these authors – as evidence that, for Barthes, it is Proust who provides the decisive voice that invites (indeed permits) him to conceive of 'to write' as an intransitive verb[30] and as a personal and intimate tendency.[31] Bowie makes a similar point, in fact, suggesting that, for Barthes, 'the memory of reading Proust, the anticipation of reading him again, or even a mere side-glance at his mountainous volumes, were themselves the crucial empowerment', and that such oblique and partial encounters with Proust's work helped him to become 'the astonishing creative writer that he was in the last decades of his life, and remains twenty years after his death'.[32]

Both Bowie and Marty provide characteristically perceptive and nuanced accounts of Proust's place in several of Barthes's texts, and these are supported by some of what Barthes has to say. Nevertheless, they do not tell a lot of the story.[33] Barthes certainly does insist that he is not (a) 'Proustian'[34] and that the happiness to be found in reading Proust stems from the fact that 'from one reading to the next, one never skips the same passages' ('d'une lecture à l'autre, on ne saute jamais les mêmes passages' (*Le Plaisir du texte*, IV, 224)). He is not, then, as Bowie observes, one of 'the specialists who merely scurr[y] back and forth on the stretched skin of this immense organism [*À la recherche*]'.[35] He is not a Proustian in this sense. Indeed, as the remaining chapters of this book will demonstrate, Barthes's writing on Proust suggests the possibility of a productive alternative to more orthodox modes of academic – 'schematic' – criticism which, in Barthes's view, smother and conceal the vital mobility of Proust's writing as they remain fixated upon the identification and interpretation of thematic patterns. Furthermore, his engagements with Proust's novel, I will argue, serve to shield *À la recherche* not only from the interpretative habits of the 'Proustian', but also from the influence of a still burgeoning field of 'Proustiana', which interposes layers of material between the novel and its (potential) readers and is in danger of offering them little more than reassuring – but lifeless – trophies.

Barthes's oeuvre is also, as Bowie suggests, peppered with generalizing, non-specialist critical engagements with *À la recherche*, and his writing on Proust frequently takes the form of what Marty calls mere 'sketches', 'notes' or 'brief annotations'.[36] Nevertheless, it is not the case that he has 'little to say about the fibrous fabric of Proust's writing' or that, in relation to Proust, he (always) abstains 'from varieties of textual analysis in which he elsewhere excelled'.[37] Barthes's unpublished notes for a series of seminars delivered in Morocco between September 1969 and August 1970, in which he analyses the workings of the Proustian sentence ('la phrase proustienne') and of Proustian discourse ('le discours proustien'), and the two companion seminars – on what he calls the 'Charlus-Discourse' ('Discours-Charlus') – to *Comment vivre ensemble,* his lecture course at the Collège de France between 1976 and 1977, provide evidence of a lot more than co-opting side glances in the direction of Proust's novel, and they are too detailed and substantial to be passed off (or over) as cursory notes. Proust is indisputably the direct object of Barthes's – often systematic – analysis in these texts.[38] Furthermore, while Barthes's more strenuous attempts to write about Proust have received remarkably scant scholarly attention, it is in these that he presents an image of Proust's work that makes sense of the punctual form and of the inconsistency of his engagements with *À la recherche* from the 1950s onwards. Read in conjunction with some of his other work (not all of it on Proust), these texts also help us to unpack the metaphors he deploys at the Proust round table in 1972 concerning the intermittent lighting of *À la recherche*'s décor and the diffraction of themes within variations.

À la recherche is discussed frequently in Barthes's work from the 1950s to 1980. Nevertheless, his views of the novel are by no means consistent. Indeed, there are striking discrepancies between them. Proust's presence in Barthes's oeuvre is thus not only punctual (in brief and localized critical spaces): it is also quite messy. Instead of viewing the fluctuations and scattered contradictions in his writing on Proust as signs of straightforward changes of mind, of forgetfulness, even of intellectual idleness, or simply as a function of evolutionary pressures internal to his own notoriously mobile[39] critical practice (and remembering his response to

Genette at the round table concerning the role of the critic as operator), I will argue that they are all *rewritings* of Proust's variations. They are erratic and incomplete operations performed on – and creatively in keeping with – the diffuse and inconsistent body of *À la recherche*. As such, the discursive structure of Barthes's reading of Proust is, as Leslie Hill puts it, 'like so many layers of a palimpsest, not because any one of these versions provides a definitive translation for any of the others, merely its abyssal re-enactment, its musical repetition, and constant propensity for variation'.[40] It is thus Barthes's Proust variations that make the critical difference: they suggest new and productive possibilities for criticism as they bring him very close to Proust's own variations, set him apart from other critics who have written on *À la recherche*, and play some part in resisting a society of the spectacle in which Proust's novel approaches the condition of a commodity fetish.

In the third and final installment of a series of radio broadcasts made with Jean Montalbetti in 1978, entitled 'Un homme, une ville: Marcel Proust à Paris avec Roland Barthes', Barthes suggests that the uniquely changeable texture of Proust's work prevents us from speaking about it exhaustively or eidetically.[41] The memory of reading Proust can thus only ever be partial and fragmentary: it is necessarily incomplete. This suggestion clearly echoes Barthes's description of *À la recherche* at the round table in 1972 as a material that is inexhaustible because it is 'always displaced when it returns' ('en ce qu'il revient toujours déplacé').[42] As a consequence of this inexhaustibility, he tells Montalbetti, to say what we think about Proust ('ce que l'on pense de Proust') and to be satisfied that we have said all we can is necessarily something of an illusion ('un peu une illusion'):

> It is such a kaleidoscopic and polyvalent work, which diffuses with such vitality and in so many directions that, in reality, we cannot speak about the Proustian work unless we choose a certain relevance ['pertinence'], a certain point of view, and, naturally, this point of view changes. In a word, we can choose this or that point of view.[43]

Barthes's remarks to Montalbetti suggest that his inconsistency is both a reflection of his own shifting desires as a writer and a necessary consequence of the polyvalent fabric of *À la recherche*, and that the stilling by critics (including Barthes himself) of the novel's kaleidoscopic turns – through the choice of a single, dogmatic relevance or point of view – is to be viewed either as provisional or as a reductive sleight of hand. In light of these observations and of the other metaphors Barthes uses to describe the tireless mobility of Proust's work, and in order to elucidate his suggestion that research on Proust's variations never really comes to an end, the chapters in this book confront the variegated materials of which both *À la recherche* and Barthes's writing on it between 1950 and 1980 are made. They do not perform the dull task of providing an exhaustive account of Barthes's work on Proust across his oeuvre (they do not even discuss every text in which Barthes refers explicitly to Proust). Instead, they work through his writing across three decades more or less chronologically, identifying not only overlaps but – perhaps more interestingly – also ruptures, discontinuities and reawakenings in his encounters with Proust. Moreover, while we will look briefly at those aspects of Barthes's engagement with Proust on which several other critics have focused in some detail (at Barthes's identification with 'Marcel' as a writerly figure and as a creative subject, for example),[44] we will also discuss works by Barthes and passages from Proust's novel that have received relatively little attention in critical writing on the relationship between Barthes and Proust. We will thus examine some of Barthes's more univocal and dogmatic assertions regarding Proust's treatment of objects in Chapter One; the workings of a literary eros in Proust's work in Chapter Two; the place of music and its relation to various forms of discourse in *À la recherche* in Chapter Three; and the nuanced neutrality of Proust's novel in Chapter Four. In each case, we will also consider the limitations of Barthes's punctual observations by identifying viewpoints in *À la recherche* that are at odds with the specific 'pertinences' he selects, and by exploring other texts by Barthes in which these – and related – viewpoints are presented in a significantly different (sometimes contradictory) light. We will thus follow the wanderings of Barthes's dogmatism and reflect on the dependability of his ideas regarding the diffuseness and variety of Proust's novel. Moreover, by discovering and discussing the manifold ways in which Proust mattered to Barthes, we will also learn that while Barthes's trajectory is unique, the implications of that trajectory for the future of criticism are far-reaching. Indeed, Barthes's writing on Proust's work across three decades of a shifting critical landscape emerges as a caution to the numbing stasis that ensures the reassuring consumption or veneration of the Proust-fetish (as often to be found in 'Proustiana' and sometimes lurking in the activity of the 'Proustian'): it proposes that all critical work should embrace inconsistency, insecurity and variation as endemic, vital and essential to its creative power and indeed its value.

Notes

1 Adam Watt observes that 'those wishing to be more demonstrative in their devotion to the author can wear their affiliation across their chest (or elsewhere) by going online and choosing from a range of inexpensive and readily available t-shirts, pin-badges, aprons, even underwear bearing stock quotations and, more often, the moustachioed visage of the author. Mugs, clocks, bumper stickers and various other items are similarly to be had at the click of a mouse' (*The Cambridge Introduction to Marcel Proust* (Cambridge: Cambridge University Press, 2011), p. 116).

2 See, for example, Anne Borrel's, Alain Senderens's and Jean-Bernard Naudin's *Proust, la cuisine retrouvée* (Paris: Éditions du chêne, 1991), Alain de Botton's *How Proust Can Change Your Life* (London: Picador, 1997) and Jonah Lehrer's *Proust Was a Neuroscientist* (Edinburgh and London: Cannongate, 2007).

3 André Benhaïm, 'Preamble', in *The Strange M. Proust*, ed. André Benhaïm (Oxford: Legenda, 2009), pp. 1–11 (p. 5).

4 Proust is variously a focus and an example in the work of several post-war theorists and philosophers in France and elsewhere, including Theodor Adorno, Giorgio Agamben, Georges Bataille, Walter Benjamin, Maurice Blanchot, Jacques Bouveresse, Gilles Deleuze, Gérard Genette, Félix Guattari, Julia Kristeva, Emmanuel Levinas, Maurice Merleau-Ponty, Martha Nussbaum, Jacques Rancière, Paul Ricœur, Richard Rorty and Jean-Paul Sartre. Anne Simon discusses Proust's circulation in a wider intellectual context in France (and also in Barthes's late work) in *Trafics de Proust: Merleau-Ponty, Sartre, Deleuze, Barthes* (Paris: Hermann, 2016).

5 Malcolm Bowie, 'Barthes on Proust', *The Yale Journal of Criticism*, 14/2 (2001), pp. 513–18 (p. 518). Or, as Barthes puts it in *Le Plaisir du texte* (1973), 'Proust's work, for myself at least, is the reference work, the general *mathesis*, the *mandala* of the entire literary cosmogony' ('l'œuvre de Proust est, du moins pour moi, l'œuvre de référence, la *mathésis* générale, le *mandala* de toute la cosmogonie littéraire' (IV, 217–64 (p. 240)). I have taken – and occasionally modified – translations of this work from the following edition: Roland Barthes, *The Pleasure of the Text*, trans. Richard Miller (New York: Hill and Wang, 1975).

6 For Leslie Hill, 'Barthes came to embody [from the early 1950s till his death in 1980], one after the other, sometimes even simultaneously, a multiplicity of divergent and seemingly irreconcilable approaches to texts', and he placed a view of 'textuality itself as a paradoxical domain [...] where meaning itself was perpetually disappointed, interrupted, suspended' at the centre of critical debate ('Roland Barthes', in *Radical Indecision: Barthes, Blanchot, Derrida and the Future of Criticism* (Notre Dame: University of Notre Dame Press, 2010), pp. 71–153 (pp. 72–73)). In *Critique et vérité* (1966), for example, Barthes

contrasts his own analysis of the structures of possible meanings (and of the dynamics of reading) with a more conventional – academic – approach to criticism, which reduces the literary text to an objective, univocal meaning that constitutes its 'truth' (see II, 759–801). We will examine his approach to criticism in this work (and elsewhere) in Chapter One. As for Proust, Joshua Landy suggests that the pleasure we derive from reading *À la recherche* is not just 'a matter of digesting a set of illuminating doctrines' but also of 'being seduced by delusions along the way, being forced to wait for the truth' (*Philosophy as Fiction: Self, Deception, and Knowledge in Proust* (Oxford: Oxford University Press, 2004), p. 34)). For a recent discussion of the relationship between ethics and literature, see, for example, Nora Hämäläinen, *Literature and Moral Theory* (London and New York: Bloomsbury Academic, 2016).

7 Kathrin Yacavone, for example, argues that 'in Barthes's late texts, dating from the mid-to-late 1970s, the French novelist [Proust] emerges as a powerful intellectual influence and as a model writer upon whom Barthes projects his literary ambition as well as aspects of his personal life' ('Reading through Photography: Roland Barthes's Last Seminar "Proust et la photographie"', *French Forum*, 34/1 (2009), pp. 97–112 (pp. 98–99)). In addition to Yacavone's text, and with some notable exceptions (Malcolm Bowie's 'Barthes on Proust' and Antoine Compagnon's '"Proust et moi"', <http://www.college-de-france.fr/site/antoine-compagnon/articles_en_ligne.htm> [accessed 1 June, 2019], for example), the majority of critical essays on Barthes and Proust produced over the last three decades or so has focused almost exclusively on Barthes's work after 1970 – predominantly on *La Chambre claire: note sur la photographie* (1980) and, more recently, on the diary kept by Barthes for two years after his mother's death (*Journal de deuil: 26 octobre 1977–15 septembre 1979*, ed. Nathalie Léger (Paris: Seuil: IMEC, 2009)) and *La Préparation du roman I et II*, ed. Nathalie Léger (Paris: Seuil/IMEC, 2003), his lecture series and seminars delivered at the Collège de France between 1978 and 1980. See, for example: Steven Ungar, 'Circular Memories', in *Roland Barthes: The Professor of Desire* (Lincoln, NE and London: University of Nebraska Press, 1983), pp. 135–51; Diana Knight, 'Roland Barthes, or The Woman Without a Shadow', in *Writing the Image after Roland Barthes*, ed. Jean-Michel Rabaté (Philadelphia: University of Pennsylvania Press, 1997), pp. 132–43; Éric Marty, 'Marcel Proust dans "la chambre claire"', *Proust en devenir*, ed. Luc Fraisse, *L'Esprit Créateur* (Special Issue), 46/4 (2006), pp. 125–33; Kathrin Yacavone, 'Barthes et Proust: *La Recherche* comme aventure photographique', *L'Écrivain préféré, Fabula LHT (Littérature, histoire, théorie)*, 4 (March 2008), <http://www.fabula.org/lht/4/Yacavone.html> [accessed 1 June, 2019]; Kathrin Yacavone, 'The "Scattered" Proust: On Barthes's Reading of the *Recherche*', in *'When familiar meanings dissolve …': Essays in French Studies in Memory of Malcolm Bowie*, ed. Naomi Segal and Gill Rye (Bern and Oxford: Peter Lang, 2011), pp. 219–31; Hill, 'Roland Barthes', especially pp. 137–53; Katja Haustein, *Regarding Lost*

Time: Photography, Identity and Affect in Proust, Benjamin and Barthes
(Oxford: Legenda, 2012); Chapter Two of Lucy O'Meara's *Roland Barthes at
the Collège de France* (Liverpool: Liverpool University Press, 2012), pp. 52–86
(which focuses on *Leçon* (1978) and '"Longtemps, je me suis couché de bonne
heure"' (1978)); Adam Watt, 'Reading Proust in Barthes's *Journal de deuil*',
Writing, Reading, Grieving: Essays in Memory of Suzanne Dow, ed. Ruth
Cruickshank and Adam Watt, *Nottingham French Studies* (Special Issue),
53/1 (Spring 2014), pp. 102–12; Diana Knight, 'What Turns the Writer into a
Great Writer? The Conversion Narrative of Barthes's *Vita nova*', *What's So
Great About Roland Barthes?*, ed. Thomas Baldwin, Katja Haustein and Lucy
O'Meara, *L'Esprit Créateur* (Special Issue), 55/4 (Winter 2015), pp. 165–80;
Anne Simon, 'Le Moi idéal', in *Trafics de Proust: Merleau-Ponty, Sartre,
Deleuze, Barthes* (Paris: Hermann, 2016), pp. 155–94.

8 See Roland Barthes et al., 'Table ronde sur Proust', in Gilles Deleuze,
Deux régimes de fous: textes et entretiens 1975–1995, ed. David Lapoujade
(Paris: Minuit, 2003), pp. 29–55 (p. 29). This text is not included in the *Œuvres
complètes*.

9 Barthes, 'Table ronde sur Proust', p. 29.

10 'À mon avis, la *Recherche du temps perdu* [...] ne peut provoquer que des
idées de recherche et non pas des recherches. Dans ce sens-là, le texte proustien
est une substance superbe pour le désir critique. C'est un véritable objet de
désir pour le critique, car tout s'épuise dans le fantasme de la recherche, dans
l'idée de chercher quelque chose chez Proust, et, par là même, aussi, tout rend
illusoire l'idée d'un résultat de cette recherche. La singularité de Proust c'est
qu'il ne nous laisse rien d'autre à faire que ceci: *le réécrire*, qui est le contraire
même de l'épuiser' (Barthes, 'Table ronde sur Proust', pp. 29–30). Emphasis in
original. Unless otherwise indicated, all emphasis is in the original text.

11 Barthes declares that there may be nothing to say about writerly texts
('des textes scriptibles, il n'y a peut-être rien à dire') and that, unlike the
readerly ('lisible'), the writerly 'can be written (rewritten) today' ('peut-être
aujourd'hui écrit (ré-écrit)' (*S/Z*, III, 120–345 (p. 122)). I have taken – and
occasionally modified – translations of this work from the following edition:
Roland Barthes, *S/Z*, trans. Richard Miller (Oxford: Blackwell, 1990).

12 Barthes, 'Table ronde sur Proust', p. 29.

13 'par des lumières qui obéiraient à une sorte de rhéostat variable et
feraient passer graduellement, et inlassablement aussi, le décor par différentes
volumes, par différents niveaux de perception, par différentes intelligibilités'
(Barthes, 'Table ronde sur Proust', p. 29).

14 Gérard Genette, 'Table ronde sur Proust', p. 34.

15 See Barthes, 'Table ronde sur Proust', p. 42, and André Boucourechliev,
Beethoven (Paris: Seuil, 1963). Barthes's 'galaxy' metaphor chimes with both
Boucourechliev's description of Beethoven's *Diabelli Variations* (1819–23) as
'a galaxy in which each star is of the same "size" and equidistant from all the

others' ('une galaxie où chaque étoile, de même "grandeur", est équidistante de toutes les autres' (Boucourechliev, *Beethoven*, p. 87)) and with his own suggestion in *S/Z* that the writerly text is a galaxy of signifiers rather than a structure of signifieds (see III, 123).

16 Barthes, 'Table ronde sur Proust', p. 42.

17 See Barthes, 'Table ronde sur Proust', p. 42: 'You can see that we are dealing with thirty-three variations without a theme. [...] The theme is diffracted entirely in the variations and there is no longer a varied treatment of a theme' ('On s'aperçoit que là on a affaire à trente-trois variations sans thème. [...] Le thème se diffracte entièrement dans les variations et il n'y a plus de traitement varié d'un thème').

18 See Barthes, 'Table ronde sur Proust', p. 35. As far as I am aware, the only text by Barthes called 'Variations' is his posthumously published 1973 piece 'Variations sur l'écriture' (see IV, 267–316).

19 Barthes, 'Table ronde sur Proust', p. 35. Barthes indicates that his definition of 'herméneutique' takes its cue from an 'opposition between "hermeneutics" and "semiology" posited by Foucault' ('opposition qui avait été posée par Foucault entre "herméneutique" et "sémiologie"' ('Table ronde sur Proust', p. 35)). He seems, however, to have confused Foucault's terms here. In 'Nietzsche, Freud, Marx' (1964), for example, Foucault argues that hermeneutics and semiology are *'two ferocious enemies'* (*'deux farouches ennemis'*), adding that a 'hermeneutic that winds itself around a semiology believes in the absolute existence of signs: it gives up the violence, the incompleteness, the infinity of interpretations, so as to create a reign of terror where the indexical mark rules and to make language suspect. [...] On the other hand, a hermeneutic that wraps itself around itself enters into the domain of languages that never stop implicating themselves, which is an intermediate region between madness and pure language' ('[u]ne herméneutique qui se replie en effet sur une sémiologie croit à l'existence absolue des signes: elle abandonne la violence, l'inachevé, l'infinité des interprétations, pour faire régner la terreur de l'indice, et suspecter le langage. [...] Au contraire, une herméneutique qui s'enveloppe sur elle-même, entre dans le domaine des langages qui ne cessent de s'impliquer eux-mêmes, cette région mitoyenne de la folie et du pur langage' ('Nietzsche, Freud, Marx', in *Nietzsche*, ed. Gilles Deleuze (Paris: Minuit, 1964), pp. 183–92 (p. 192)). On Foucault's analysis, then, a critic who follows 'a vertical climb towards a central object', as Barthes puts it, is held entirely within a hermeneutic that winds itself around a semiology rather than within a hermeneutic *tout court*. Barthes's approach to 'herméneutique' here is closer to his description of the inventory of the hermeneutic code in *S/Z* than it is to Foucault's understanding of the term: 'to identify the different (formal) terms around which an enigma is centred and by which that enigma is formulated, held in suspense, and finally disclosed' ('distinguer les différents termes (formels), au gré desquels une énigme se centre, se pose, se formule, puis se retarde et enfin se dévoile' (III, 133)).

20 See Barthes, 'Table ronde sur Proust', p. 48. We will return to Barthes's allergy to 'le plan' in Chapters Three and Four.

21 See Barthes, 'Table ronde sur Proust', p. 29: 'C'est un discours non seulement *digressé* [...], mais c'est, de plus, un discours troué et déconstruit'. This anticipates a view of Gustave Flaubert's work that appears in *Le Plaisir du texte*: like Flaubert, Proust has ways of cutting and of making holes in narrative discourse (see IV, 223). We will discuss the relationship between Barthes's Flaubert and Barthes's Proust in Chapters Two and Three. Pierre Bayard examines the role of digression in *À la recherche* in *Le Hors-sujet: Proust et la digression* (Paris: Minuit, 1996).

22 For a discussion of Barthes's identification with 'Marcel' (of what he calls 'Marcellisme'), see, for example: Kathrin Yacavone's 'Barthes et Proust', 'Reading through Photography' and 'The "Scattered" Proust'; Leslie Hill's chapter on Barthes in *Radical Indecision*; Chapter Two of Lucy O'Meara's *Roland Barthes at the Collège de France*; Diana Knight's 'What Turns the Writer into a Great Writer?'; and, more recently, Chapter Five of Anne Simon's *Trafics de Proust* (pp. 155–94). We will return briefly to Barthes's 'Marcellisme' in Chapter Four.

23 Bowie, 'Barthes on Proust', p. 513.

24 Bowie, 'Barthes on Proust', p. 518.

25 Bowie, 'Barthes on Proust', p. 513. Bowie is forcing things a little here, of course: while Barthes suggests that the mental and physical processes associated with involuntary memory imply a kind of idleness ('une sorte de paresse'), he also says that, even for Proust, writing is not an idle activity: 'écrire n'est pas une activité paresseuse' ('Osons être paresseux', V, 760–66 (p. 765)).

26 Bowie, 'Barthes on Proust', p. 514.

27 Bowie, 'Barthes on Proust', p. 514.

28 Marty, 'Marcel Proust dans "la chambre claire"', p. 125. Marty refers to the following essays: 'Une idée de recherche' (1971), 'Proust et les noms' (1972), 'Ça prend' (1979), '"Longtemps, je me suis couché de bonne heure"'. He also discusses *La Chambre claire* and mentions Barthes's seminars on the 'Charlus-Discourse', which appear at the end of *Comment vivre ensemble: simulations romanesques de quelques espaces quotidiens. Cours et séminaires au Collège de France 1976–1977*, ed. Claude Coste (Paris: Seuil/IMEC, 2002), pp. 203–20 (all subsequent references are to this edition and are given after quotations in the text). While Marty says that there is only one session dedicated to the 'Charlus-Discourse', there are in fact two (dated 23 and 30 March 1977).

29 Marty, 'Marcel Proust dans "la chambre claire"', p. 126. See also Barthes, 'Sur la lecture', IV, 927–36 (p. 934).

30 See Marty, 'Marcel Proust dans "la chambre claire"', p. 126. See also Barthes, 'Écrire, verbe intransitif', III, 617–26.

31 See *Préparation*, p. 200: 'as a *Tendency*, *Writing* easily fits the image

of a natural, physiological Need, as it were independent of any intention or deliberation on the part of the subject' ('comme *Tendance*, *Écrire* coïncide facilement avec l'image d'un Besoin naturel, physiologique, comme indépendant de la délibération, de la visée du sujet'). All subsequent references are to this edition and are given after quotations in the text. I have taken – and occasionally modified – translations of this work from the following edition: Roland Barthes, *The Preparation of the Novel. Lecture Courses and Seminars at the Collège de France (1978–1979 and 1979–1980)*, trans. Kate Briggs (New York: Columbia University Press, 2011).

32 Bowie, 'Barthes on Proust', p. 518.

33 Bowie refers to *La Chambre claire* but did not have access to the published versions of either *Comment vivre ensemble* or *La Préparation du roman* in 2001. He also discusses a selection of direct references to Proust in *Essais critiques* (1964); *Critique et vérité*; *Système de la mode* (1967); *L'Empire des signes* (1970); *Le Plaisir du texte*; *Fragments d'un discours amoureux* (1977); and *Le Grain de la voix* (1981). While I refer to a number of these texts in what follows, I also examine several others, including a number of Barthes's essays from the fifties.

34 Barthes says 'je ne suis pas "proustien"' in an interview with Claude Jannoud published in *Le Figaro* (27 July 1974) under the title 'Roland Barthes contre les idées reçues' (see IV, 564–69 (p. 569)). This is repeated in *La Préparation du roman* (see p. 391). Barthes's assertion is ambiguous, of course: it means either that he is not 'Proustian' or that he is not 'a Proustian' (i.e. a Proust specialist).

35 Bowie, 'Barthes on Proust', p. 518.

36 'de simples esquisses [...], des notes ou notules' (Marty, 'Marcel Proust dans "la chambre claire"', p. 125). A 'notule' is defined in the *Trésor de la langue française informatisé* as a 'brief annotation to a text' ('courte annotation à un texte'), a 'brief note' ('petite note'). Barthes discusses the difference between *notula* (a word that reminds him of an idea) and *nota* (a note, a piece of paper) in *La Préparation du roman* (p. 137).

37 Bowie, 'Barthes on Proust', p. 517.

38 In 'The "Scattered" Proust', Yacavone suggests that 'although omnipresent, he [Proust] is never the direct object of sustained and systematic investigation [in Barthes's work]' (p. 219). The Rabat seminar notes and the companion seminars to *Comment vivre ensemble* (on the 'Charlus-Discourse') remain almost entirely unexplored in the critical literature on either Barthes or Proust. To my knowledge, the only study of the seminar notes is Claude Coste's brief essay 'Notes de cours pour le Maroc', in *Roland Barthes au Maroc*, ed. Ridha Boulaâbi, Claude Coste and Mohamed Lehdahda (Meknès: Publications de l'Université Moulay Ismaïl, 2013), pp. 9–22.

39 In her 2012 biographical essay, *Roland Barthes: au lieu de la vie* (Paris: Flammarion, 2012), for example, Marie Gil describes Barthes as an

'oscillateur'. Andy Stafford discusses Gil's use of this term (and its limitations in relation to Barthes's critical activity) in '*Classé, Surclasser, Déclassé*, or, Roland Barthes, Classification without Class', *What's So Great About Roland Barthes?*, ed. Thomas Baldwin, Katja Haustein and Lucy O'Meara, *L'Esprit Créateur* (Special Issue), 55/4 (Winter 2015), pp. 148–64.

40 Hill, 'Roland Barthes', p. 143.

41 See Roland Barthes (with Jean Montalbetti), 'Un homme, une ville: Marcel Proust à Paris avec Roland Barthes', *Cassettes Radio France*, 3 episodes (Paris: Radio France, 1978), III, 28 mins (13:50).

42 Barthes, 'Table ronde sur Proust', p. 29.

43 'C'est une œuvre kaléidoscopique, polyvalente, qui diffuse avec tellement de vitalité, dans tellement de directions, qu'en réalité on ne peut parler de l'œuvre proustienne que si on choisit une certaine pertinence, un certain point de vue, et naturellement, ce point de vue change. Enfin, on peut choisir tel ou tel point de vue' (Barthes, 'Un homme, une ville', III, 13:20–45).

44 See note 22 above.

CHAPTER ONE

Objects

On a now defunct Wikipedia page, Barthes was included in a list of writers influenced by Proust.[1] The selection criteria for this eclectic set are unclear: it may come as a surprise to some that Proust should be – or have been – thought of as an influence on John Updike and not, for example, on Jean-Paul Sartre. In any case, while Proust is indisputably an important reference in Barthes's oeuvre, and while Wikipedia's web designers and contributors may continue to believe that lists of who influenced whom are of use,[2] the inclusion of Barthes's name in this hodgepodge of novelists, literary theorists and philosophers was probably more contentious than its author(s) imagined.

Barthes himself was not keen on 'influence'. In a tetchy interview with Renaud Matignon published in *France-Observateur* in 1964, he says that he does not believe in influences.[3] Rather than ideas, Barthes declares, it is languages, understood as formal containers that we can 'fill differently' ('des formes que l'on peut remplir différemment' (II, 616)), that are transmitted between texts. Consequently, and since books are more like 'currencies' than 'forces', the notion of circulation, he argues, is more accurate than that of 'influence'.[4] In the course of the same interview, Barthes mentions Proust, among others, in defending himself against Matignon's provocation that his work has had a bothersome, or even impoverishing, influence on certain of his contemporaries:

> I would be quite happy to admit to a 'negative' influence, because I do not think that a 'negative' attitude, as far as literature is concerned, is necessarily an 'impoverishing' one; reflecting on the limits, on the detection or on the impossibilities of writing is an essential part of literary creation. For one hundred years, from Mallarmé to Blanchot, important works have been written out of this *hollow*; even Proust's work, which seems so positive, so liberating, is born explicitly of a book that is impossible to write. (II, 616)[5]

These remarks echo a number of Barthes's slightly less defensive observations in earlier essays on the negativity of Proust's writing and on the search for an 'impossible' literature by which, Barthes contends, modernity is inaugurated.[6] Before discussing the circulation of this particular Proustian currency within his work, though, I want to remain with Barthes on the relation of 'influence', and to look briefly at what he says about the task of the critic in his discussion with Matignon and in two other texts from the 1960s. Later in the *France-Observateur* interview, he characterizes his own criticism of the work of contemporary writers (including Michel Butor, Jean Cayrol and Alain Robbe-Grillet) in the following terms:

> However, and I repeat, negative or not, I do not believe in influences; I may have lent – temporarily, partially, and not without misunderstanding – an intellectual voice – or even an intellectualist one – to a number of my contemporaries' creative preoccupations, but this has only ever been a contact between languages. (II, 617)[7]

In *Critique et vérité*, Barthes describes linguistic touching of this kind as a productive rewriting, as a 'doubling'[8] by virtue of which a second writing ('une seconde écriture') makes contact with 'the first writing of the work' ('la première écriture de l'œuvre' (II, 761)). Moreover, in 'Qu'est-ce que la critique?' (1963), he argues that the critic as rewriter – of Proust or any other author – is required to adjust his or her own language, understood as a formal system of logical constraints at a given historical moment, to the author's, 'like a good carpenter, who brings two parts of a complicated item of furniture together by groping "intelligently"'.[9] For Barthes, as Bowie observes, the critic is a 'mechanism for the articulation of rhetorical character in literary texts',[10] and the purely formal nature of his or her critical carpentry is a guarantee of its universality. Critical proof, Barthes says, is tautological[11] rather than of a truth-oriented ('aléthique') order:

> It is not for criticism to say whether Proust has spoken the 'truth', whether the Baron de Charlus was indeed the Count de Montesquiou, whether Françoise was Céleste, or even, more generally, whether the society he described reproduces accurately the historical conditions of the nobility's disappearance at the end of the nineteenth century; its role is solely to elaborate a language whose coherence, logic [...] can collect or better still can 'integrate' (in the mathematical sense of the term) the greatest possible quantity of Proustian language. (II, 505)[12]

Rewriting is not correction, imitation or exhaustive interpretation:[13] the task of the critic is not to unearth and reveal truths about authors or their works,[14] or to produce precise replicas of literary texts, but to bring about linguistic intimacy, a creative rubbing ('frottement' (II, 505)), through 'integration'. Indeed, for Barthes, criticism seeks not to discover the work in question, but 'to *cover* it as completely as possible in its own language' ('la *couvrir* le plus complètement possible par son propre langage' (II, 505)).

How, then, can the coherence or logic of Barthes's language be said to rub against, to collect, to integrate (with) or to cover the language of *À la recherche*? We might ask what 'couvrir' – which Barthes italicizes – signifies here, and to what extent integration in the mathematical sense of the term is useful for an understanding of the critic's rubbing and covering.[15] Does the critic place his or her own language over that of the work, with the effect of hiding it from view, protecting it or somehow enclosing it? Is the covering in fact a cover-up – a kind of censorship? Does the critic's task require him or her to 'cover a distance from end to end' or to 'take in a certain period of time in one go' ('embrasser d'un seul tenant une certaine période de temps')?[16] If so, is his or her 'parcours' or 'embrace' as unserious or ephemeral as it might sound ('parcourir' means both to pass through or to read through, to skim read)? More improbably, rather than simply approach it like a carpenter, groping or rubbing intelligently, does the critic copulate with the work in order to produce something new (as a stallion covers a mare, for example)? How much covering up or concealment can there be in a fleeting dalliance? In what, precisely, does Barthes's integration and covering – his rewriting – of Proust consist?

As we have already seen, for Bowie, Barthes co-opts Proust's work 'in the form of an eloquent excerpt, to underwrite an argument or to reinforce an assertion'.[17] Nevertheless, Proust's text is also, as Bowie acknowledges, Barthes's paradigmatic example of the *livre à venir* (the book to come).[18] For example, in *Le Degré zéro de l'écriture*, published eleven years before the interview with Matignon, he writes:

> the greater modern works linger as long as possible, in a sort of miraculous stasis, on the threshold of Literature, in this anticipatory state in which the breadth of life is given, stretched but not destroyed by this crowning phase, an order of signs. For instance, we have the first person in Proust, whose whole work rests on a slow and protracted effort towards Literature. (I, 194)[19]

Proust's narrative remains this side of convention for as long as it can: whereas Balzac's use of the third-person (masculine) singular pronoun brings about 'a kind of algebraic state of the action, in which existence plays the smallest part possible' ('une sorte d'état algébrique de l'action, où l'existence a le moins de part possible' (I, 193)), Proust's first-person narrator inhabits a liminal world in which life is yet to be transformed into a destiny ('un destin'), in which memory is yet to take on a practical or utilitarian function (to become an 'acte utile'), and in which duration is yet to be lived as an 'orientated and meaningful time' ('un temps dirigé et significatif' (I, 194)). Similarly, while authors' use of the simple past tense within the realm of belles-lettres is to reduce reality to a 'point of time' ('un point') and to abstract a meaningful verbal act (an 'acte verbal pur') from a multiplicity of superimposed experiences, the dense temporal convolutions and superimpositions of *À la recherche* are surely more in keeping with the modern novel's terrifying, limitless expression (its 'parole sans limite' (I, 190)).[20]

For Barthes, then, Proust's text is a (modern) place in which an existential density is deposited rather than signified: it is a depositary of the 'thickness' of existence rather than of its 'signification' ('l'épaisseur de l'existence, et non de sa signification' (I, 191)). In a similar vein, Proust's novel is heralded in 'Pré-romans', published one year after *Le Degré zéro de l'écriture*, as the first example of a work in which 'la Littérature' flees, refuses and kills itself:

> throughout his immense work, Proust is always on the point of writing. He has the traditional literary act in his sights, but constantly puts it off. It is at the end of this *never-fulfilled* wait that the work is constructed in spite of itself: it is the waiting that has made up the thickness of a work whose *suspended* character was enough to serve as a basis for the writer's expression. (I, 500)[21]

While Proust is presented in 'Pré-romans' as a first, as a unique event in the history of writing (one that paves the way for the work of Cayrol, Jean Duvignaud and Robbe-Grillet, for example), Barthes does not make him abscond from all literary convention – from the reassuringly ordered forms of 'la Littérature' (I, 190). Instead, he argues both here and in *Le Degré zéro de l'écriture* that Proust's novel is formed out of borders and thresholds: the suspension of tradition, a 'miraculous stasis' on the edge of classical convention and 'euphorie' (I, 190), is the very stuff of which, for Barthes, *À la recherche* itself is made. In 1953 and 1954, then, *À la recherche* is described as something like a hinge.

While it is the impossibility of writing a novel (or being the preparation of a future novel)[22] that makes up the density of Proust's work, and while this may be a necessary condition for the development – or even the possibility – of the modern novel (of the *nouveau roman*),[23] *À la recherche* is not fully detached from the nineteenth-century novel's stable regimes of signification.

Covering Proust

Barthes does not always take this nuanced view. In fact, on a number of occasions in the 1950s (and at other times, as we shall see in later chapters), he draws a line between *À la recherche* and the modern novel. He also presents Proust's text as something relatively homogeneous. For example, in 'Littérature objective' (1954), he compares Proust and Robbe-Grillet:

> In order to grasp the temporal nature of the object in Robbe-Grillet, we must observe the mutations he makes it undergo, and here again contrast the revolutionary nature of his attempt with the norms of classical description. The latter, certainly, has managed to submit its objects to forces of decay. But precisely, it was as if the object, long since constituted in its space or substance, thereafter encountered a Necessity descended from the empyrean; classical time has no other figure than that of a destroyer of perfection (Chronos and his scythe). In Balzac, in Flaubert, in Baudelaire, even in Proust (but in an inverted mode), the object is the vehicle of melodrama; it decays, vanishes, or recovers a final glory, participates in short in a veritable eschatology of matter. One might say that the classical object is never anything but the archetype of its own ruin, which means setting against the object's spatial essence a subsequent (hence external) time that functions as a destiny and not as an internal dimension. Classical time never encounters the object except as its catastrophe or deliquescence. (II, 299)[24]

Even though Proust's eschatology of matter inverts Balzac's, Flaubert's and Baudelaire's,[25] he (or, rather, even he) also fails to escape from a classical melodrama in which objects encounter time as an external, destructive force: as their destiny. Proust thus effects an inversion of the temporal nature of the object as it appears in the work of his nineteenth-century predecessors, but he cannot be said to have abandoned it altogether. While classical time has been twisted or manipulated, it is not entirely out of joint. In contrast, for Barthes, Robbe-Grillet's treatment of material objects – his *chosisme* – constitutes a definitive rejection of classical norms:

> Robbe-Grillet gives his objects an entirely different type of mutability. It is a mutability whose process is invisible: an object, first described at a moment of novelistic continuity, reappears later on, endowed with a scarcely perceptible difference. This difference is of a spatial, situational order (for instance, what was on the right is now on the left). Time dislocates space and constitutes the object as a series of slices that almost completely overlap each other: in that spatial 'almost' lies the object's temporal dimension. This is a type of variation that we find in a cruder version in the movement of magic lantern slides or of animated comic strips. (II, 299)[26]

The minute spatial mutations in Robbe-Grillet's revolutionary fictional worlds conspire, then, to produce an image of the object as an aggregate of superimposed layers. The gaps and edges formed by these overlappings are the spaces in which the operations of time become visible. Moreover, according to Barthes, the restitution of objects in Robbe-Grillet's work occurs at a purely optical level, and their mutations are a function of dislocation rather than – as is the case in classical (nineteenth-century) novels and poetry – decomposition: sight, he says, is the only sense in which 'the continuous is an addition of tiny but integral fields; space can only tolerate *completed* variations: man never participates visually in the internal process of decay' (II, 300).[27]

It is surprising that Barthes should try to map the coordinates of the *nouveau-romancier*'s break with tradition (represented in this example by Proust, among others) in this way. There may be some important differences between Proust's and Robbe-Grillet's way with objects, but there is also something decidedly Proustian about the superimposed mutability of Robbe-Grillet's objects as Barthes describes it. Indeed, if we read Proust instead of simply taking Barthes's word for it, we can begin to see something problematic here: Proust's novel does not quite fall in with the paradigmatic distinctions on which Barthes's analysis rests.

First, on a purely linguistic level, it is difficult not to hear echoes of Proust in Barthes's reference to magic lantern slides. Second, on a more symbolic level, the magic lantern is one of several optical instruments (others include the kaleidoscope, microscope and telescope) that the narrator of À *la recherche* associates with the mutability of objects: in 'Combray', the images of Golo and Geneviève de Brabant projected onto the narrator's bedroom walls, curtain and door, for example, serve to reconfigure spatial and temporal relations between material things. The narrator's room is transformed into a medieval scene; the objects of habit it contains become a landscape through which Golo rides. These objects are also transformed into his 'ossature' in an act of 'transverté-bration' (*ALR*, I, 10). A further example is to be found in the narrator's descriptions of the work of the artist Elstir, which, he says, is 'the projection, the way of seeing things peculiar to that great painter' ('la projection de la manière de voir particulière à ce grand peintre' (*ALR*, II, 712)). In the following passage, Elstir's head is compared to a magic lantern:

> The parts of the walls that were covered by his paintings, all homogeneous with one another, were like the luminous images of a magic lantern, which would have been in this instance the head of the artist, and the strangeness of which one could never have suspected so long as one had known only the man, which was like seeing the iron lantern housing its lamp before any coloured slide had been slid into its groove. Among these paintings several of the kind that seemed most absurd to ordinary people interested me more than the rest because they recreated those optical illusions which prove to us that we should never succeed in identifying objects if we did not make reason intervene. (*ALR*, II, 712)[28]

In Elstir's paintings, the projections of the magic lantern break words and things apart and set objects in new relations with one another. They stimulate a reappraisal of 'that aggregate of impressions we call vision' ('cet agrégat de raisonnements que nous appelons vision' (*ALR*, II, 713)), the abandonment of a form of Cratylism[29] and a 'metamorphosis of the things represented, analogous to what in poetry we call metaphor' ('métamorphose des choses représentées, analogue à celle qu'en poésie on nomme métaphore' (*ALR*, II, 191)).[30]

Third, there are clear points of contact between Robbe-Grillet's (or rather Barthes's) temporal regime, which dislocates space and constitutes the object as a series of overlapping slices, and Marcel's experience before the haggard faces of the dying socialites present at the 'Bal de têtes' in *Le Temps retrouvé*.[31] In both Proust and Robbe-Grillet, the contemporary moment is envisaged as a dense *feuilleté* of temporalities. The term 'transversale' is first used in *Du côté de chez Swann* to describe the 'artificial line' ('ligne artificielle') constructed by the narrator in an effort to match the man he has just encountered – Charles Swann – with one he used to know in Combray (see *ALR*, I, 400). It recurs in *Le Temps retrouvé*, for similar purposes of identification, when Marcel meets Mlle de Saint-Loup:

> Here there was a new transversal, for my great-uncle's footman who had announced me that day and who, by the gift of a photograph, had enabled me to identify the lady in pink, was the uncle of the young man whom not only M. de Charlus but also Mlle de Saint-Loup's father had loved and on whose account her mother had been made unhappy. (*ALR*, IV, 607)[32]

Here and elsewhere during the Princesse de Guermantes's matinee, a vast network of indirect communications, made up of superimposed layers of experience, composes a vitreous laminate in which objects (including parts of people and places) are associated with different temporal 'altitudes' (see *ALR*, IV, 449).[33] These are juxtaposed in a series of 'levels' ('plans'), which, in creating for the narrator a sense of depth, must be read simultaneously (see *ALR*, IV, 503). As he reads into the 'profondeurs' of the tired faces before him, the narrator experiences something close to the process of mutability that Barthes describes. Thus, whereas the dislocation of objects in Robbe-Grillet is, according to Barthes, free from degradation, the narrator's encounter with faces in *Le Temps retrouvé* is arguably one that involves both the object's dislocation and its internal (biological) degeneration. Although this may be a crucial difference between Robbe-Grillet and Proust, Barthes nevertheless makes contact with and integrates the language of Proust as he describes the physical transformations of objects in Robbe-Grillet's work.[34]

Finally, variation is a fundamental creative force in Proust's novel as Barthes understands it.[35] As we have already seen, he suggests that *À la recherche*, like Beethoven's *Diabelli Variations*, is made of theme-less variations. He also contends that this form of variation constitutes a destruction of metaphor, or at least of 'the origin of metaphor' ('l'origine de la métaphore').[36] Bringing each of these points together, we might ask how Barthes's views on variation as a destroyer of origins in Proust can be brought to bear upon our understanding of the mutability of Robbe-Grillet's objects and of Elstir's metaphor-like metamorphoses. It is unclear, for example, whether the tiny, almost imperceptible spatial shifts in Robbe-Grillet's work, its '*completed* variations' (II, 300), which Barthes views as revolutionary, are the sign of an unconventional, Proust-style 'theme of variation' ('thème de la variation'),[37] or whether they in fact imply a more canonical approach.

What, then, does this tell us about Barthes's integration, rubbing against, rewriting or 'covering' of Proust? How might we characterize the linguistic contact between Barthes and Proust on this occasion? For Bowie, Barthes's criticism is pricked and punctured by Proust's novel even as he conceives of it as a literary cosmogony and as a paradigmatic example of the *livre à venir*. What explains this critical complexity, he says, is Barthes's 'refusal of interpretation [...], an unlimited recalcitrance towards the efforts of criticism'.[38] According to Bowie, Barthes's deployment of bits of Proustian language can be understood as an integration in so far as it achieves the 'silence and the expressionless neutrality of an equation'.[39] Bowie continues:

> Remembering the very first word of *Moby Dick*, its first chapter-title, we could say that Proust's book mattered to Barthes more in its generalized 'loomings' than in the copious and artful individual sentences by which other critics have been so readily seduced. The memory of reading Proust, the anticipation of reading him again, or even a mere side-glance at his mountainous volumes, were themselves the crucial empowerment. (p. 518)

Barthes's 'covering' of Proust in the passages we have examined thus far does entail co-opting side glances and generalizing, non-specialist critical engagements, and this may be a way of covering Proust up – of making the material work written by Proust 'disappear from view' (or certainly quieten down).[40] However, the examples we have looked at so far demonstrate that Proust's presence in Barthes's work is even more disconcerting, more paradoxical, than Bowie allows. Barthes's collection or integration of 'the greatest possible quantity of Proustian language' (II, 505) is not limited to passages where he describes Proust's innovations or where he cites Proust in order to shore up or to underwrite an argument. The gleam of the magic lantern is visible through the covering that Barthes places over it. Or to put it another way: Barthes *covers* (in both the concealing and generative senses of the word) Proust to make Robbe-Grillet. He makes Proustian language and forms circulate – loom large – even as he endeavours to describe a language that is, he claims, thoroughly un-Proustian: he brings the languages of Proust and Robbe-Grillet, the 'classical' and the 'modern', into irritable contact even as he seeks to trace their lines of demarcation.

How to live with objects

In 'Jean Cayrol et ses romans' (1952), which appeared two years before the essay on Robbe-Grillet's 'objective' literature, Barthes argues that classical art ('l'art classique') reduces the world to a 'structure of relations' ('une structure de rapports' (I, 151)). Things, he says, do not matter:

> If we consider a great novel of the eighteenth century, *Dangerous Liaisons*, for example, we see that there are no objects to be found in it: its characters circulate in a space without matter; their gaze only ever rests upon meanings; it would appear that this gaze is not short enough to reach objects. (I, 151)[41]

As is the classical novel, so is eighteenth-century painting: objects that appear in Chardin's still lifes, for example, have been submitted to a compositional law, and composition, according to Barthes, implies a movement away, a 'suppression of real and threatening space in favour of an ideally human distance' ('suppression de l'espace réel et menaçant, au profit d'une distance idéalement humaine' (I, 151)). In what Barthes calls 'le complexe classico-romantique' (I, 152), the material stuff of the world is experienced as a distant spectacle rather than as part of a human environment, and humanity (or at least a good amount of Western humanity) is blind to objects until they are organized within a composition, their matter concealed 'behind an order' ('derrière un ordre' (I, 152)). The matter of objects, of *tangibilia*, is thus kept at a safe distance:

> every effort is made to remove man from direct conflict with space, in order to place a salutary delay between man and his milieu, during which space is constructed, matter moves away and loses the unusual and bothersome character of objects that do not keep their distance. (I, 152)[42]

Things are very different in Cayrol's 'modern' novels, where matter misbehaves and overcomes a classical, ideal distance. Human subjects now inhabit a world of objects that they see and touch – that have acquired 'the necessary form of a familiarity' ('la forme nécessaire d'une familiarité' (I, 152)). The human participates directly, with the entire surface of his or her body, in the 'pression' and 'mouvement' (I, 152) of things, and he or she feels space as a 'worrying juxtaposition of surfaces' ('une juxtaposition inquiétante de surfaces' (I, 153)) rather than as a series of neatly ordered depths. The modern object, Barthes says elsewhere, is 'either suffocation (Ionesco) or nausea (Sartre)'.[43] Furthermore, whereas objects are represented in the plates of the *Encyclopédie* – at least in their vignettes – as things that are subjected to a human gaze (and are to that extent '*signed* by man' (IV, 45)),[44] the ontological tables are turned in the modern novel: humanity becomes spectacle as it is beset by the stubborn gaze of the objects – the surfaces – that surround it.

Barthes does not refer to Proust in the articles on Cayrol or on the plates of the *Enyclopédie*. Nevertheless, given his alignment of Proust elsewhere with both classical and modern authors (including Cayrol),[45] we might enquire if the distinctions he draws in these articles can nevertheless be made to bear upon Proust's work. To what extent does the material substance of objects matter to Proust's narrator? Is he more like Cayrol than Laclos? In other words, does Marcel perceive the world as a milieu or as a distant spectacle? What role does the surface of his body (and that of the objects he encounters) play in his experience of the world? How short or long is his gaze? Does he touch what he sees?

Looking and touching in Proust: distance and proxemics

On several occasions, the narrator of Proust's novel is uncomfortably aware of a distance between himself and the objects (including people and places) under his gaze. His first sight of Balbec, for example, is a source of bitter disappointment for him: Swann's and Legrandin's descriptions of the town have led to the formation of a particular image of it in his mind, and the reality does not live up to it. Everything that is realized, he says, is 'sterilizing' ('stérilisant' (*ALR*, II, 26)). This painful deflation is nothing, however, compared to the paroxysms of fear he feels at the sight of his new room in Balbec's Grand-Hotel, where he is to spend the holidays with his grandmother. This enormous Pandora's box ('boîte de Pandore' (*ALR*, II, 27)) contains several faces and things with which he is not familiar:

> There was no space for me in my bedroom (mine in name only) at Balbec; it was full of things that did not know me, that shot back at me the distrustful glance I shot at them, and, without taking any notice of my existence, showed that I was interrupting the humdrum course of theirs. [...] I was tormented by the presence of some little bookcases with glass fronts that ran along the walls, but especially by a large cheval-glass that stood across one corner and before the departure of which I felt there could be no possibility of rest for me there. (*ALR*, II, 27)[46]

Why should such mundane objects, the surfaces of which are often shiny or reflective, hold such a terror for him? One answer seems to lie in their being different from the things in his room in Paris (they are not his). His feeling of comfort and relaxation in the company of the latter is also expressed in terms of their relative connectedness to – we could even say oneness with – his eyes and body. They trouble him as little as his own pupils, he says, 'for they were merely extensions of my organs, an enlargement of myself' ('car ils n'étaient plus que des annexes de mes organes, un agrandissement de moi-même' (*ALR*, II, 27)). While the objects in Paris are almost proprioceptively his own, and are to that extent invisible to him, those he encounters in Balbec are entirely visible yet radically apart from his cowering body. The Parisian objects are part of a milieu in which Marcel feels secure; those in Balbec make an unhomely spectacle.

In his hotel room in Balbec, the narrator undergoes what Barthes, in *Comment vivre ensemble*, and without direct reference to Proust, calls 'proxemic ordeals' ('des épreuves de proxémie'): 'At the hotel: bad bedside lamp, no desktop lamp, darkness without familiarity ≠ artificial and sophisticated reconstitution of a proxemy'.[47] For Marcel, Paris is relatively proxemic: it is a 'space of the familiar gaze' ('espace du regard familier'), of 'sleep, rest, sedentary work at home: the sphere of the "automatic gesture"'.[48] By contrast, the world of Balbec – the narrator's experience of the objects and people he sees there – can be understood as a series of distressing proxemic experiments in which objects look back. The unfamiliar objects in Balbec dismiss Marcel by returning, in the form of a reflection, the suspicious glance he directs towards them. This is a mirrored glance that does not acknowledge his existence and is not 'signé par l'homme' (see IV, 45): a glance that excludes him. The most troubling thing, the large cheval-glass, supplies nothing more than what is to him a frightening surface in or through which he can view his body – a mirror image that is in danger of returning his gaze.

While Marcel persists in the conviction that his fear of this object is somehow due to its distinctness in relation to his body, a radical sense of otherness is also expressed here not in terms of absolute proprioceptive loss, but in terms of the self-visibility that its untouchably reflective surface affords him. The distrustful glance of the cheval-glass is a reflection of the uncomfortable gaze he directs towards it (rather than something generated by or within the object itself). Why should the sight of oneself – a making-visible of oneself to oneself – be so threatening? In Marcel's case, the sight of himself seeing himself in the surface of this object produces a sense of absolute alterity – a sterilizing *Unheimlichkeit* – in relation to his surroundings. A sense of otherness thus arises out of feelings of (or a desire for) self-identity (albeit superficial) rather than of difference. The flat, reflective object suppresses any sense of being-at-home. Coupled with his desire to be fully part of its world, it presents an image that, insofar as it reflects his body, is always already distant from it (there is a genetic relation between the two, but the reflected image of the body is necessarily detached from the object it reflects and by which it is seen). It is for this reason, perhaps, that Marcel cannot view the glass-fronted bookcases and the mirror as an annex of his own organs: what he sees is the annexation – a taking away and a distancing – by the glassy surfaces of his bodily organs only to be *seen*, and while they are emphatically recognizable as his own, he is denied by them the power of proprioceptive or proxemic feeling (his own power of annexation). While, for Barthes, Aunt Léonie's proxemic bed is a site of 'fantasmatic expansion' ('foyer d'expansion fantasmatique du sujet'),[49] the reflective proxemy of an inhabitual, mirrored surface promises no such self-enlargement to the petrified narrator.[50]

Balbec does have its proxemic pleasures, though. Marcel encounters another set of irradiant objects on the promenade outside his hotel, in the form of a young cyclist's eyes. On this occasion, he is a voyeur of eyeballs:

> If we thought that the eyes of a girl like that were merely two glittering sequins of mica, we should not be eager to know her and to unite her life to ours. But we feel that what shines in those reflecting discs is not due solely to their material composition; that it is, unknown to us, the dark shadows of the ideas that this being is conceiving, relative to the people and places that she knows [...]. I knew that I would never possess this young cyclist if I did not possess also what was in her eyes. And it was consequently her whole life that filled me with desire; a painful desire because I felt that it was not to be realised, but exhilarating, because what had hitherto been my life, having ceased suddenly to be my whole life, being no more now than a little part of the space stretching out before me, which I was burning to cover and which was composed of the lives of these girls, offered me that prolongation, that possible multiplication of oneself which is happiness. (*ALR*, II, 152)[51]

In seeing Albertine's eyes (he seems, in fact, to see something 'beyond' the mere surface of these organs), Marcel could be said to apprehend what Sartre calls the 'gaze' ('le regard'). For Sartre, the gaze of the 'Other' engenders a making-visible to the subject of his or her own body and of his or her desire in relation to the 'Other'. The subject is stripped of a 'presence without distance' ('présence sans distance') to his or her own world and is afflicted by a 'distance from others' ('distance à autrui').[52] In Proust's text, the distance created by the gaze is figured in the space that stretches out before Marcel as he looks at Albertine's eyes and over which he longs to travel. The flat surfaces of the mirror and bookcase fronts in his room reveal that he is other – that he does not belong in the room (or to himself). Here, the stretched-out 'space that was made of the life of Albertine' ('espace [...] qui était fait de la vie d'Albertine' (*ALR*, II, 152)) is a further sign of his exile – a reminder that he can only wander across its surface and may never penetrate its depths. He is a tiny speck in the corner of her brilliant, shining eye. In spite of the sense of exclusion they both produce, there is an important difference between the two experiences in Balbec: the objects in Marcel's hotel room may reflect his body, but they do not permit a fantasmatic self-expansion; while Albertine's eyes of mica are not felt as something attached to his own organs, they nevertheless bring about a happy multiplication of the self as they promise a secret, untouched futurity.

There are further proxemic ordeals beyond Balbec, of course. Marcel frequently expresses his sense of exclusion in relation to objects and people in terms that describe resistant surfaces. In *A l'ombre des jeunes filles en fleurs*, for example, the Swanns' home is surrounded by a kind of carapace – 'a cool and pink glaze' ('un rose et frais glacis' (*ALR*, I, 517)). This is the expression of social and psychological limits. The narrator has long desired to enter the Swann household but has been able to observe this strangely glazed place only at its edges. This is partly as a result of the snooty disapproval of his family. The *couches sociales* of Combray are not easily penetrated. Moreover, in referring to objects or scenes as paintings, as mediated spectacles, Proust's narrator makes a distinction between the worlds inhabited by the spectator (the narrator himself) and by the objects he perceives.[53] Here we encounter a further complication, or rather neutralization, of Barthes's classical/modern paradigm. In *S/Z*, he says that

> realism (badly named, at any rate often badly interpreted) consists not in copying the real but in copying a (depicted) copy of the real: this famous real, as though suffering from a fearfulness which keeps it from being touched directly, *is set further away*, postponed, or at least captured through the pictorial matrix in which it has been steeped before being put into words. (III, 164)[54]

The world is left untouched in Laclos and Balzac: in the work of the former, it is already composed as a spectacle; in Balzac's, it is to be organized within a 'tableau' before it is described in words.[55] For Barthes, 'writers' dream of painting' ('[l]e rêve de peinture des écrivains' (II, 164)) has been dead for some time – at least since Mallarmé. Nevertheless, the 'model of painting' ('modèle de la peinture' (III, 163)) lives on in À la recherche, but in modified – literalized – form: Marcel does not, unlike his 'classical' predecessors, de-depict the real (remove it from its picture) before putting it into words. The model of painting is thus allowed to show itself within the virtual world of the text. On several occasions, Proust's narrator crosses and recrosses the boundaries between mimetic description and ekphrasis so that the artificial effects of pictures and picturing fall upon the natural effects of observation.[56] There is occasionally an edge that separates the one from the other (usually, one has to look hard for tiny flashes reflecting such things), but in À la recherche we are forced to occupy, or to multiply, a threshold between the two. Marcel's experience of objects is thus one that oscillates dramatically between the modern tactility (vision) and eighteenth-century or realist distance (blindness) that Barthes describes.[57]

Marcel reflects on the mediated insecurities of our encounters with objects (which may include the surfaces of human bodies as well as things like boots and spoons) and the matter of which they are made. His sense of alienation is expressed most explicitly in *Du côté de chez Swann*: 'When I saw any external object, my consciousness that I was seeing it would remain between me and it, enclosing it in a slender, incorporeal outline that prevented me from ever coming directly in contact with its matter' (*ALR*, I, 83).[58] In spite (or perhaps even because) of this avowed phenomenological limitation, Marcel occasionally feels very close to the stuff of things, and this is experienced as a sense of fullness. For example, in *Le Côté de Guermantes*, he has some time to kill before he meets Robert de Saint-Loup for dinner, and he decides to return to his lodgings to read for a couple of hours. There, he observes:

> I kept, when I was in my room, the same fullness of sensation that I had felt outside. It gave such an apparent convexity of surface to things that as a rule seem flat and empty, to the yellow flame of the fire, the coarse blue paper on the ceiling, on which the setting sun had scribbled corkscrews and whirligigs, like a schoolboy with a piece of red chalk, the curiously patterned cloth on the round table, on which a ream of essay paper and an inkpot lay in readiness for me, with one of Bergotte's novels, that ever since then these things have continued to seem to me to be enriched with a wholly special kind of existence. (*ALR*, II, 394)[59]

The menace of this transformation is both sexual and spatial. It is also framed by pleasure. The flat and unreflective surfaces of these everyday things have acquired a swollen convexity ('bombait'). The carpet, table and block of paper are inflated by the intensity of feeling in Marcel's gaze. This is not a hapticity born merely of physical closeness, but from fullness of feeling. The surfaces of these objects have expanded into the form of the lens that is directed at them. The flat surface-now-become-lens-become-eye of the object swells and looks back into the narrator's eye. The expansion is certainly cartoon-like (recalling Tex Avery, for example), and it approaches schizophrenia as it is described by Deleuze and Guattari: Marcel is approaching 'that unbearable point at which the mind touches matter and lives each intensity, consumes it'.[60] His Dionysian fullness of feeling engenders a near contiguity of otherwise separate, albeit asymptotic surfaces.[61] What the object presents to the eye, then, is the sensation of touch as much as sight. Can we conclude from this that the distance between subject and object has been overcome, or does it create a new possibility of distance?

Proust's description also suggests an augmentation of Keplerean optics. The object is not only inscribed onto the surface of the retina, the inner surface at the back of the eye, but threatens to press itself against the external (frontal) surface of the eyeball.[62] If we look carefully at the language of the bedtime drama in Combray, we see something similar. Marcel's gaze, like his mind, becomes distended and reaches out to touch the surface of his mother: 'my mind [...], rendered convex like the look which I shot at my mother' ('mon esprit [...], rendu convexe comme le regard que je dardais sur ma mère' (*ALR*, I, 24)). In both cases, the distance between subject and object certainly seems to have been eliminated, or substantially reduced.

In another passage, however, the narrator feels so good (having seen Albertine's naked neck and pink cheeks) that the surface of his eye grows to such an extent that it hardly feels the weight of a world that is not vast enough to fill it:

> The sea, which was visible through the window as well as the valley, the swelling breasts of the first of the Maineville cliffs, the sky in which the moon had not yet climbed to the zenith – all this seemed less than a featherweight on my eyeballs, which between their lids I could feel dilated, resistant, ready to bear far greater burdens, all the mountains of the world, upon their fragile surface. Their orb no longer found even the sphere of the horizon adequate to fill it. (*ALR*, II, 285)[63]

The breasts of the Maineville cliffs seen through the hotel window may be swollen (like the surfaces of the contents of the narrator's room in Paris) and pressed onto the surface of the eyeball, but this surface is so immense a frame that areas of it remain unmarked, empty or unused. This is not to say that Proust has forever forsworn a conventional view of visual causality. The role of the retina in vision is not denied. It is rather that fullness of feeling concentrates the world on the surface of the eye, where it is framed and where it is also the recipient of an ocular touch. Marcel's Nietzschean fullness of feeling is such that while he seems to set aside the Keplerean connection between retina and external objects, confining his impression to the surface of the eye as both bearer of their weight – what Barthes, as we saw earlier, might call their 'pression' (see I, 152) – and containing frame, his ocular surface tissue has grown so vast that those objects cannot reach out and touch every part of it. It might seem, then, that the paradox of touch and vision has been obliquely resolved. At the same time, we must be cautious in assuming that the touch of the eye represents an overcoming or resolution of Marcel's sense of alienation: frightening distance as much as haptic joy may be aspects bestowed on sight by the very things that vision itself constructs and comprehends.

Returning to Barthes's observations about distance and proximity in Cayrol, we might say that, at times, 'matter moves away' ('la matière s'éloigne' (I, 152)) in *À la recherche*. At others, however, it is intoxicatingly close. Marcel can thus be said to experience the matter of objects both at a classical distance and within a pleasurable version of Cayrol's modern closeness. However, things are stranger – more varied – than this. The distancing of matter in Proust does not imply, as it seems to in 'classical' art (at least for Barthes), a view of 'spatiality' ('la spatialité') as 'a series of depths' ('un enchaînement de profondeurs' (I, 153)). While it might be conventional to assume that perception, experience and consciousness are not fully separable, Marcel describes consciousness as if it were somehow a hindrance to perception, that is to say, as the condition of a distance between subject and object (narrator and world). Objects acquire an impenetrable surface – a spiritual outline or edging (a 'mince liséré'). Marcel's world is full of objects, but he is not a (simple) describer of objects that happen to be quite complex things. His is a world that includes the describer as well as the external objects he describes. He uses a range of devices and masks that seem to hide the external world behind teasing phenomenological thresholds. The text conjures glimpses or flashes of pictorial surfaces, for example, to show that consciousness is limited and oblique. Classical distance is thus combined with a 'worrying juxtaposition of surfaces' ('juxtaposition inquiétante de surfaces' (I, 153)) that is, for Barthes, unique to the modern novel. Similarly, the narrator's fullness of feeling and sense of closeness to objects is infected at its edges with contradiction: while eye and object are brought closer together in spatial terms, to have the eye reach out to touch the surface of another object is to have it do what is categorially alien to it. In Proust's dialectic, vision and touch are synthesized as the same, but the surface of a table (for example) also expands to touch the eye and in doing so threatens to blind it. The narrator's fullness of feeling and sense of closeness to objects is thus always at risk of loss. The modern gaze that is short enough to reach objects ('assez court pour atteindre des objets' (I, 151)) is almost no gaze at all – or is at least a seriously handicapped one. The (classical) distance of objects figures prominently in Proust's work, then, but it does so, paradoxically, as a consequence of extreme perceptual proximity.

Proust's treatment of objects thus makes Barthes's classical/modern distinction a bit problematic. In the following well-known passage, we encounter further difficulties as Marcel compares the effects of recent photographic innovations and his experience of approaching and kissing Albertine's cheek:

> Apart from the most recent applications of the art of photography – which set crouching at the foot of a cathedral all the houses which, time and again, when we stood near them, have appeared to us to reach almost to the height of the towers, drill and deploy like a regiment, in file, in open order, in mass, the same famous and familiar structures, bring into actual contact the two columns on the Piazzetta which a moment ago were so far apart, thrust away the adjoining dome of the Salute, and in a pale and toneless background manage to include a whole immense horizon within the span of a bridge, in the embrasure of a window, among the leaves of a tree that stands in the foreground and is portrayed in a more vigorous tone, give successively as setting to the same church the arched walls of all the others – I can think of nothing that can so effectively as a kiss evoke from what we believe to be a thing with one definite aspect, the hundred other things which it may equally well be since each is related to a view of it that is no less legitimate. (ALR, II, 660)[64]

In *Proust et les signes*, Deleuze heralds the disparate shifting fragments of Albertine's face as a sign of the 'final blur in which the face is released and undone' ('brouillage final où le visage [...] se déboîte et se défait').[65] Moving closer to an object, either with Marcel's puckered lips or with Cayrol's outstretched arm,[66] brings about a 'worrying juxtaposition of surfaces' by virtue of which a thing with one definite aspect, in this case Albertine, is no longer visible: she has exploded into 'dix Albertines' (*ALR*, II, 660). The object (or face) that is close does not possess, as it does in Cayrol, the 'necessary form of a familiarity' ('forme nécessaire d'une familiarité' (I, 152)). For Marcel, the fascination of the photograph stems from its capacity simultaneously to represent real objects and – like kissing – to disrupt our sense that this is a reality in which we feel at home.[67] Its effect is uncanny. The familiar things and places that are known to us may be reconfigured as places and things known only to – or within – the entity of the image. In the passage above, the columns of the Piazzetta come together in an image that seems both to emanate from the real and to set real objects in new relations with each other; the latter retain their identity whilst taking on new aspects. In reflecting on the mutability of objects in this way, Proust moves away from Cayrol and in doing so comes closer to Robbe-Grillet.

Given Proust's domination of the French literary scene of the twentieth century (and arguably of the twenty-first), we might expect his treatment of objects to sit comfortably alongside that of 'modern' writers such as Cayrol and Robbe-Grillet. As Barthes understands such creatures, however, Proust is neither an 'homme moderne' nor an 'homme classique' – at least not fully. This is not to say that Proust's way with objects is simply different from Cayrol's (that Proust is more classical than the modern Cayrol, for example), but rather that his descriptions of objects allow us to add phenomenological complexity to rigid distinctions between classical art and modernity – that Marcel's encounters with objects, his proxemic ordeals, can be understood as a convoluted negotiation between the extremes that Barthes identifies. In the currency of Barthes, then, Proust's novel is not quite between two centuries,[68] but rather an unstable middle ground, a shifting mediation ('mitoyenneté') between literary phenomenologies which, for Barthes, are fundamentally opposed.[69] *À la recherche* is a work in which what we might dare to call influence, understood as a circulation of languages or as contact between them, is played out. Its liminal rhythms rub off on Barthes: he integrates the language of Proust within the *nouveau-roman*'s revolutionary 'chosisme' in order, paradoxically, to describe the ontological distances by which they are separated.

Notes

1   See <http://en.wikipedia.org/wiki/Marcel_Proust> [accessed 1 June 2019]. The others were John Banville, Samuel Beckett, Truman Capote, Jean Cocteau, Gilles Deleuze, Graham Greene, Jack Kerouac, Eric de Kuyper, Naguib Mahfouz, Manuel Mujica Láinez, Iris Murdoch, Vladimir Nabokov, Orhan Pamuk, John Updike, Edmund White and Virginia Woolf. The page also included a list of 'influences'.

2   A list of Barthes's various 'influences' remains (Proust is not included): see <http://en.wikipedia.org/wiki/Roland_Barthes> [accessed 1 June 2019].

3   The interview was, in fact, published under this very title: 'Je ne crois pas aux influences' (see II, 615–19). Jacques Derrida shares Barthes's hostility to the notion. In *L'Écriture et la différence* (1967), for example, we read the following: 'Here, I am talking about convergences, not influence: first of all, because that is a notion whose philosophical meaning is not clear to me' ('Nous parlons ici de convergences et non d'influence; d'abord parce que c'est là une notion dont le sens philosophique ne nous est pas clair') ('Violence et métaphysique', in *L'Écriture et la différence* (Paris: Seuil, 1967), pp. 117–228 (p. 164)).

4   See II, 616: 'la notion de *circulation* me paraît plus juste que celle d'*influence*; les livres sont plutôt des "monnaies" que des "forces"'.

5   'Je ne demanderais pas mieux que d'avouer une influence "négative", car je ne pense pas qu'en littérature une attitude "negative" soit forcément "appauvrissante"; la réflexion sur les limites, les détections ou les impossibilités de l'écriture est un élément essentiel de la création littéraire, et, depuis cent ans, de Mallarmé à Blanchot, il s'est écrit de très grandes œuvres à partir de ce *creux*; même l'œuvre de Proust, qui nous paraît si positive, si libérante, est née explicitement d'un livre impossible à écrire'.

6   See, for example, *Le Degré zéro de l'écriture*, I, 194.

7   'Cependant, je le répète, négatives ou non, je ne crois pas aux influences; il se peut que j'aie donné – passagèrement, partiellement et au prix peut-être de quelques malentendus – une voix intellectuelle – et même intellectualiste – à certaines préoccupations créatrices de certains contemporains; mais ce n'a jamais été qu'un contact de langages'. Fanny Lorent explores the 'adventure of a contact' ('l'aventure d'un contact') between Barthes, Robbe-Grillet and Cayrol in *Barthes et Robbe-Grillet: un dialogue critique* (Brussels: Les Impressions nouvelles, 2015), p. 7.

8   See II, 776: 'double this work with a second act of speech' ('doubler cette œuvre d'une autre parole').

9   'comme un bon menuisier qui rapproche en tâtonnant "intelligemment" deux pièces d'un meuble compliqué' (II, 505).

10   Bowie, 'Barthes on Proust', p. 516.

11   See II, 505: 'Proust, c'est Proust'.

12 'La critique n'a pas à dire si Proust a dit "vrai", si le baron de Charlus était bien le comte de Montesquiou, si Françoise était Céleste, ou même, d'une façon plus générale, si la société qu'il a décrite reproduisait avec exactitude les conditions historiques d'élimination de la noblesse à la fin du XIXe siècle; son rôle est uniquement d'élaborer elle-même un langage dont la cohérence, la logique [...] puisse recueillir, ou mieux "intégrer" (au sens mathématique du terme) la plus grande quantité de langage proustien'. I have taken – and occasionally modified – translations of this work from the following edition: Roland Barthes, 'What Is Criticism?', in *Critical Essays*, trans. Richard Howard (Evanston: Northwestern University Press, 1972), pp. 255–60.

13 As we saw in the Introduction, Barthes says that Proust is singular to the extent that 'all he leaves us to do is *rewrite him*, which is the exact contrary of exhausting him' ('il ne nous laisse rien d'autre à faire que ceci: *le réécrire*, qui est le contraire même de l'épuiser' ('Table ronde sur Proust', p. 30)).

14 This is not to say, of course, that readers are not lured into seeking such pleasures. In *La Préparation du roman*, Barthes views the pursuit of 'keys' ('clefs') as an activity that *À la recherche* both stimulates and problematizes: 'the Keys are of the order of a deceptive *illusion*, but that illusion functions as a Surplus-Value of Reading [...] illusion is the very foundation of reading' ('les Clefs sont de l'ordre du *leurre*, mais ce leurre fonctionne comme une Plus-Value de la Lecture [...] le leurre est le fondement même de la lecture' (p. 396)).

15 Even if we accept that, for Barthes, the meta-language of critical discourse should move towards 'the silence and the expressionless neutrality of an equation' (Bowie, 'Barthes on Proust', p. 516), this does not explain his reference to mathematical integration. While Alan Sokal, Jean Bricmont or Jacques Bouveresse would almost certainly not approve, an attempt to describe what Barthes could mean by integration 'in the mathematical sense of the term' in the context of a critical analysis of Proust (and using terms that may be formally instructive or heuristic rather than mathematically rigorous) might read as follows (I am indebted to Dr Jim Baldwin for this summary): let us identify with Proust's text our variable, call it x. And let us identify with our conclusion some other variable, y, which could be described loosely as a function or functional of x. One could argue that y is built in the following way: while x is continuous, we can chop it into pieces. Each piece can be made smaller and smaller until its width limits to zero. It approaches zero but never gets there: it is infinitely thin. Let us call each tiny piece δx. Our y, naturally, is a sum of other arguments and sub-conclusions, each of which is a function of the text, and these arguments we will call $f(x)$. We can associate each δx with a function of each piece: '$f(\delta x)$'. If we were to add up all of these '$f(\delta x)$'s, we would arrive at y. Integration is precisely this summing up. In 'Introduction à l'analyse structurale des récits' (1966), Barthes is not far from suggesting that the slicings, functions and associations at work in structural analysis amount to 'integration' understood in this way. He writes: '[s]ince any

system can be defined as a combination of units pertaining to certain known classes, the first step is to break down the narrative and determine whatever segments of narrative discourse can be distributed into a limited number of classes; in other words, to define the smallest narrative units. According to the integrative perspective defined here, a purely distributional definition of units will not do: meaning must be, from the very first, the criterion by which units are determined. It is the functional character of certain segments of the story that makes units of them, hence the name of "functions" that was immediately attributed to those first units' ('[t]out système étant la combinaison d'unités dont les classes sont connues, il faut d'abord découper le récit et déterminer les segments du discours narratif que l'on puisse distribuer dans un petit nombre de classes; en un mot, il faut définir les plus petites unités narratives. Selon la perspective intégrative qui a été définie ici, l'analyse ne peut se contenter d'une définition purement distributionnelle des unités: il faut que le sens soit dès l'abord le critère d'unité: c'est le caractère fonctionnel de certains segments de l'histoire qui en fait des unités: d'où le nom de "fonctions" que l'on a tout de suite donné à ces premières unités' (II, 835–36)). The translation of this passage is taken from the following edition: Roland Barthes, 'An Introduction to the Structural Analysis of Narrative', trans. Lionel Duisit, *New Literary History*, 6/2 (Winter 1975), pp. 237–72 (p. 244).

16   These are definitions of 'couvrir' in the *Trésor de la langue française informatisé*.

17   Bowie, 'Barthes on Proust', p. 514.

18   Maurice Blanchot's *Le Livre à venir*, which contains an essay entitled 'L'Expérience de Proust', was published in 1959. 'L'Expérience de Proust' first appeared under the title 'Proust' in *La Nouvelle Revue française* in 1954.

19   'les plus grandes œuvres de la modernité s'arrêtent-elles le plus longtemps possible, par une sorte de tenue miraculeuse, au seuil de la Littérature, dans cet état vestibulaire où l'épaisseur de la vie est donnée, étirée sans pourtant être encore détruite par le couronnement d'un ordre des signes: par exemple, il y a la première personne de Proust, dont toute l'œuvre tient à un effort, prolongé et retardé vers la Littérature'. I have taken – and occasionally modified – translations of this work from the following edition: Roland Barthes, *Writing Degree Zero*, trans. Annette Lavers and Colin Smith (London: Jonathan Cape, 1967).

20   For a detailed analysis of the role of 'superposition' in Proust's work, see Malcolm Bowie, 'Reading Proust between the Lines', in *The Strange M. Proust*, ed. André Benhaïm (Oxford: Legenda, 2009), pp. 125–34.

21   'tout au long de son œuvre immense, Proust est toujours sur le point d'écrire, il vise à l'acte littéraire traditionnel, mais le remet sans cesse, et c'est au terme de cette attente *jamais honorée* que l'œuvre se trouve construite malgré elle: c'est l'attente elle-même qui a formé l'épaisseur d'une œuvre dont le caractère *suspendu* a suffi à fonder la parole de l'écrivain'. Barthes confuses

author and narrator here and elsewhere (see II, 616 or I, 500, for example). As Simon suggests, '[u]nlike the narrator of the *Recherche*, Proust, who devoted fifteen years of his life to the writing of his work, is absolutely not bound by a Blanchovian procrastination or rhetoric of the "book to come"' ('Proust, contrairement au narrateur de la *Recherche*, n'est absolument pas dans le dilatoire ni dans la rhétorique blanchotienne du "livre à venir" lorsque, pendant quinze ans, il consacre sa vie à l'écriture de son œuvre' (*Trafics de Proust*, p. 178)).

22 As Barthes puts it in *La Préparation du roman*: 'the Novel remains at the level of [...] its Preparation' ('le Roman en reste à [...] sa Préparation' (p. 49)). We will return to the relationship between *À la recherche* and Barthes's conception of 'le Roman' – and its preparation – in Chapter Four.

23 See I, 500: 'The most conscious forms of novel-writing today are all part of this Proustian movement by which the writer sets his novel going before our eyes and then consigns it to silence at a point when, a hundred years earlier, he would have barely begun to speak' ('Aujourd'hui, les états les plus conscients de la création romanesque participent tous à ce mouvement proustien par lequel l'écrivain institue son roman devant nous et le renverse dans le silence au moment où cent ans plus tôt il aurait à peine commencé à parler').

24 'Pour saisir la nature temporelle de l'objet chez Robbe-Grillet, il faut observer les mutations qu'il lui fait subir, et ici encore opposer la nature révolutionnaire de sa tentative aux normes de la description classique. Celle-ci, sans doute, a su soumettre ses objets à des forces de dégradation. Mais précisément, c'était comme si l'objet, depuis longtemps constitué dans son espace ou sa substance, rencontrait ultérieurement une Nécessité descendue de l'empyrée; le Temps classique n'a d'autre figure que celle d'un destructeur de perfection (Chronos et sa faux). Chez Balzac, chez Flaubert, chez Baudelaire, chez Proust même (mais sur un mode inversé), l'objet est porteur d'un mélodrame; il se dégrade, disparaît ou retrouve une gloire dernière, participe en somme à une véritable eschatologie de la matière. On pourrait dire que l'objet classique n'est jamais que l'archétype de sa propre ruine, ce qui revient à opposer à l'essence spatiale de l'objet, un Temps ultérieur (donc extérieur) qui fonctionnerait comme un destin et non comme une dimension interne. Le temps classique ne rencontre jamais l'objet que pour lui être catastrophe ou déliquescence'. I have taken – and occasionally modified – translations of this work from the following edition: Roland Barthes, 'Objective Literature', in *Critical Essays*, trans. Richard Howard (Evanston: Northwestern University Press, 1972), pp. 13–24.

25 It is not entirely clear why this should be the case. Is it because *À la recherche* begins, more or less, with the glory of the madeleine episode? Or could it be because the destructive effects of time on the object are somehow redeemed in involuntary memory and its 'translation' into writing?

26 'Robbe-Grillet donne à ses objets un tout autre type de mutabilité. C'est une mutabilité dont le processus est invisible: un objet, décrit une première fois

à un moment du continu romanesque, reparaît plus tard, muni d'une différence à peine perceptible. Cette différence est d'ordre spatial, situationnel (par exemple, ce qui était à droite, se trouve à gauche). Le temps déboîte l'espace et constitue l'objet comme une suite de tranches qui se recouvrent presque complètement les unes les autres: c'est dans ce "presque" spatial que gît la dimension temporelle de l'objet. Il s'agit donc d'un type de variation que l'on retrouve grossièrement dans le mouvement des plaques d'une lanterne magique ou des bandes de "Comics"'.

27 'la vue est le seul sens où le continu soit addition de champs minuscules mais entiers: l'espace ne peut supporter que des variations *accomplies*: l'homme ne participe jamais visuellement au processus interne d'une dégradation'.

28 'Les parties du mur couvertes de peintures de lui, toutes homogènes les unes aux autres, étaient comme les images lumineuses d'une lanterne magique laquelle eût été, dans le cas présent, la tête de l'artiste et dont on n'eût pu soupçonner l'étrangeté tant qu'on n'aurait fait que connaître l'homme, c'est-à-dire tant qu'on n'eût fait que voir la lanterne coiffant la lampe, avant qu'aucun verre coloré eût encore été placé. Parmi ces tableaux, quelques-uns de ceux qui semblaient le plus ridicules aux gens du monde m'intéressaient plus que les autres en ce qu'ils recréaient ces illusions d'optique qui nous prouvent que nous n'identifierions pas les objets si nous ne faisions pas intervenir le raisonnement'.

29 See *ALR*, II, 712: 'surfaces and volumes are in reality independent of the names of objects that our memory imposes on them after we have recognized them' ('les surfaces et les volumes sont en réalité indépendants des noms d'objets que notre mémoire leur impose').

30 J. Theodore Johnson, Jr. has suggested that Elstir's studio appears like a giant magic lantern, and that the artist personifies the light source and projects the images. As Johnson notes, Proust himself makes this connection elsewhere in the novel (see Johnson, 'La Lanterne Magique: Proust's Metaphorical Toy', *L'Esprit Créateur*, 11/1 (Spring 1971), pp. 17–31 (especially pp. 28–30)). For a more recent examination of the significance of the magic lantern (as a means of exploring the relationship between subjectivity and embodiment), see Johanna Malt, 'The Blob and the Magic Lantern: On Subjectivity, Faciality and Projection', *Paragraph*, 36/3 (2013), pp. 305–23.

31 See *ALR*, IV, 496–531. In what follows, I occasionally use the name Marcel to refer to the narrator of *À la recherche*. As we shall see in Chapter Four, Barthes identifies with a different 'Marcel' in two texts from the late 1970s.

32 'Nouvelle transversale ici, car le valet de chambre de ce grand-oncle, qui m'avait introduit ce jour-là et qui plus tard m'avait par le don d'une photographie permis d'identifier la Dame en rose, était le père du jeune homme que non seulement M. de Charlus, mais le père même de Mlle de Saint-Loup avait aimé, pour qui il avait rendu sa mère malheureuse'.

33 According to Gilles Deleuze, there is a system of transversals at work in

Proust's text that enables movement from one worldly fragment or multiple to the next 'without ever reducing the multiple to the One' ('sans jamais ramener le multiple à l'Un'). See *Proust et les signes* (Paris: PUF, 1996), p. 153.

34 Unlike Barthes, Deleuze identifies similarities between the 'methods of describing the object' ('méthodes de description de l'objet' (*Proust et les signes*, p. 44, n. 1)) in the *nouveau roman* and in *À la recherche*. Both, he suggests, 'remain under the sign of hieroglyphs and implied truths' ('reste[nt] sous le signe des hiéroglyphes et des vérités impliquées' (p. 44, n. 1)).

35 We will return to the significance of variation in Barthes's understanding of the role of the critic in later chapters.

36 Barthes, 'Table ronde sur Proust', pp. 42–43.

37 Barthes, 'Table ronde sur Proust', p. 42.

38 Bowie, 'Barthes on Proust', p. 516.

39 Bowie, 'Barthes on Proust', p. 516.

40 Bowie, 'Barthes on Proust', p. 516.

41 'Que l'on pense à un grand roman du XVIIIe siècle, aux *Liaisons dangereuses,* par exemple, on n'y trouvera aucun objet: les personnages circulent dans un espace sans matière, [...] leur regard ne se pose jamais que sur des significations; on dirait que ce regard n'est pas assez court pour atteindre des objets'. Barthes makes similar claims elsewhere. In 'Les Planches de l'*Encyclopédie*' (1964), he observes that '[t]he object [...], humanly, is a very ambiguous thing; we have noted that for a long time our literature did not acknowledge it' ('[l]'objet [...], humainement, est une chose très ambigüe; on a vu que pendant longtemps notre littérature ne l'a pas reconnu' (IV, 44)), and in *La Préparation du roman*, he discusses the rarity of tangible objects in 'classical' texts such as Laclos's ('rareté des *tangibilia* dans le texte (par exemple *Les Liaisons dangereuses*)' (p. 94)).

42 'tout est fait pour écarter l'homme de la lutte directe avec l'espace, pour interposer, entre l'homme et son milieu, un retard salutaire pendant lequel l'espace se construit, la matière s'éloigne et perd ce caractère insolite et gênant des objets privés de recul'.

43 'ou bien l'étouffement (Ionesco), ou bien la nausée (Sartre)' ('Les Planches de l'*Encyclopédie*', IV, 44).

44 'Signé[s] par l'homme'. As far as the plates of the *Encyclopédie* are concerned, the 'vignette' is the name given to the 'large-scale *tableau-vivant*' ('grande scène vivante' (IV, 41–42)) in which objects are represented in a human context.

45 See I, 194, for example.

46 'De la place, il n'y en avait pas pour moi dans ma chambre de Balbec (mienne de nom seulement), elle était pleine de choses qui ne me connaissaient pas, me rendirent le coup d'œil méfiant que je leur jetai et sans tenir aucun compte de mon existence, témoignèrent que je dérangeais le train-train de la leur. [...] J'étais tourmenté par la présence de bibliothèques à vitrines, qui

couraient le long des murs, mais surtout par une grande glace à pieds, arrêtée en travers de la pièce et avant le départ de laquelle je sentais qu'il n'y aurait pas pour moi de détente possible'.

47 'À l'hôtel: mauvaise lampe de chevet, pas de lampe de travail, obscurité sans familiarité ≠ reconstitution artificielle et sophistiquée d'une proxémie' (*Comment vivre ensemble*, p. 157). I have taken – and occasionally modified – translations of this work from the following edition: Roland Barthes, *How to Live Together: Novelistic Simulations of Some Everyday Spaces. Notes for a Lecture Course and Seminar at the Collège de France (1976–1977)*, trans. Kate Briggs (New York: Columbia University Press, 2013). Marcel's tormentors are not a lousy bedside lamp or an unhomely darkness, of course, but an unfamiliar clock, curtains, bookcases and mirror. For Barthes, the ill person's bed is marked by 'the most powerful proxemy' ('la proxémie la plus forte'), and the prime example of a proxemic bed is that of Aunt Léonie (see *Comment vivre ensemble*, p. 157). Just like the objects of habit in Marcel's Parisian nest, his aunt's bed 'is, as it were, part of the body; bodily prosthesis, like a fifth limb' ('fait en quelque sorte partie du corps; protèse du corps, comme un cinquième membre' (*Comment vivre ensemble*, p. 157)). A number of Barthes's examples of proxemy have a distinctly Proustian ring to them. Indeed, the first reads like a truncated rewrite of the descriptions of sleep and habit in the opening pages of 'Combray': 'Evening: I go to bed, I turn out the light, I disappear beneath the covers to sleep. But I need to blow my nose. I stretch out my arm in the darkness and, without fail, I locate the top drawer of the bedside table, and in this drawer, no less infallibly, I find a handkerchief that is on the right. I put it back and close the drawer again just as infallibly' ('Soir: je me couche, j'éteins, je m'enfonce sous les couvertures pour dormir. Mais j'ai envie de me moucher. Dans l'obscurité, j'allonge le bras, j'atteins sans me tromper le premier tiroir de la table de nuit, et dans ce tiroir, non moins infailliblement, un mouchoir qui est à droite. Je repose et je referme aussi infailliblement' (p. 155)).

48 'sommeil, repos, du travail sédentaire chez soi: la sphère du "geste immédiat"' (*Comment vivre ensemble*, p. 155).

49 *Comment vivre ensemble*, p. 158.

50 Barthes discusses the proxemy of his own bed (in a sanatorium) in *La Préparation du roman* (see p. 307).

51 'Si nous pensions que les yeux d'une telle fille ne sont qu'une brillante rondelle de mica, nous ne serions pas avides de connaître et d'unir à nous sa vie. Mais nous sentons que ce qui luit dans ce disque réfléchissant n'est pas dû uniquement à sa composition matérielle; que ce sont, inconnues de nous, les noires ombres des idées que cet être se fait, relativement aux gens et aux lieux qu'il connaît [...]. Je savais que je ne posséderais pas cette jeune cycliste si je ne possédais aussi ce qu'il y avait dans ses yeux. Et c'était par conséquent toute sa vie qui m'inspirait du désir; désir douloureux, parce que je le sentais

irréalisable, mais enivrant, parce que ce qui avait été jusque-là ma vie ayant brusquement cessé d'être ma vie totale, n'étant plus qu'une petite partie de l'espace étendu devant moi que je brûlais de couvrir, et qui était fait de la vie de ces jeunes filles, m'offrait ce prolongement, cette multiplication possible de soi-même, qui est le bonheur'.

52　Jean-Paul Sartre, *L'Être et le néant* (Paris: Gallimard, 1943), p. 309. According to Sartre, my fundamental relation to others is always tinged with anxiety. A necessary condition of 'Being' is vulnerability. I must constantly come to terms with the possibility of being seen by the 'Other'. When the 'Other' looks at me, I am immediately objectified. It is 'in and through the revelation of my being-as-object for the Other that I must be able to grasp the presence of his or her being-as-subject' ('dans et par la révélation de mon être-objet pour autrui que je dois pouvoir saisir la présence de son être-sujet' (p. 296)). I thus experience the gaze of the 'Other' as an intrusion, a haemorrhage within the 'centre' of my world (p. 294).

53　For a discussion of the role of pictures and picturing in Proust's novel, see Thomas Baldwin, *The Picture as Spectre in Diderot, Proust and Deleuze* (Oxford: Legenda, 2011).

54　'le réalisme (bien mal nommé, en tout cas souvent mal interprété) consiste, non à copier le réel, mais à copier une copie (peinte) du réel: ce fameux réel, comme sous l'effet d'une peur qui interdirait de le toucher directement, *est remis plus loin*, différé, ou du moins saisi à travers la gangue picturale dont on l'enduit avant de le soumettre à la parole'.

55　In 1971, Barthes expresses the same view about Eugène Fromentin's *Dominique* of 1862: 'This pure subject who lives in a world untouched by triviality: everyday objects only exist for him if they are part of a painting, a "composition"' ('Ce sujet pur vit dans un monde sans trivialité: les objets quotidiens n'existent pour lui que s'ils peuvent faire partie d'un tableau, d'une "composition"' ('Fromentin: *Dominique*', IV, 96)).

56　I discuss boundary crossing of this kind in Chapter Two of *The Picture as Spectre in Diderot, Proust and Deleuze* (pp. 67–96).

57　For further analysis of the 'model of painting' as it pertains to Balzac's artist stories (including *Sarrasine*), see Diana Knight, *Balzac and the Model of Painting: Artist Stories in 'La Comédie humaine'* (Oxford: Legenda, 2007).

58　'quand je voyais un objet extérieur, la conscience que je le voyais restait entre moi et lui, le bordait d'un mince liséré spirituel qui m'empêchait de jamais toucher directement sa matière'.

59　'Je gardais, dans mon logis, la même plénitude de sensation que j'avais eue dehors. Elle bombait de telle façon l'apparence de surfaces qui nous semblent si souvent plates et vides, la flamme jaune du feu, le papier gros bleu du ciel sur lequel le soir avait brouillonné, comme un collégien, les tire-bouchons d'un crayonnage rose, le tapis à dessin singulier de la table ronde sur laquelle une rame de papier écolier m'attendaient avec un roman de Bergotte, que, depuis, ces choses ont continué à me sembler riches de toute une sorte particulière d'existence'.

60 'ce point insupportable où l'esprit touche la matière et en vit chaque intensité, la consomme' (Gilles Deleuze and Félix Guattari, *Capitalisme et schizophrénie I. L'Anti-Œdipe* (Paris: Minuit, 1972–73), p. 26).

61 It is likely that, some years before he came to write of swelling things, Proust read the following passage from *Twilight of the Idols* (1889), in which Nietzsche describes a state of Dionysian ecstasy in terms that look very much like Proust's: 'In this state [of "intoxication"] we enrich everything out of our own *plenitude*: whatever we see, whatever we want, we see swollen, crammed, strong, supercharged with energy. Man in this state transforms things until they reflect his power – until they are reflections of his perfection' (*Twilight of the Idols*, trans. Duncan Large (Oxford: Oxford University Press, 1998), p. 47). Significantly, Proust contributed an article entitled 'L'Irréligion d'état' to the May 1892 edition of *Le Banquet*, which also contained an article by Dreyfus on *Twilight of the Idols* entitled 'La Philosophie du marteau' (see Duncan Large, *Nietzsche and Proust* (Oxford: Oxford University Press, 2001), p. 66, n. 12). In *Nietzsche and Proust*, Duncan Large suggests that '[w]hether or not Proust intended it to be the case, [...] his "débuts littéraires" were closely bound up with the fate of the foremost Nietzschean journal of his time. When *Le Banquet* folded in 1893, Proust, Dreyfus and Halévy all moved over to *La Revue blanche*, each to continue publishing in a similar vein to before. Moreover, Proust also contributed to other journals and newspapers which carried pieces on Nietzsche over the same period' (pp. 66–67).

62 For a discussion of Keplerean optics, see Svetlana Alpers, *The Art of Describing: Dutch Art in the Seventeenth Century* (Chicago: University of Chicago Press, 1983). It should be noted that while Proust is talking about a convexity of surface, Kepler refers to the image that is formed on the concave surface of the retina.

63 'La mer, que j'apercevais à côté de la vallée dans la fenêtre, les seins bombés des premières falaises de Maineville, le ciel où la lune n'était pas encore montée au zénith, tout cela semblait plus léger à porter pour les globes de mes prunelles qu'entre mes paupières je sentais dilatés, résistants, prêts à soulever bien d'autres fardeaux, toutes les montagnes du monde, sur leur surface délicate. Leur orbe ne se trouvait pas suffisamment rempli par la sphère même de l'horizon'.

64 'Les dernières applications de la photographie – qui couchent au pied d'une cathédrale toutes les maisons qui nous parurent si souvent, de près, presque aussi hautes que les tours, font successivement manœuvrer comme un régiment, par files, en ordre dispersé, en masses serrées, les mêmes monuments, rapprochent l'une contre l'autre les deux colonnes de la Piazzetta tout à l'heure si distantes, éloignent la proche Salute et dans un fond pâle et dégradé réussissent à faire tenir un horizon immense sous l'arche d'un pont, dans

l'embrasure d'une fenêtre, entre les feuilles d'un arbre situé au premier plan et d'un ton plus vigoureux, donnent successivement pour cadre à une même église les arcades de toutes les autres – je ne vois que cela qui puisse, autant que le baiser, faire surgir de ce que nous croyions une chose à aspect défini, les cent autres choses qu'elle est tout aussi bien, puisque chacune est relative à une perspective non moins légitime'.

65 Deleuze, *Proust et les signes*, p. 212.

66 See I, 153: 'as soon as an author extends his arm in the direction of an object' ('dès qu'un auteur étend son bras vers un objet').

67 Áine Larkin examines the role of photographs and photography in *À la recherche* in *Proust Writing Photography: Fixing the Fugitive in 'À la recherche du temps perdu'* (Oxford: Legenda, 2011), and both Marty and Yacavone have discussed the relationship between Proust and photography as Barthes understands it (see Marty, 'Marcel Proust dans "la chambre claire"', and Yacavone, 'Reading through Photography' and 'Barthes et Proust').

68 See Antoine Compagnon, *Proust entre deux siècles* (Paris: Seuil, 1989).

69 See *S/Z*, III, 141: 'mediation upsets the rhetorical – or paradigmatic – harmony of Antithesis' ('La mitoyenneté trouble l'harmonie rhétorique – ou paradigmatique – de l'Antithèse').

CHAPTER TWO

Eros, Rhythm

In *Le Plaisir du texte*, Barthes distinguishes two regimes of reading. The first, he says, goes 'straight to the articulations of the anecdote' and 'considers the extent of the text, ignores the play of language' (IV, 225).[1] I lose discourse ('Je perds du discours' (IV, 225)), and yet my reading is not, Barthes argues, 'fascinated by any verbal loss – in the speleological sense of that word' (IV, 225).[2] In contrast, the second regime is enthralled by such linguistic playfulness and loss (the speleological connotations of which we shall return to in a moment):

> The other reading skips nothing; it weighs, it sticks to the text, it reads, so to speak, with application and transport, grasps at every point in the text the asyndeton that cuts languages – and not the anecdote: it is not (logical) extension that captivates it, the winnowing-out of truths, but the layering of *signifiance*. (IV, 225)[3]

While Barthes's first reading diet is more suited to consumers of the classics,[4] the second is prescribed for readers of modern texts. I do not devour the modern work. I take my time: I 'graze' ('brouter').[5] There is pleasure in both regimes of reading, of course, but it is only the second that is, for Barthes, the source of truly erotic bliss.

How, then, does Barthes understand the erotic? In an interview with Hasumi Shiguéhiko in 1972, he contends that he is moving away from what concerned him in his 'scientific' past (while refusing nevertheless to deny its value). His semiological fantasy ('fantasme') has given way to the solicitations of a 'theory of the signifier, of the literary erotic' ('théorie du signifiant, de l'érotique littéraire').[6] In what does this new theory of the signifier consist, and how is it connected to the erotic in literary texts (and, more specifically, in Proust's novel)? A partial response to this question is provided in the following passage from 'Texte (théorie du)', first published in 1973, one year after the interview with Shiguéhiko and in the same year as *Le Plaisir du texte*:

> *Signifiance*, contrary to signification, cannot be reduced to communication, representation, expression: it places the subject (of the writer, of the reader) in the text, not as a projection, even if that projection is fantasmatic (there is no 'transport' of a constituted subject), but as a 'loss' (in the speleological sense of the word); hence its identification with *jouissance*; it is by virtue of the concept of *signifiance* that the text becomes erotic (it is in no way required to represent erotic 'scenes' in order to do this). (IV, 450)[7]

Conventionally erotic moments (of seduction, sex or whatever) are thus not a necessary condition of textual eroticism: a text can only be viewed as erotic, in fact, if it engages in what Barthes calls the 'radical work' ('travail radical' (IV, 450)) of *signifiance*. In both this passage and the section on the two regimes of reading in *Le Plaisir du texte*, the operations of *signifiance* are identified with 'loss' in the speleological sense of the word, which refers to 'a place in which a flow of water disappears, only to reappear further along'.[8] 'Perte' is not to be understood as absolute loss: the stream of *signifiance* comes and goes and, for Barthes, it is precisely in such intermittence that the erotic is to be found.

In 'Le Troisième Sens' (1970), Barthes aligns *signifiance* with what he calls 'obtuse' meaning ('le sens obtus'). *Signifiance* is to signification what obtuse meaning is to 'obvious' meaning ('le sens obvie'). Barthes describes the obvious meaning of certain film stills taken from the work of Sergei Eisenstein as a purely symbolic signification:

> It [obvious meaning] is intentional (it is what the author wanted to say) and it is taken from a kind of common, general lexicon of symbols; it is a meaning that seeks me out, me, the recipient of the message, the subject of the reading, a meaning that starts with S.M.E. [Sergei Mikhailovich Eisenstein] and that goes on *ahead of me*: evident certainly [...], but closed in its evidence, held in a complete system of destination. (III, 488)[9]

In contrast to obvious or symbolic meaning, which is endowed with a '"natural" clarity' ('clarté "naturelle"' (III, 488)) and is therefore easy to read, an obtuse, third meaning or *signifiance* is a 'supplement that my intellectual understanding cannot succeed in absorbing, at once persistent and fleeting, smooth and elusive' (III, 488).[10] It is a pathos-supplement, 'an emotion value, an evaluation' ('une émotion valeur, une évaluation' (III, 493)) within a logos-driven system of intentionality. Its 'érotisme' (III, 498), Barthes says, brings about a breakdown in the codes of signification, effecting the 'blunting' ('l'émoussement') of meaning, its 'drifting' ('dérive' (III, 498)).

Barthes's sense of the erotic as an obtuse supplement of affect will be crucial for our reading of Barthes's seminars on Proust's 'Charlus-Discourse' later in this chapter. For the time being, though, I want to work through his suggestion that *signifiance* is able to blast open 'the field of meaning totally, that is infinitely' ('le champ du sens totalement, c'est-à-dire infiniment' (III, 488)).

Erotic meaning in more detail

While *signifiance* is a scandal that disrupts and suspends the reasoned work of obvious signification, blurring the limit that separates 'natural' expression from disguise and trickery (see III, 492), it is also a *'non-negating derision* of expression' ('*dérision non-négatrice* de l'expression'), a 'postiche' that does not renounce the good faith of its referent (III, 493). Thus, while the critic who believes that a text possesses a global and secret significance ('un signifié global et secret' ('Texte (théorie du)', IV, 449)) will be confused by, or simply blind to, the infinite workings of *signifiance*, narrative logic and signification have not been abandoned altogether: 'the *contemporary* problem is not to destroy the narrative but to subvert it: today's task is to dissociate subversion from destruction' (III, 502).[11] Geological metaphors and images of superimposition abound in Barthes's attempts to describe the drifting intermittences of the erotic text. Here, in 'Le Troisième Sens', *signifiance* is understood as a laminate or multilayering, a 'feuilleté', of meaning 'that always lets the previous meaning continue, as in a geological formation' ('qui laisse toujours subsister le sens précédent, comme dans une construction géologique' (III, 493)).

This view of *signifiance* as layering, a signifying form that outplays signification without constituting an absolute elsewhere of meaning ('*ailleurs* du sens' (III, 501)), is taken up again in *Le Plaisir du texte*, where Barthes suggests that there is a psychological duality in the very apprehension of the work of art. He counters a certain structuralist rigour – the organizing decorum of a previous incarnation, perhaps – by reintroducing the shifting attentions of the reader, the source of a vicarious pleasure in the content of the text:

> There are those who want a text (an art, a painting) without a shadow, without the 'dominant ideology'; but this is to want a text without

fecundity, without productivity, a sterile text (see the myth of the Woman Without a Shadow). The text needs its shadow: this shadow is *a bit* of ideology, *a bit* of representation, *a bit* of subject: ghosts, pockets, traces, necessary clouds: subversion must produce its own *chiaroscuro*. (IV, 238)[12]

The artwork is understood here as non-presence, or rather as incomplete presence: *a bit* of presence. For Barthes, Flaubert is the creator of an underhand, perverse form of writing, and he (like Proust) possesses a means of cutting ('couper') and making holes ('trouer') in discourse without rendering it 'meaningless' ('insensé' (IV, 223)). He succeeds in producing a narrative discourse which is torn apart – made out of bits – but which is also never reduced to apparently meaningless babble. What is so strange about Flaubert, Barthes argues, is his ability to maintain the mimesis of language (a primary source of 'immense pleasures' ('grands plaisirs')) in a state of such ambiguity that it can never be fully reduced to a stable 'good conscience' ('bonne conscience') or even 'parodie' (IV, 223): the discourse of his texts is almost untenable – almost, but not fully. Famously, Barthes illustrates the notion of signifying intermittence rather than plenitude using a metaphor of the semi-clothed body and its powers of seduction:

> Is not the most erotic portion of a body *where the clothing gapes*? In perversion (which is the realm of textual pleasure) there are no erogenous zones (a foolish expression, besides); it is intermittence, as psychoanalysis has so rightly stated, that is erotic: the intermittence of skin flashing between two articles of clothing (trousers and sweater), between two edges (the open-necked shirt, the glove and the sleeve). (IV, 223)[13]

The reader of the erotic text is engaged in a syncopic game of participation and retraction, seduced by the flashes, the intermittent light of a gaping *entre-deux*: 'it is this flash itself that seduces, or rather: the staging of an appearance-disappearance' ('c'est ce scintillement même qui séduit, ou encore: la mise en scène d'une apparition-disparition' (IV, 223)). Barthes invites us here to think of reading in terms of incompletion: appearing is thought with disappearing, showing with hiding, the lure of mimetic stability and visibility with a sudden invisibility and textual instability. The eroticism of reading is understood as a delicate balancing act, requiring a special liking for textual subtlety, a taste for a non-negating and intermittent derision of logical expression – for ruptures that are controlled ('surveillées'), conformities ('conformismes') that are faked ('truqués') and 'déstructions' that are always 'indirectes' (IV, 223).

Where, then, are the 'erotic places' ('lieux érotiques' (IV, 254)) of *À la recherche*? In trying to answer this question, we will shed light on the amenability of Proust's novel not only to the semiological fantasy of structural analysis but also to a theory of the literary erotic.

Becoming erotic

In 'Une idée de recherche', first published in 1971 and one of a small number of stand-alone texts by Barthes on Proust, Proust's novel is identified as 'one of those great cosmogonies' ('l'une de ces grandes cosmogonies') whose infinite explorability 'shifts our critical work far away from any illusion of achieving a "result"' ('déporte le travail critique loin de toute illusion de "résultat"' (III, 918)).[14] We will return to this aspect of Barthes's understanding of *À la recherche* in the next chapter, in order to consider the possibility that the novel as infinite 'galaxie' (see III, 918) is a paradigm example of the writerly text. For now, though, I want to move the focus away from Barthes's views on the universe of *À la recherche* as a whole and more squarely onto his appreciation – in 'Une idée de recherche' and elsewhere – of the individual stars and constellations of which it is made. For Barthes, Proust's novel is governed by a law of reversal, an interchangeability of functions and agents that modulates throughout the book:

> Every feature is required to reverse itself, by an implacable movement of rotation: endowed with an aristocratic language, Swann can only, at a certain moment, invert it into bourgeois language. This constraint is so statutory that it renders futile, Proust says, any observation of manners: one can readily deduce them from the law of inversion. (III, 920)[15]

Barthes provides numerous examples of such rotations or reversals in 'Une idée de recherche', ranging from the solitary, vulgar, ugly old lady on the little train in Balbec, whom the narrator takes for the madam of a brothel but who turns out to be none other than Princess Sherbatoff (see III, 917), to 'the scene of the hornet' ('la scène du frelon') at the beginning of *Sodome et Gomorrhe*, during which the narrator discovers 'the Woman under the Baron de Charlus' ('la Femme sous le baron de Charlus' (III, 920)). For Barthes, it is important not to view Proust's enantiology – his discourse of reversal – as a moralistic reduction ruled by the logic of an 'only' and according to which the princess is really only a vulgar little old lady and the baron is really only a woman. If we do so, Barthes argues, we run the risk of ignoring 'the flowerings of form' ('les efflorescences de la forme') in which a metaphorical concomitance, an 'is also', is at work: 'the princess *is also* a madam' ('la princesse *est aussi* une maîtresse de bordel' (III, 921)). It could thus be argued that Proust's Marcel shares with Melville's Ishmael a 'tolerant inclusiveness', a 'disinclination for rigid partial versions and sectarian monocularity', and an 'erotized and playful porousness to the wholeness of life'.[16] Indeed, for Barthes, the play of opposites in Proust's work 'can only derive from an erotics (of discourse), as if its occasion was the very moment in which Proust came to delight in writing: studded all through the great continuum of the quest, inversion is the *supplement-bliss* of narrative, of language' (III, 919).[17]

How erotic, though, are Proust's supplements of reversal – at least as Barthes describes them? The Proustian pandemic of inversion 'conjoins two absolutely antipathetic states in one and the same object and radically reverses an appearance into its contrary' ('conjoint dans un même objet deux états absolument antipathiques et renverse radicalement une apparence en son contraire' (III, 917)). Reversal is effected according to an 'exact figure, as if a god – a *fatum* – were maliciously presiding over the trajectory that leads the princess to coincide with her geometrically determined absolute contrary' (III, 919),[18] and it controls 'the very becoming of the main characters, [which is] subject to "exact" elevations and falls' (III, 919).[19] The structural exactness – the law – of such binary contradictions is at odds with the intermittent, erotic flicker of *signifiance*: a precise, rhythmical game of contraries is out of kilter, it seems, with the wanderings of the obtuse by virtue of which a tightly packed and occasionally unglued laminate of meaning is created.

It is revealing in this regard to compare Barthes's understanding of the encounter between Charlus and Jupien in *Sodome et Gomorrhe* ('the scene of the hornet') with that of Deleuze and Guattari, for whom this meeting is the primordial example of a 'true becoming' ('véritable devenir').[20] Proust's Marcel considers the result of apomixis in plants to be similar to that of human inbreeding. Both can lead, he says, to degeneracy and sterility (see *ALR*, III, 5). In contrast, the 'crossing effected by insects gives to subsequent generations of the same species a vigour unknown to their predecessors' ('croisement opéré par les insectes donne aux générations suivantes de la même espèce une vigueur inconnue de leurs ainées' (*ALR*, III, 5)). Nevertheless, the to-ing and fro-ing of certain insects can cause the plant species to develop out of all proportion, in which case 'as an anti-toxin protects us against disease, as the thyroid gland regulates our adiposity [...], so an exceptional act of self-fertilization comes at a given point to apply its turn of the screw, to put its foot on the brake, brings back within normal limits the flower that has exaggerated its transgression of them' (*ALR*, III, 5).[21] In the language of Deleuze and Guattari, the pollen-carrying insect becomes orchid, effecting a 'becoming-orchid' of the wasp ('devenir-orchidée de la guêpe'), and the orchid becomes insect, in a 'becoming-wasp' of the orchid ('devenir-guêpe de l'orchidée').[22] The reterritorializing, braking act of the orchid's apomixis thus counters the deterritorializing effects of the insect's promiscuous consumption, which itself is understood, in the first instance, as a deterritorialization of the flower's self-pollination. In *Francis Bacon: logique de la sensation* (1981), Deleuze argues that the becoming-animal of 'l'homme' in the work of Bacon is not 'an arrangement between man and animal, nor a resemblance, but a deep identity, a zone of indiscernibility more profound than any sentimental identification'.[23] In other words, a 'devenir-animal' is not a combination of human and animal forms but 'the common fact of man and amimal' ('le fait commun de l'homme et de l'animal').[24] In becoming animal, then, the human being does not imitate or resemble an animal.[25] Instead, becoming is thought as an explosion of heterogeneous series 'on the line of flight composed by a common rhizome that can no longer be attributed to or subjugated by anything that signifies'.[26] A zone of indiscernibility between man and animal is created by a force of becoming that permits the 'évolution aparallèle'[27] of otherwise unrelated series. Thus, for Deleuze and for Guattari, becoming is the site of a heterogeneous encounter, a subtle *rencontre* rather than a straightforward fusion of disparate or precisely reversed entities.

Barthes is certainly aware of this – typically Nietzschean – take on becoming (or of something very close to it), and he aligns it explicitly with the workings of loss and *signifiance*. In the final paragraph of 'Texte (théorie du)', for example, he writes:

> the text is never *appropriated*, it situates itself within the infinite *intercourse* of codes [...] it is a science of *jouissance*, as every 'textual' text (one that has entered the field of *signifiance*) tends ultimately to provoke or to live the *loss of consciousness* (the cancellation) assumed by the subject in erotic jouissance, and it is a science of becoming (of a *subtle* becoming, the perception of which must take place, for Nietzsche, beyond the crude form of things): '[...] we are not *subtle* enough to perceive what is probably an *absolute flow* of *becoming*; the *permanent* exists only thanks to our crude organs, which summarize things and

reduce them to common levels, when in fact nothing exists *in that form*. The tree is at each instant a new thing; we assert *form* because we do not grasp the subtlety of an absolute moment'. (IV, 458–59)[28]

Barthes's view of 'the very becoming of the main characters' ('le devenir même des principaux personnages' (III, 919)) in Proust's novel as a process of exact reversals depends on a relatively unsubtle, and consequently un-erotic, approach to becoming, which is in danger of seeing only the binary stasis of arboreal, binary structures and of remaining blind to the 'écoulement' ('flow') – note the aquatic metaphor in Nietzsche as he is quoted by Barthes – of *signifiance*.

There are further difficulties when we consider how Barthes reads the narrator's encounter with the dusty faces of ageing socialites at the Princesse de Guermantes's matinee in *Le Temps retrouvé*:

> Yet there is a moment in the novel when the great inverting form no longer functions. [...] We know that all of Proust's characters come together in the last volume of the work [...]; in what condition? Not in the least inverted, but on the contrary *prolonged, paralysed* (even more than aged), *preserved*, and – the neologism is warranted – '*persevered*'. In reprieved life, inversion no longer takes: the narrative has nothing left to do but come to an end – the book has nothing left to do but begin. (III, 921)[29]

It is worth pausing for a moment here to consider Marcel's descriptions of M. d'Argencourt, one of the gentlefolk present at the matinee:

> The most extraordinary of all was my personal enemy M. d'Argencourt; he was the veritable *clou* of the party. Not only had he replaced a barely silvered beard by one of incredible whiteness, he had so tricked himself out by those little material changes which reconstitute and exaggerate personality and, more than that, apparently modify character, that this man, whose pompous and starchy stiffness still lingered in my memory, had changed into an old beggar who inspired no respect, an aged valetudinarian so authentic that his limbs trembled and the swollen features, once so arrogant, kept on smiling with silly beatitude. Pushed to this degree, the art of disguise becomes something more, it becomes a complete transformation of personality. (*ALR*, IV, 500)[30]

It is surprising that Barthes should locate the end of the great work of inversion in *À la recherche* at a moment when it appears to be at the very height of its power.[31] If there is an erotic enantiology in Proust's work, it is certainly not absent from the final pages. Moreover, while Barthes's understanding of inversion suggests an un-erotic stability and lack of subtlety, Marcel's observations concerning the creepiness of M. d'Argencourt's appearance resonate powerfully with Barthes's analysis of *signifiance* in 'Le Troisième Sens'. In that essay, commenting on a still from *Battleship Potemkin* (1925) in which a crying woman is pictured, Barthes observes that its obtuse meaning emanates from certain details – 'the funny headdress, the old woman, the squinting eyelids, the fish'[32] – that belong to 'a somewhat low language' ('un langage un peu bas'), namely that of 'a rather pitiful disguise' ('un déguisement assez pitoyable' (III, 492)). This language is combined in Eisenstein's image with an obvious meaning (noble suffering), and together they form 'a dialogism so tenuous that there is no guarantee of its intentionality' ('un dialogisme si ténu [...] qu'on ne peut en garantir l'intentionnalité' (III, 492)). Marcel suggests that M. d'Argencourt's transformation is the consequence of the art of disguise taken to its extreme. On the face of it, it seems that such out-and-out metamorphosis cannot function erotically (in accordance with a principle of obtuseness or *signifiance*) insofar as it serves to counteract the effects of a theatrical dialogism on which, for Barthes, the erotic depends. The narrator's suggestion that 'to compare him with an actor was an overstatement for, having no conscious mind at all, he was like a shaky doll with a woollen beard stuck on his face pottering around the room' (*ALR*, IV, 502)[33] could be said to reinforce this view. Nevertheless, his lack of credentials as an actor notwithstanding, the figure of the doddery old automaton presents the narrator with a difficult task of reading. While the beard may look false, Marcel also knows that it is real, and he is able to make out past identities beneath the layers of the extreme makeover: 'Puppets that one could only identify as those one had known previously by reading simultaneously across several levels that were situated behind them and that gave them depth' (*ALR*, IV, 503).[34] The narrator thus encounters M. d'Argencourt's face as an erotic multilayering of meaning, a geological construction in which the contemporary puppet is to be envisaged – read – in all of its temporal thickness.

The narrator's reading provides a model for our own reading of *À la recherche* itself, which cannot ignore the 'instances of layering', the 'uncanny repetitions and whispered refrains' that, as Malcolm Bowie has shown, are a key element of the 'strangeness' of Proust's book.[35] While, in 'Une idée de recherche', Barthes reduces the variations and superimpositions in Proust's work to an exact game of reversals played out between binary opposites, his approach elsewhere is more in keeping with the erotic, intermittent flow of its *signifiance*. During the 1972 round-table discussion on Proust cited in previous chapters, Barthes invites Genette to reconsider his insistence on the need for an 'extreme attention to the temporal/spatial disposition of thematic signifiers'[36] in *À la recherche*, which implies, problematically for Barthes, that 'in analysing variations, one seeks a theme' and that 'one is entirely within a hermeneutic'.[37] He observes:

> we must not forget that in the history of music, there is a great work that pretends to use the 'theme and variations' structure but in fact undoes it: Beethoven's variations on a waltz by Diabelli [...]. You can see that we are dealing with thirty-three variations without a theme. And there is a theme that is given at the beginning, which is a very silly theme, but one that is given precisely, to some extent, for the sake of derision. I would say that Beethoven's variations here function a little like Proust's work.[38]

Thus, for Barthes, instead of referring back to an object that would be their ultimate cause, the variations of metaphor in Proust set in motion what Paul de Man calls 'an imaging activity that refers to no object in particular'.[39] The sense of 'derision' that informs Barthes's understanding of erotic *signifiance* is also in evidence here. It might be argued, however, that in destroying the origin of metaphor,[40] Proust's variations are not the purveyors of a tenuous dialogism between signification and *signifiance*. Nevertheless, Barthes seems to have moderated his views in this regard in *Comment vivre ensemble*, where he considers the possibility of a 'new rhetoric (of non-method)' ('nouvelle rhétorique (de la non-méthode)') in which there would be an 'unlimited right to digression' (droit illimité à la digression' (p. 182)). Further on, he suggests that 'we could even imagine, tendentiously, a work, a lecture series, which would be made up only of digressions [...]. *Cf.* the *Diabelli Variations*: the theme is more or less inexistent, an extremely vague memory flashes through the thirty variations, all of which are thus an absolute digression' (p. 182).[41] The oeuvre Barthes has in mind, some five years after the Proust round table, is clearly *À la recherche*. The variations and digressions of Proust's novel, which Barthes aligns quietly with those of his own work (his lecture series) on this occasion, are now understood not as an outright destruction of origin but as a non-negating derision: a vague bit, an erotic flash of origin.[42]

Erotic rhythm

There are significant affinities between Barthes's analysis of Proust's variations and Deleuze's work on 'transversals' in *Proust et les signes*. First published in 1964, *Proust et les signes* is the only book by Deleuze to focus specifically on Proust. Félix Guattari's voice is also discernible in the updated versions of 1970 and 1976, especially in their treatment of transversals.[43] His concept of 'transversalité' is designed to describe 'the communications and relations of the unconscious'.[44] Transversals are also essential, Guattari believes, for a full appreciation of the manner in which hermetically sealed worlds might be drawn, collaged or assembled together whilst preserving, nevertheless, the respective singularity of each. Or, in the words of Deleuze, '[i]t is transversality that constitutes the singular unity and totality of the Méséglise Way and of the Guermantes Way, without suppressing their difference or distance: "between these routes certain transversals were established"'.[45] Just as, for Barthes, the flow of Proust's metaphorical variations cannot be reduced to a single common origin or theme (which nevertheless traverses them as an intermittent flash), so too, for Deleuze, the singular monads of Proust's world can only come into contact transversally: the multiple cannot be reduced to the 'One'.[46]

Proust's variations and transversals appear to obey an idiorrhythmic principle: they allow for contact at a distance.[47] In *Comment vivre ensemble*, Barthes uses the term 'idiorrhythmia' ('idiorrythmie') to describe a fluid balance between the rhythms of individuals and of communities. He draws on Émile Benveniste's distinction between *rythmos*, implying rigid patterns and regular cadence, and *rhuthmos*, which is described as follows:

> supple, open, mobile rhythm; momentary form but form all the same. *Cf.* in music, metronomic rhythm ≠ *rhuthmos*. *Rhuthmos* = *swing* [...]. *Rhuthmos* is rhythm that admits one more or one less, an imperfection, a supplement, a lack, an *idios*: that which does not enter the structure, or enters it by force. Remember Casals's saying: *rhuthmos* is delay. (p. 69)[48]

The suppleness and mobility of the form of *rhuthmos* is a variation on the intermittent flow, the loss, of *signifiance*. As a delayed, mobile, momentary supplement (among other things), *rhuthmos* is protected by idiorrhythmia.[49] It is not surprising, therefore, that Barthes should identify idiorrhythmia as the 'constitutive dimension of Eros' ('dimension constitutive d'Eros') and suggest that 'the more idiorrhythmia is foreclosed, the more Eros is driven away' ('plus l'idiorrythmie est forclose, plus Eros est chassé' (p. 72)). In order to illustrate this point, he refers to the work of the Marquis de Sade:

> Another *Telos* (banal paradigm): Eros. Text: Sade: Sainte-Marie-des-Bois, and the castle in the *120 journées de Sodome*. An eccentric example, since idiorrhythmia is foreclosed. No *rhuthmos*, neither for the victims (of course), nor the libertines: meticulous timetables, obsessional rites, implacable rhythm = the *coenobium*, the convent, not an idiorrhythmic space. (p. 81)[50]

Sade's grinding text lacks idiorrhythmia, *rhuthmos*, and therefore eroticism. Texts in which eros is the object of implacable faith or obsession are not erotic: the cenobitic rhythm of both victims and persecutors ignores the 'diffuse, vague, uncertain Cause, the floating *Telos*, the fantasy' ('Cause diffuse, vague, incertaine, *Télos* flottant, fantasme' (p. 81)) of an erotic *rhuthmos*, just as faith in the permanence and development of an underlying theme is immune to the theme-less variations of Beethoven's *Diabelli Variations* and of Proust's *À la recherche*. There is thus a 'discourse […] of arrogance' ('discours […] de l'arrogance' (p. 81)) in Sade, and this is anathema to an idiorrhythmic effort, which requires a form of *époché*, or 'non-discourse, the suspension of the discourse of *It goes without saying*' ('le non-discours, la suspension du discours du *Il va de soi*' (p. 81)). For Barthes, idiorrhythmic non-discourse is also a non-method, since method, in accordance with Nietzsche's much-cited distinction between method and culture (*paideia*), is a fetishization of 'the goal as privileged place, to the detriment of other possible places' ('le but comme lieu privilégié, au détriment d'autres lieux possibles' (p. 180)).[51]

Barthes's teaching duties at the Collège de France between 1976 and 1977 involved both weekly lectures concerned with idiorrhythmia and companion seminars entitled 'Qu'est-ce que tenir un discours? Recherche sur la parole investie'. The focus of Barthes's seminars on 23 and 30 March 1977 was what he calls the 'Charlus-Discourse', which refers to a heated and perplexing verbal exchange between Marcel and the Baron de Charlus in *Le Côté de Guermantes*. Before the encounter with the Baron, the narrator attends a dinner at the Guermantes's mansion. Mme de Guermantes quotes isolated lines of early poems by Victor Hugo in which, the narrator observes, there is a 'romantisme intermittent' (*ALR*, II, 838). Her conversation is peppered with poetic bits and pieces from which the 'richly articulated rhymes' ('des rimes richement articulées'

(*ALR*, II, 838)) of Hugo's later work are entirely absent. The narrator is sent into an electric frenzy (suggesting, perhaps, the magnetic attractiveness of poetic intermittence, fragmentation and *rhuthmos*):

> The lines that had entered or returned to my mind during this dinner magnetized in turn, summoned to themselves with such force the poems in the heart of which they were normally embedded, that my magnetized hands could not hold out for longer than forty-eight hours against the force that drew them towards the volume in which were bound up *Les Orientales* and *Les Chants du crépuscule*. (*ALR*, II, 838)[52]

The narrator's excitement as he recalls his evening with the Guermantes soon gives way to violent frustration and incomprehension during his encounter with the Baron de Charlus. He must wait two days before being able to see Mme de Guermantes's fragments of Hugo returned to their habitual location; his thirty-five-minute wait before setting eyes on a reclining and aloof Charlus may be brief in comparison, but Charlus's subsequent discourse – his speech – affords nothing but a further series of delays and deferrals that hold the narrator in a state of insecurity, unsure as to the precise nature of the Baron's grievance against him. Indeed, after a lengthy conversation in which the Baron repeatedly asks (recommends) the narrator to leave only to implore him in the next breath to stay, Marcel returns home none the wiser. If, as Deleuze suggests, *À la recherche* is an apprenticeship in the reading and interpretation of signs, this apprenticeship is surely in trouble here.[53] Marcel does not quite know why he has been invited and cannot fully understand what is going on. He is never really sure what Charlus is talking about. Part of the narrator's confusion stems from his suspicion that he is a player in Charlus's dramatic *mise en scène* (see *ALR*, II, 842). But he, like the reader of Proust's text, is never certain of this. While Marcel is confident, at times, that he is indeed such a player (when he bumps into two footmen who have been eavesdropping, for example, the encounter seems to confirm that a 'spectacle' (*ALR*, II, 847) is what they have come to expect), he nevertheless continues to respond as best he can to the Baron's elusive accusations and does not quite know why Charlus should have footmen on hand outside to protect him. The reader might wonder (and the narrator does not tell) as to the significance of the fact that the Baron's hat is replaced immediately by his servants after Marcel destroys it in a fit of rage (and this is a hat which, the narrator observes, had been left on a chair with a cape, '*as though* the Baron had but recently come in').[54] Is it a prop, an object of theatrical use? Whatever it is, neither the narrator nor the reader is afforded a reassuring 'spasm of the signified' ('spasme du signifié') here:[55] they witness spasms of an entirely different kind.

The limits of the structural: Charlus and pathos

Deleuze describes Charlus as an 'enormous flickering sign'[56] ('énorme signe clignotant') that cannot be reduced to a single, overarching signified. Indeed, while he is, for Deleuze, 'the apparent master of the Logos' ('le maître apparent du Logos')[57] and would, the narrator suggests, be able to convince others that he was justified in committing murder 'by force of logic and beautiful language' ('à force de logique et de beau langage' (*ALR*, II, 844)), the regular cadence – the stable rhythm – of his discourse is disturbed by the shifting, mobile rhythm (the *rhuthmos*) of 'involuntary signs that resist the sovereign organization of language and cannot be mastered in words and phrases, but put the logos to flight and involve us in another realm'.[58] The modulations in tone and volume in the Baron's speech carry him from apoplexy to extreme gentleness: no sooner has he smiled disdainfully ('avec dédain'), raised his voice to the supreme pitch of its highest registers ('plus extrêmes registres') and attacked 'without strain, the shrillest and most insolent note' ('avec douceur la note la plus aiguë et la plus insolente' (*ALR*, II, 844)), than he returns, in a measured manner ('avec une extrême lenteur'), to 'une intonation naturelle' (*ALR*, II, 845). The narrator is confronted by the manipulative master of logic and a linguistic aesthete who emits, either in spite or because of his powers, 'signs of violence and madness' ('[des] signes de violence et de folie').[59] For Deleuze, these signs constitute a stunning pathos, and Charlus's pathos is an eminently idiorrhythmic class of singularities that can only communicate indirectly: pathos, he says, is a 'vegetal realm consisting of cellular elements [...]. It is a schizoid universe of closed vessels, of cellular regions, where contiguity itself is a distance'.[60]

Pathos is a powerful presence – a force – in Proust's 'Charlus-Discourse' as Barthes understands it,[61] and supplies a link to the analysis he offers in 'Le Troisième Sens', where, as we saw earlier, *signifiance* is viewed as an erotic supplement that 'my intellectual understanding cannot succeed in absorbing, at once persistent and fleeting, smooth and elusive' ('mon intellection ne parvient pas bien à absorber, à la fois têtu et fuyant, lisse et échappé' (III, 488)). Having suggested that the

'Charlus-Discourse' is atypical insofar as it cannot be organized along the traditional lines of structural analysis ('selon les voies classiques de l'analyse structurale' (p. 204)), Barthes immediately compares Proust and Balzac and refers to his own work on *Sarrasine*:

> the codes in the 'Charlus-Discourse' cannot be considered from the same perspective (to be of the same 'order') as the ones in *Sarrasine* – and this has nothing to do with the distinctiveness of *Sarrasine* as a narrative. If Balzac refers to a cultural code (allusions to art, for instance): dull units are denoted (as it were), it is the being-there, the naturality of culture that is presented: a use of the code, but without connotation. ≠ Charlus: cultural code (style of seats, for example) + an affective, emotive, enunciative supplement. [...] 'Charlus-Discourse': a banal interweaving of codes (*cf. Sarrasine*) + some supplements. Culture, for instance, is not simply a reference, an origin (Balzac), it is a space of enunciation. (pp. 204–05)[62]

It has become something of a critical commonplace to identify *S/Z* as marking a 'brutal and declared break with structuralism',[63] but Barthes indicates here that *À la recherche* poses problems for structuralism in a way that Balzac's text does not. While it may be true, as Marty argues, that Barthes's aim in *S/Z* is to 'deconstruct' *Sarrasine* rather than to establish it 'as one' ('comme un'),[64] Balzac's text, as least as it is understood by Barthes in *Comment vivre ensemble*, remains amenable to a traditional form of 'l'analyse structurale' (p. 205) insofar as its 'banal' interweaving of codes (p. 205), its 'dull units' ('unités mates' (p. 204)), pose little difficulty for a 'locating of units, of the morphemes of discourse' ('repérage d'unités, de morphèmes du discours' (p. 205)). In Proust's work, Charlus's direct references to Velázquez's *Las Lanzas* (1634–35) and Wagner's *Walküre* (1856), for example, are similarly unproblematic. The same is not true, however, of the 'ensemble' (p. 204) of the 'Charlus-Discourse'. Charlus's dull units, unlike those to be found in *Sarrasine*, are supplemented by an extreme force of enunciation, an 'affective shimmering' ('moire affective' (p. 209)) that is so changeable, so capricious, that it can shift gear without warning: the matte is supplemented by the mottled. Just as *signifiance* acts as an erotic pathos-supplement to obvious meaning, it is the 'forces of discourse' ('forces de discours' (p. 209)) that constitute a regime that is 'less well known' ('moins connu' (p. 205)) for structural analysis.[65] From the moment that textual analysis takes the erotic force of a supplement of enunciation, of affect (a subject who speaks 'while being affected'),[66] into account, it can no longer be – only – 'planimetrical, tabular' ('planimétrique, tabulaire' (p. 219)). It seems safe to say that this is not a form of criticism that could be described as an 'ultra-structuralisme'.[67] Indeed, while Barthes's approach in *S/Z* may constitute what François Dosse calls a major turning point ('tournant majeur') in his critical practice, the moment at which he deconstructs 'his own conceptual grid and gives freer rein to his literary intuition' ('sa propre grille conceptuelle pour laisser davantage de liberté à son intuition littéraire'),[68] his reading of Proust in *Comment vivre ensemble* marks a further critical variation, another turn away from the tenets of structuralism, which, in its most abstract and radically anti-humanist forms, demands the evacuation of the subject of enunciation in order to satisfy its claims to scientificity. Nevertheless, Barthes's observations in *Comment vivre ensemble* also suggest that in both *S/Z* and his work on the 'Charlus-Discourse', the erstwhile structural analyst is unable simply to abandon what in 1972 he characterizes as a semiological fantasy. Thus, for Barthes, in the wake of structuralism, the form of literary criticism is fissiparous: a movement beyond the dead ends of structuralism – through a reading either of Balzac in 1970 or of Proust in 1977 – does not entail their complete interment.

Barthes's understanding of force is informed by his reading of Nietzsche (and, as we saw earlier, of Deleuze on Nietzsche). For Nietzsche, as Barthes puts it in *Comment vivre ensemble*, force is a 'begetting of a difference'[69] and is tied closely to his conception of culture (*paideia*). While method, as we have already seen, 'always supposes the good will of the thinker, a "premeditated decision"' ('suppose toujours une bonne volonté du penseur, une "décision préméditée"' (p. 33)), culture is associated with a 'violence to which thought is subjected' ('violence subie par la pensée' (p. 33)) and requires a 'listening to forces' ('écoute des forces' (p. 34)). We might be tempted, then, to call the 'Charlus-Discourse' a 'non-discourse on non-method'. Nevertheless, Barthes warns against viewing his original 'non' as an absolute negation:

> I said 'non-method' at the beginning. As usual, the 'non' is too simple. It would have been better to say: pre-method. It is as if I were preparing materials for a methodical analysis: as if I were not worried, really, about the method that will take hold of them. Nevertheless – and this is where I want to finish – this preparation of a method is infinite, infinitely expansive. It is a preparation whose accomplishment is continually put off. Method is only acceptable as a mirage: it belongs to the order of the *Later*. (p. 183)[70]

The 'Charlus-Discourse' is thus neither a non-discourse nor a non-method, but an erotic 'field, a play of forces, of mobile intensities' ('champ, un jeu de forces, d'intensités mobiles' (p. 216)) in which a reassuring spasm of the signified is always put off until later.

Barthes says that Charlus 'grazes on/judders discourse' ('broute le discours' (p. 208)). He speaks 'like a lawnmower, a pneumatic drill: he grazes voraciously on discourse/judders discourse voraciously' ('comme une tondeuse, un marteau-piqueur: il broute voracement le discours' (p. 208)). Barthes's double use of 'brouter' here allows us to return, with some caution, to the starting point of this chapter, namely Barthes's distinction in *Le Plaisir du texte* between two diets of reading. In French as in English, 'grazing' is the consumption of grass and other green stuff by animals, suggesting an activity that is relatively leisurely and casual. In colloquial English, it can also refer more generally to acts of eating 'informally, taking small quantities of food at frequent but usually irregular intervals' (*OED*), and in French, as noted earlier, *brouter* can also be used to describe the reciprocating or juddering motion of certain tools and mechanical devices (among other things). While the second definition in English might suggest an intermittence or haphazardness of sorts, this sense is clearly more prominent in the second definition of the French verb. Now, the reader of modern texts may graze or 'mow' ('tondre') in order to rediscover 'the leisure of bygone readings' ('le loisir des anciennes lectures'), but he or she does so 'scrupulously' ('avec minutie' (*Le Plaisir du texte*, IV, 225)). This reader reads – grazes – at his or her leisure, without falling into what Barthes refers to elsewhere as 'idleness' (*S/Z*, III, 122). A minute and scrupulous attention to textual detail affords him or her access to the erotic enchantment of the signifier and 'the voluptuousness of writing' ('la volupté de l'écriture' (III, 122)). The rich polysemy of the French verb is important in *Comment vivre ensemble*, where Barthes explains what he means by *brouter*: 'when speaking of certain tools, to cut jerkily, in relation to a brake, a clutch, a machine, to jerk violently'.[71] He says nothing about feeding. Nevertheless, 'voraciously' ('il broute voracement le discours' (p. 208)) suggests a particularly ravenous oral consumption on Charlus's part: feeding and jerking combined (furthermore, as Barthes was no doubt aware, *brouter* also means to engage in cunnilingus (to lick or to eat out)). Bearing each of these possibilities in mind, we may see them touch. As they do this, we also see that Charlus, the reader and Marcel are all engaged in *broutement*, and that this can be understood as something erotic. Or as Jean-François Lyotard observes in *Discours, Figure* (1971):

'Discourse is thick. It does not merely signify, but expresses [...] it, too, has something trembling, movement and force, stored within it [...] it too opens itself up to grazing'.[72] We take our time, and in doing so we build deferrals. Neither the 'Charlus-Discourse' nor the act of reading it could ever be said to amount to an idly methodical process that is oriented exclusively towards a single, stable goal or 'obvious' meaning (a theme), or to constitute what Barthes calls a 'protocol of operations' designed to obtain a closed signification or single result ('protocole d'opérations pour obtenir un résultat' (*Comment vivre ensemble*, p. 33)). The discourse of Charlus the Jackhammer is a violently intermittent, shimmering of signs, a voluptuous patchiness and layering of *signifiance*. It is also a microcosm that encapsulates the 'discourse' of Proust's text as Barthes apprehends it. Indeed, as we shall see in the next chapter, the 'culture' of Proust's novel is such that, for Barthes, critical engagements with it require a 'listening to forces'.[73] They must be creatively alive to – operate variations upon – the force of its musical *broutement* rather than remain fixed solely upon the identification and development of well-formed or stable themes and conclusions.

Charlus is not Barthes's only *brouteur*, of course. In 1954, some twenty-three years before his seminars on the 'Charlus-Discourse', Barthes says that the historian Jules Michelet (1798–1874) does not simply consume history. He also '"grazes" on it, which is to say he passes over it and at the same time he swallows it' (*Michelet*, I, 304).[74] Thus, in the course of his historical Romantic journey ('voyage romantique'), which is to be distinguished from a hasty – and purely ocular – modern itinerary,[75] Michelet behaves more like a reader of a *texte de jouissance* than the consumer of a classical work.[76] As a walker and a swimmer (a 'marcheur' and a 'nageur' (I, 304)), he too proceeds slowly and patiently. He gets stuck in.[77] Furthermore, the patchy interpolations in his writing – which, as Barthes observes, are described by Proust using a musical metaphor (see *ALR*, III, 666) – serve to interrupt its steady rhetorical march towards logical resolution. They bring Michelet's discourse close to Charlus's voluptuous, erotic flickering and separate him from the likes of Chateaubriand and other 'sliding' writers ('écrivains "glisseurs"' (I, 306)):

Michelet's discourse – what is usually called style – is precisely that kind of concerted navigation which brings side by side, like a shark and its prey, History and its narrator. Michelet is one of those predatory writers (Pascal, Rimbaud) who cannot write without constantly devouring their discourse. This voration consists for Michelet in substituting for the oratorical cadence of noble art certain abrupt interpolations, certain peremptory remarks such as 'let us say', 'you will have', 'I shall return to this', 'I suppose', 'I should say', 'it must be said'. And the preface, the note or the postface are to the discourse what the interpolation is to the sentence: Michelet's recurrent glances into his work are frequent (what Proust, a propos of Michelet himself, called his musician's cadences). (I, 306)[78]

Michelet is a predator and a devourer ('vorateur') who feeds on his own discourse at every instant, and his ravenous style cannot nourish a regime of reading that is alert only to a text's anecdotal articulations (see IV, 225). Whereas sliders 'spread discourse, accompany it without interrupting it, and gradually manoeuvre the sentence towards a final euphoria',[79] hungry writers like Michelet constantly 'pierce it with unfinished gestures, like the obsessive movements of an owner who swiftly reassures himself of the presence of his property' (I, 306).[80] The exhilaration of a final cadence, which, in the work of Chateaubriand, is brought about by a measured progression within and across individual sentences, is thus punctured[81] in Michelet's work by what is described by Barthes as a series of brief, frequent plunges ('plongées') and rhetorical breaks ('ruptures d'euphorie rhétorique' (I, 306)) – by what, as we saw at the beginning of this chapter, he refers to in later works as a form of loss.[82] In contrast to Chateaubriand's 'phrase', which progresses smoothly and self-consciously towards neat, polished conclusions,[83] the Micheletist sentence is thus profoundly Charlus-like in its muscular eruptions, incomplete gestures and abrupt swallowings:[84] its body judders and jerks to the discontinuous rhythm of *signifiance*.

It is important to consider the context in which Proust's narrator refers to the musical cadences of Michelet's style. As he waits for Albertine and Françoise to return home from shopping, his jealousy momentarily assuaged by a confidence in the former's 'docilité' (*ALR*, III, 664) (he knows, in other words, precisely what Albertine is doing and does not suspect that her companion is a homosexual), Marcel plays the composer Vinteuil's sonata on the piano. Almost immediately, he is struck by a passage of music with which he is familiar, but which he now also views in an entirely new light.[85] As he works his way through Vinteuil's composition, he is reminded of Wagner (more specifically, of *Tristan und Isolde* (1859)), and, using a vivid corporeal metaphor, he reflects on the nervous to-ing and fro-ing of themes in Wagner's work:

those insistent, fleeting themes that visit an act, withdraw only to return, and, sometimes distant, drowsy, almost detached, are at other moments, while remaining vague, so pressing and so near, so internal, so organic, so visceral, that one would call them the resumption not so much of a musical motif as of an attack of neuralgia. (*ALR*, III, 665)[86]

It is, paradoxically, the painfully vital, bodily nature of Wagner's themes that most appeals to a relaxed Marcel: their recurrent yet brief visitations in a variety of physical forms and at different intensities contribute to his sense of the 'reality' of the composer's art.[87] It is unsurprising, then, that Barthes should draw on another section from this passage to reinforce his own view of Michelet's predatory devourings, which are the source of the small ruptures – the rhetorical gulps – in the body of the historian's discourse.

Later, Marcel dwells upon the simultaneous incompleteness and retrospective unity – and attendant beauty – of several nineteenth-century works of art, and among them he includes Michelet's history books:

> I thought how markedly, all the same, these works participate in that quality of being – albeit marvellously – always incomplete, which is the peculiarity of all the great works of the nineteenth century, with which the greatest writers of that century have stamped their books, but, watching themselves at work as though they were at once author and critic, have derived from this self-contemplation a novel beauty, exterior and superior to the work itself, imposing upon it retrospectively a unity, a greatness that it does not possess [...] the greatest beauties in Michelet are to be sought not so much in his work itself as in the attitudes that he adopts when he is considering his work, not in his *History of France* nor in his *History of the Revolution*, but in his prefaces to his books. Prefaces, that is to say pages written after the books themselves, in which he considers the books, and with which we must include here and there certain phrases beginning as a rule with a 'Shall I say?', which is not a scholar's precaution but a musician's cadence. (*ALR*, III, 666)[88]

According to Marcel, the unity of such incomplete works is effected by a retroactive 'illumination' (*ALR*, III, 667) that inspires artists to see that their works would be better brought together in a cycle in which the same characters reappear.[89] This special kind of artistic togetherness is born, he says, of a transformative process that, in terms of the genesis and growth of the work of art, inverts conventional approaches to themes and variations on them:

> A unity that was ulterior, not fictitious [...]. Not fictitious, perhaps indeed all the more real for being ulterior, for being born of a moment of

enthusiasm when it is discovered among fragments which need only to be joined together. A unity that has been unaware of itself, therefore vital and not logical, that has not banned variety, chilled execution. It emerges (only applying itself this time to the work as a whole) like a fragment composed separately, born of an inspiration, not required by the artificial development of a theme, which comes in to form an integral part of the rest. (*ALR*, III, 667)[90]

It is in this sense, for Proust's narrator, that certain nineteenth-century writers and musicians (such as Balzac, Michelet or Wagner) are able to produce what might be called 'variations without a theme'. In so doing, they abandon what Barthes describes as an academic and canonical form of variation in which the theme is given first and the variations follow.[91] Like intelligence for the writer, the theme comes afterwards:[92] an ulterior thematic unity is conferred by the inspired artist on a series of previously unrelated fragments in a process that sees those fragments made into variations. The great nineteenth-century work of art, be it textual or musical, is made of *variety* rather than variations on a theme: it is not to be understood as the logical systematization – the development – of a motif viewed as its transcendental origin.

Barthes thus redeploys Proust's musical metaphor as he describes the effects of Michelet's Charlus-like consumption of his own discourse. His reference to *À la recherche* in *Michelet* suggests an affinity between the art of *broutement*, of textual *signifiance* and *jouissance*, and a conception of thematic unity and variation in nineteenth-century musical and literary works which, as we have just seen, Proust's narrator discusses in a lengthy digression on the significance of Vinteuil's little phrase. Nevertheless, this resonance should not be read as an unequivocal endorsement of Proust's approach to music.

Notes

1 'droit aux articulations de l'anecdote, elle considère l'étendue du texte, ignore les jeux de langage'.

2 'fascinée par aucune perte verbale – au sens que ce mot peut avoir en spéléologie'.

3 'L'autre lecture ne passe rien; elle pèse, colle au texte, elle lit, si l'on peut dire, avec application et emportement, saisit en chaque point du texte l'asyndète qui coupe les langages – et non l'anecdote: ce n'est pas l'extension (logique) qui la captive, l'effeuillement des vérités, mais le feuilleté de la signifiance'.

4 Barthes's examples on this occasion are the novels of Jules Verne and Émile Zola (see IV, 225).

5 See IV, 225. We will return to the meaning of *brouter* later on. According to *Le Petit Robert*, the term refers to the act of feeding on 'grass, shoots, leaves' ('l'herbe, les pousses, les feuilles') and to the movement of either a 'sharp-edged tool [...] or a mechanical device (clutch) which operates in an irregular and jerky manner' ('un outil tranchant [...] ou d'un organe mécanique (embrayage) qui fonctionne de manière irrégulière et saccadée').

6 'Pour la libération d'une pensée pluraliste', IV, 469–82 (p. 482).

7 'La signifiance, contrairement à la signification, ne saurait donc se réduire à la communication, à la représentation, à l'expression: elle place le sujet (de l'écrivain, du lecteur) dans le texte, non comme une projection, fût-elle fantasmatique (il n'y a pas "transport" d'un sujet constitué), mais comme une "perte" (au sens que ce mot peut avoir en spéléologie); d'où son identification à la jouissance; c'est par le concept de signifiance que le texte devient érotique (pour cela, il n'a donc nullement à représenter des "scènes" érotiques)'.

8 'lieu où disparaît un cours d'eau, qui réapparaît plus loin'. This is the 'geological' definition of 'perte' in *Le Petit Robert*.

9 'Il est intentionnel (c'est ce qu'a voulu dire l'auteur) et il est prélevé dans une sorte de lexique général, commun, des symboles; c'est un sens qui me cherche, moi, destinataire du message, sujet de la lecture, un sujet qui part de S.M.E. et qui va *au-devant de moi*: évident, certes [...], mais d'une évidence fermée, prise dans un système complet de destination'. I have taken – and occasionally modified – translations of this work from the following edition: Roland Barthes, 'The Third Meaning', in *The Responsibility of Forms: Critical Essays on Music, Art and Representation*, trans. Richard Howard (Oxford: Blackwell, 1986), pp. 41–62.

10 'supplément que mon intellection ne parvient pas bien à absorber, à la fois têtu et fuyant, lisse et échappé'.

11 'le problème *actuel* n'est pas de détruire le récit, mais de le subvertir: dissocier la subversion de la destruction, telle serait aujourd'hui la tâche'.

12 'Certains veulent un texte (un art, une peinture) sans ombre, coupé de l'"idéologie dominante"; mais c'est vouloir un texte sans fécondité, sans productivité, un texte stérile (voyez le mythe de la Femme sans Ombre). Le texte a besoin de son ombre: cette ombre, c'est *un peu* d'idéologie, *un peu* de représentation, *un peu* de sujet: fantômes, poches, trainées, nuages nécessaires: la subversion doit produire son propre *clair-obscur*'.

13 'L'endroit le plus érotique d'un corps n'est-il pas *là où le vêtement bâille*? Dans la perversion (qui est le régime du plaisir textuel) il n'y a pas de "zones érogènes" (expression au reste assez casse-pieds); c'est l'intermittence, comme l'a bien dit la psychanalyse, qui est érotique: celle de la peau qui scintille entre deux pièces (le pantalon et le tricot), entre deux bords (la chemise entrouverte, le gant et la manche)'.

14   I have taken – and occasionally modified – translations of this work from the following edition: Roland Barthes, 'An Idea of Research', in *The Rustle of Language*, trans. Richard Howard (Berkeley and Los Angeles: University of California Press, 1989), pp. 271–76.

15   'Tout trait est appelé à se renverser, par un mouvement de rotation implacable: pourvu d'un langage aristocratique, Swann ne peut, à un certain moment, que l'inverser en langue bourgeoise. Cette contrainte est si légale qu'elle rend inutile, dit Proust, l'observation des mœurs: on peut très bien les déduire de la loi d'inversion'.

16   Tony Tanner, 'Introduction', in Herman Melville, *Moby Dick* (Oxford: Oxford University Press, 1988), pp. vii–xxvi (p. xxv).

17   'ne peut visiblement relever que d'une érotique (du discours), comme si le tracé du renversement était le moment même où Proust jouit d'écrire: c'est, piqué ici et là dans le grand continuum de la quête, le *plus-à-jouir* du récit, du langage'.

18   'une figure exacte, comme si un dieu – un *fatum* – présidait avec malice au trajet qui conduit la princesse à coïncider avec son contraire absolu, déterminé géométriquement'.

19   'le devenir même des principaux personnages, soumis à des élévations et à des chutes "exactes"'.

20   Gilles Deleuze and Félix Guattari, *Capitalisme et schizophrénie II. Mille plateaux* (Paris: Minuit, 1980), p. 17.

21   'comme une antitoxine défend contre la maladie, comme le corps thyroïde règle notre embonpoint [...], ainsi un acte exceptionnel d'autofécondation vient à point nommé donner son tour de vis, son coup de frein, fait rentrer dans la norme la fleur qui en était exagérément sortie'.

22   Deleuze and Guattari, *Mille plateaux*, p. 17. With greater entomological plausibility, Proust calls the insect a 'bourdon' ('bumblebee' (*ALR*, III, 6)) rather than a wasp or a hornet.

23   'un arrangement de l'homme et de la bête, ce n'est pas une ressemblance, c'est une identité de fond, c'est une zone d'indiscernabilité plus profonde que toute identification sentimentale' (Gilles Deleuze, *Francis Bacon: logique de la sensation* (Paris: Seuil, 2002), p. 30).

24   Deleuze, *Francis Bacon*, p. 28.

25   The implicit distinction on which Deleuze's observations depend has been rusticated by an approach to the relationship between man and animal that is less informed by ecclesiastical convention. See, for example, Jacques Derrida's seminars on *La Bête et le souverain, volume I (2001–2002)* (Paris: Galilée, 2008).

26   'dans la ligne de fuite composée d'un rhizome commun qui ne peut plus être attribué, ni soumis à quoi que ce soit de signifiant' (Deleuze and Guattari, *Mille plateaux*, p. 17).

27   Deleuze and Guattari, *Mille plateaux*, p. 17.

28 'le texte n'est jamais *approprié*, il se situe dans l'*intercourse* infinie des codes [...] c'est une science de la *jouissance*, car tout texte "textuel" (entré dans le champ de la signifiance) tend à la limite à provoquer ou à vivre la *perte de conscience* (l'annulation) que le sujet assume pleinement dans la jouissance érotique, et c'est une science du devenir (de ce devenir *subtil* dont Nietzsche réclamait la perception par-delà la forme grossière des choses): "[...] nous ne sommes pas assez *subtils* pour apercevoir l'*écoulement* probablement *absolu* du *devenir*: le *permanent* n'existe que grâce à nos organes grossiers qui résument et ramènent les choses à des plans communs, alors que rien n'existe *sous cette forme*. L'arbre est à chaque instant une chose neuve, nous affirmons la *forme* parce que nous ne saisissons pas la subtilité d'un mouvement absolu"'.

29 'Il y a cependant un moment, dans la *Recherche*, où la grande forme inversante ne fonctionne plus. [...] On sait que tous les personnages de Proust se retrouvent dans le volume final de l'œuvre [...]; dans quel état? Nullement inversés [...], mais au contraire *prolongés*, *figés* (plus encore que vieillis), *préservés*, et l'on voudrait pouvoir dire: "*persévérés*". Dans la vie sursitaire, l'inversion ne prend plus: le récit n'a plus qu'à finir: le livre n'a plus qu'à commencer'.

30 'Le plus extraordinaire de tous était mon ennemi personnel, M. d'Argencourt, le véritable clou de la matinée. Non seulement, au lieu de sa barbe à peine poivre et sel, il s'était affublé d'une extraordinaire barbe d'une invraisemblable blancheur, mais encore (tant de petits changements matériels peuvent rapetisser, élargir un personnage, et bien plus, changer son caractère apparent, sa personnalité) c'était un vieux mendiant qui n'inspirait plus aucun respect qu'était devenu cet homme dont la solennité, la raideur empesée étaient encore présentes à mon souvenir et qui donnait à son personnage de vieux gâteux une telle vérité que ses membres tremblotaient, que les traits détendus de sa figure, habituellement hautaine, ne cessaient de sourire avec une niaise béatitude. Poussé à ce degré, l'art du déguisement devient quelque chose de plus, une transformation complète de la personnalité'.

31 There are numerous further examples. See, for example, *ALR*, IV, 504: 'the hard, scraggy girl had become a buxom, generous dowager' ('la sèche et maigre jeune fille était devenue une vaste et indulgente douairière').

32 'la coiffe loustic, la vieillarde, les paupières qui louchent, le poisson'.

33 'c'était trop de parler d'un acteur et, débarrassé qu'il était de toute âme consciente, c'est comme une poupée trépidante, à la barbe postiche de laine blanche, que je le voyais agité, promené dans ce salon'.

34 'Des poupées, mais que pour les identifier à celui qu'on avait connu, il fallait lire sur plusieurs plans à la fois, situés derrière elles et qui leur donnaient de la profondeur'.

35 Bowie, 'Reading Proust between the Lines', p. 129.

36 'extrême attention à la disposition chrono-topologique des signifiants thématiques' (Genette, 'Table ronde sur Proust', p. 34).

37 'en analysant les variations, on cherche un thème, on se situe complètement dans une herméneutique' (Barthes, 'Table ronde sur Proust', p. 35).

38 'il ne faut pas oublier que dans l'histoire de la musique, il y a une grande œuvre qui feint de prendre la structure "thème et variations" mais en réalité la défait; ce sont les variations de Beethoven sur une valse de Diabelli [...]. On s'aperçoit là qu'on a affaire à trente-trois variations sans thème. Et il y a un thème qui est donné au début, qui est un thème très bête, mais qui est donné justement, un peu, à titre de dérision. Je dirais que ces variations de Beethoven fonctionnent un peu comme l'œuvre de Proust' (Barthes, 'Table ronde sur Proust', p. 42).

39 Paul de Man, *Blindness and Insight: Essays in the Rhetoric of Contemporary Criticism* (London: Routledge, 1983), p. 235.

40 See Barthes, 'Table ronde sur Proust', pp. 42–43.

41 'on pourrait même imaginer, tendanciellement, une œuvre, un cours, qui ne serait fait que de digressions [...]. *Cf.* les *Variations Diabelli*: le thème est à peu près inexistant, un très vague souvenir en traverse par éclairs les trente-deux variations, dont chacune est ainsi une digression absolue'.

42 We will return to the affinities between Proust's and Barthes's variations in the next chapter. Barthes is not alone, of course, in finding 'variation' (or varied rhythm) in Proust's work. Some eighteen years before the Proust round table at the ENS, Maurice Blanchot suggests that the space of *À la recherche* 'had to come close [...] to the essence of the sphere' ('devait se rapprocher [...] de l'essence de la sphère') and that 'his entire book, his language, this style of slow curves, of fluid heaviness, of transparent density, always in movement, wonderfully made to express the infinitely varied rhythm of voluminous gyration, symbolizes the mystery and the thickness of the sphere, its movement of rotation' ('tout son livre [*À la recherche*], son langage, ce style de courbes lentes, de fluide lourdeur, de densité transparente, toujours en mouvement, merveilleusement fait pour exprimer le rythme infiniment varié de la giration volumineuse, figure le mystère et l'épaisseur de la sphère, son mouvement de rotation' ('L'Expérience de Proust', in *Le Livre à venir* (Paris: Gallimard, 1986), pp. 19–37 (p. 33); as mentioned previously, Blanchot's essay was first published in *La Nouvelle Revue française* in 1954). Barthes's understanding of 'variation' in *À la recherche* also resonates with Deleuze and Guattari's conception of the 'refrain' ('ritournelle') and of style as 'variation continue' in *Mille plateaux* (see p. 123: 'What is called a style [...] is nothing other than the procedure of a continuous variation' ('Ce qu'on appelle un style [...], c'est précisément le procédé d'une variation continue')) and elsewhere (see Guattari's 'Les Ritournelles du temps perdu', in *L'Inconscient machinique: essais de schizo-analyse* (Paris: Éditions recherches, 1979), pp. 257–364, for example). In 'De la ritournelle', the eleventh chapter of *Mille plateaux*, Deleuze and Guattari suggest that a child's 'song' ('chanson') is 'a skip: it jumps from chaos to the beginnings of order in chaos and is in danger of breaking apart at any moment'

('un saut: elle saut du chaos à un début d'ordre dans le chaos, elle risque aussi de se disloquer à chaque instant' (p. 382)). As we shall see in due course, the same can be said of Charlus's 'skipping', juddering speech.

43 This is not to suggest, like François Dosse, that Deleuze borrows the term from Guattari – or only from Guattari (see François Dosse, *Gilles Deleuze et Félix Guattari: biographie croisée* (Paris: Éditions la découverte, 2007), p. 158). Indeed, Proust uses 'transversal/e/s' on six occasions in *À la recherche*.

44 'les communications et rapports de l'inconscient' (Deleuze, *Proust et les signes*, p. 201, n. 1).

45 '[c]'est elle qui fait l'unité et la totalité singulières du côté de Méséglise et du coté de Guermantes, sans en supprimer la différence ou la distance: "entre ces routes des transversales s'établissaient"' (Deleuze, *Proust et les signes*, p. 202).

46 See Deleuze, *Proust et les signes*, p. 153: 'never reduce the multiple to the One' ('jamais ramener le multiple à l'Un').

47 Barthes refers to Deleuze's work on Proust on several occasions. See, for example, 'Les Vies parallèles' (II, 811–13): 'this paradoxical reading is in accordance with the glimpses we catch of Proust's philosophy (particularly since the publication of G. Deleuze's book on *Proust et les signes*)' ('cette lecture paradoxale est conforme à ce que nous entrevoyons de la philosophie de Proust (notamment depuis le livre de G. Deleuze sur *Proust et les signes*)' (p. 812)). For an analysis of the relationship between Barthes and Deleuze and Guattari on 'rhythm' (particularly as this pertains to the quotidian), see Michael Sheringham, 'Everyday Rhythms, Everyday Writing', in *Rhythms: Essays in French Literature, Thought, and Culture*, ed. Elizabeth Lindley and Laura McMahon (Bern and Oxford: Peter Lang, 2008), pp. 147–58.

48 'rythme souple, disponible, mobile; forme passagère, mais forme tout de même. *Cf.* en musique, rythme métronymique ≠ *rhuthmos*. *Rhuthmos* = swing [...]. *Rhuthmos*: c'est le rythme admettant un plus ou un moins, une imperfection, un supplément, un manque, un *idios*: ce qui n'entre pas dans la structure, ou y entrerait de force. Se rappeler le mot de Casals: le *rhuthmos*, c'est le retard'. Barthes in fact writes 'le rythme, c'est le retard' here. He corrected this mistake as he delivered the lecture (see *Comment vivre ensemble*, p. 69, n. 13), and I have altered the text to avoid confusion.

49 'Idiorrhythmia: protection of *rhuthmos*' ('Idiorrythmie: protection du *rhuthmos*' (*Comment vivre ensemble*, p. 69)).

50 'Autre *Télos* (paradigme banal): Eros. Texte: Sade: Sainte-Marie-des-Bois, et le château des *120 journées de Sodome*. Exemple excentrique, car il y a forclusion de l'idiorrythmie. Pas de *rhuthmos*, ni pour les victimes (bien sûr), ni pour les libertins: horaires minutieux, rites obsessionnels, rythme implacable = le *coenobium*, le couvent, non l'espace idiorrythmique'.

51 Barthes begins his lecture series with a presentation of Nietzsche's distinction as it is described by Deleuze in *Nietzsche et la philosophie* (Paris:

PUF, 1962), p. 123. It remains to be seen whether Barthes's 'non' is as absolute as it sounds.

52 'Ceux qui étaient entrés ou rentrés dans ma mémoire, au cours de ce dîner, aimantaient à leur tour, appelaient à eux avec une telle force les pièces au milieu desquelles ils avaient l'habitude d'être enclavés, que mes mains électrisées ne purent pas résister plus de quarante-huit heures à la force qui les conduisait vers le volume où étaient reliés *Les Orientales* et *Les Chants du crépuscule*'.

53 There is, of course, an important shift in Deleuze's understanding of interpretation between the first part of *Proust et les signes* (1964), in which he argues that '[t]o think is always to interpret, that is to say, to explain, develop, decipher, translate a sign' ('[p]enser, c'est toujours interpréter, c'est-à-dire expliquer, développer, déchiffrer, traduire un signe'), and part two (first published in 1970), in which he writes, 'To interpret has no unity other than the transversal' ('L'interpréter n'a pas d'autre unité que transversale'). See Deleuze, *Proust et les signes*, pp. 119 and 156.

54 'sur une chaise avec une pelisse, *comme si* le baron venait de rentrer' (*ALR*, II, 842; my emphasis).

55 See 'Le Troisième Sens', III, 502.

56 Deleuze, *Proust et les signes*, p. 207.

57 Deleuze, *Proust et les signes*, p. 209.

58 'des signes involontaires qui résistent à l'organisation souveraine du langage, qui ne se laissent pas maîtriser dans les mots et les phrases, mais font fuir le logos et nous entraînent dans un autre domaine' (Deleuze, *Proust et les signes*, p. 209).

59 Deleuze, *Proust et les signes*, p. 209.

60 'le pathos est un végétal fait de parties cloisonnées [...]. C'est l'univers schizoïde des boîtes closes, des parties cloisonnées, ou la contiguïté même est une distance' (Deleuze, *Proust et les signes*, p. 209).

61 Indeed, the 'Charlus-Discourse' carries out the 'seconde mission' that Barthes says he would entrust to the 'Novel (fantasized, and probably impossible)' ('Roman (fantasmé, et probablement impossible')), namely 'the expression of *pathos*' ('l'expression du *pathos*'): 'the Novel, as I read or desire it, is precisely that form which, in delegating the discourse of affect to characters, allows this affect to be spoken overtly: the pathetic can be enunciated' ('le Roman, tel que je le lis ou le désire, est précisément cette Forme qui, en déléguant à des personnages le discours de l'affect, permet de dire ouvertement cet affect: le pathétique y est énonçable' ('"Longtemps, je me suis couché de bonne heure"' (V, 459–70), p. 469)). Like *significance*, such expressions of pathos, or rather 'the emotion that they always reawaken in me' ('l'émotion qu'elles ravivent toujours en moi') are understood as supplements, constituting *punctum*-like 'moments of truth' ('moments de vérité') and 'the anecdote's points of *surplus value*' ('les points de *plus-value* de l'anecdote' (V, 468)). As we shall see in Chapter Four,

the pathos of the 'Charlus-Discourse' is understood in similar (but by no means identical) supplementary terms.

62 'les codes du "Discours-Charlus" ne peuvent être pris dans la même perspective (le même "ordre") que ceux de *Sarrasine* – et ceci indépendamment de la marque narrative de *Sarrasine*. Si Balzac recourt à un code culturel (allusions à l'art, par exemple): unités mates, et comme dénotées, c'est l'être-là, la naturalité de la culture qui est donnée: code manié sans connotation. ≠ Charlus: code culturel (style des sièges, par exemple) + un supplément affectif, émotif, énonciatif [...] 'Discours-Charlus': un tissu banal de codes (*cf.* *Sarrasine*) + des suppléments. La culture, par exemple, n'est pas seulement une référence, une origine (Balzac), mais une place d'énonciation'.

63 'rupture brutale et déclarée avec le structuralisme' (Éric Marty, *Roland Barthes, le métier d'écrire* (Paris: Seuil, 2006), p. 144).

64 Marty, *Roland Barthes, le metier d'écrire*, p. 147.

65 There are clear affinities between signification/*signifiance*, dull cultural units/affective supplement and *studium*/*punctum* (in separating them with a slash I do not suggest that these concepts are diametrically opposed). For a more detailed analysis of the relationship between the *punctum* and the obtuse, see Derek Attridge, 'Roland Barthes's Obtuse, Sharp Meaning', in *Writing the Image After Roland Barthes*, ed. Jean-Michel Rabaté (Philadelphia: University of Pennsylvania Press, 1997), pp. 77–89. As Attridge notes, both the *punctum* and the obtuse 'have a distinctive emotional force' and are 'associated with love and eroticism' (p. 79).

66 See *Préparation*, p. 205: '*I write, and in doing so I'm affected*; I make myself the centre and the agent of the action; I establish myself in the action, not by adopting an external position (like the priest) but an internal one, where the subject and the action form one and the same ball'('*j'écris en m'affectant*, en me faisant centre et acteur de l'action; je m'établis dans l'action, non vers l'extérieur, comme le prêtre, mais sur une position interne, où le sujet et l'action ne font qu'une seule et même boule'). While Charlus is not the self-affecting author of the text we are reading, he can nevertheless be understood as the discursive embodiment of precisely that figure – of an enunciating subject who does not only speak 'about' an external object or end, but who is also the producer of an internal diathesis (see *Préparation*, p. 205).

67 See Jacques Derrida, 'Force et signification', in *L'Écriture et la différence* (Paris: Seuil, 1967), pp. 9–49. Referring to a text by Jean Rousset, Derrida writes: 'we are dealing with an ultra-structuralism' ('on a affaire à un ultra-structuralisme' (p. 29)). More needs to be said, of course, about the relationship between Barthes's and Derrida's understanding of 'force'. A good starting point, at least as far as Derrida is concerned, would be Clare Connors's *Force from Nietzsche to Derrida* (Oxford: Legenda, 2010). Derrida's essay on Rousset, in which he has a lot to say about Rousset's analysis of Proust, appeared some ten years before Barthes's seminars on the 'Charlus-Discourse'.

For an examination of some of the 'links' between Derrida and Barthes, see, for example, Arkady Plotnitsky, 'Un-Scriptible', in *Writing the Image After Roland Barthes*, ed. Jean-Michel Rabaté (Philadelphia: University of Pennsylvania Press, 1997), pp. 243–58.

68 François Dosse, *Histoire du structuralisme*, 2 vols (Paris: Éditions la découverte, 1992), II, p. 79.

69 'engendrement d'une différence' (*Comment vivre ensemble*, p. 34).

70 'J'ai dit au début: non-méthode. Comme toujours, le non est trop simple. Il vaudrait mieux dire: pré-méthode. C'est comme si je préparais des matériaux en vue d'un traitement méthodique; comme si, à vrai dire, je ne m'inquiétais pas de quelle méthode ils vont être saisis. [...] Cependant – et c'est ici que je veux finir –, cette préparation de méthode est infinie, infiniment expansive. C'est une préparation dont l'accomplissement est sans cesse reculé. La méthode n'est acceptable qu'à titre de mirage: elle est de l'ordre du *Plus tard*'.

71 'couper par soubresauts en parlant de certains outils, agir par à-coups en parlant d'un frein, d'un embrayage, d'une machine' (*Comment vivre ensemble*, p. 208).

72 'Un discours est épais. Il ne signifie pas seulement, il exprime [...] il a lui aussi du bougé consigné en lui, du mouvement, de la force [...]. Lui aussi se donne à brouter' (Jean-François Lyotard, *Discours, figure* (Paris: Klincksieck, 1971), p. 15).

73 *Comment vivre ensemble*, p. 34.

74 'la "broute", c'est-à-dire qu'à la fois il la parcourt et il l'avale'. I have taken – and occasionally modified – translations of this work from the following edition: Roland Barthes, *Michelet*, trans. Richard Howard (Berkeley and Los Angeles: University of California Press, 1987).

75 See I, 304: 'we must remember that, for the Romantics, travel had an entirely different effect from its modern counterpart; nowadays we participate in a journey with our eyes only' ('encore faut-il se rappeler que le voyage romantique était de tout autre effet que le voyage moderne; nous ne participons jamais à un voyage que par les yeux').

76 See *Le Plaisir du texte*, IV, 225.

77 See I, 304: 'here, landscape is slowly, arduously conquered; landscape surrounds, presses in, threatens, invades – one must force one's way through it, and not only with the eyes but with the muscles and with patience' ('ici, le paysage est lentement, âprement conquis; il entoure, il presse, il envahit, il menace, il faut s'y forcer un passage, et non plus seulement par les yeux, mais par les muscles et la patience').

78 'Le discours de Michelet – ce qu'on appelle d'ordinaire le style – est précisément cette sorte de navigation concertée qui mène bord à bord, comme un poisson et sa proie, l'Histoire et son narrateur. Michelet appartient à ce genre d'écrivains prédateurs (Pascal, Rimbaud), qui ne peuvent écrire sans dévorer à tout instant leur discours. Cette voration consiste pour Michelet

à substituer aux cadences oratoires de l'art noble, des incises brusques, des interpellations du type de: "Mettez, vous aurez, j'y reviendrai, je crois, le dirais-je, il faut le dire". Et la préface, la note ou la postface sont au discours ce que l'incise est à la phrase: ces regards récurrents de Michelet dans son œuvre sont fréquents (ce que Proust appelait, à propos de Michelet lui-même, ses cadences de musicien)'.

79 'étalent le discours, l'accompagnent sans l'interrompre et dirigent insensiblement la phrase vers une euphorie finale'. We will return to Barthes's notion of 'sliding' in the next chapter, where we consider Robbe-Grillet's observation that the meaning or direction ('le sens') of Barthes's writing is located 'in sliding and not at all in the elements between which thought has slid' ('dans le glissement et non pas du tout dans les éléments entre lesquels la pensée aura glisée' (Alain Robbe-Grillet, *Pourquoi j'aime Barthes* (Paris: Christian Bourgois, 2001), p. 32)).

80 'menacés de perdre leur proie s'ils la font trop belle, la percent à tout instant de gestes inachevés, comme le mouvement maniaque d'un propriétaire qui s'assure rapidement de la présence de son bien'.

81 In this, only his second book, Barthes anticipates the language of *La Chambre claire*, the last of his books to be published during his lifetime.

82 See IV, 450, for example.

83 See I, 306: 'Chateaubriand's sentence always ends in décor' ('la phrase de Chateaubriand se termine toujours en décor') and 'listens to itself sliding' ('s'écoute glisser').

84 Barthes says that Michelet's 'phrase' 'swallows itself, [...] destroys itself' ('s'avale, [...] se détruit' (I, 306)).

85 This is, of course, the 'little phrase' ('petite phrase') that is the 'national anthem of Swann and Odette's love' ('hymne national de l'amour de Swann et d'Odette' (*ALR*, III, 878)).

86 'ces thèmes insistants et fugaces qui visitent un acte, ne s'éloignent que pour revenir, et, parfois lointains, assoupis, presque détachés, sont, à d'autres moments, tout en restant vagues, si pressants et si proches, si internes, si organiques, si viscéraux qu'on dirait la reprise moins d'un motif que d'une névralgie'.

87 See *ALR*, III, 665: 'I began to perceive how much reality there is in the work of Wagner' ('Je me rendais compte de tout ce qu'a de réel l'œuvre de Wagner').

88 'je songeais combien tout de même ces œuvres [those of Wagner] participent à ce caractère d'être – bien que merveilleusement – toujours incomplètes, qui est le caractère de toutes les grandes œuvres du XIXe siècle, du XIXe siècle dont les plus grands écrivains ont manqué leurs livres, mais, se regardant travailler comme s'ils étaient à la fois l'ouvrier et le juge, ont tiré de cette autocontemplation une beauté nouvelle extérieure et supérieure à l'œuvre, lui imposant rétroactivement une unité, une grandeur qu'elle n'a pas [...] les

plus grandes beautés de Michelet, il ne faut pas tant les chercher dans son œuvre même que dans les attitudes qu'il prend en face de son œuvre, non pas dans son *Histoire de France* ou dans son *Histoire de la Révolution*, mais dans ses préfaces à ses livres. Préfaces, c'est-à-dire pages écrites après eux, où il les considère, et auxquelles il faut joindre çà et là quelques phrases, commençant d'habitude par un "Le dirai-je" qui n'est pas une précaution de savant, mais une cadence de musicien'.

89 This clearly applies to literary works (Balzac's *Comédie humaine*, for example), but the narrator of *À la recherche* also suggests that each of the different 'musiques' that fills Wagner's individual compositions, for example, is a unique 'being' ('être' (*ALR*, III, 665)).

90 'Unité ultérieure, non factice [...]. Non factice, peut-être même plus réelle d'être ultérieure, d'être née d'un moment d'enthousiasme où elle est découverte entre des morceaux qui n'ont plus qu'à se rejoindre. Unité qui s'ignorait, donc vitale et non logique, qui n'a pas proscrit la variété, refroidi l'exécution. Elle surgit (mais s'appliquant cette fois à l'ensemble) comme tel morceau composé à part, né d'une inspiration, non exigé par le développement artificiel d'une thèse, et qui vient s'intégrer au reste'.

91 See Barthes, 'Table ronde sur Proust', p. 42.

92 See *ALR*, IV, 459: 'with the scholar the work of the intelligence precedes, and with the writer it comes afterwards' ('chez le savant le travail de l'intelligence précède et chez l'écrivain vient après').

CHAPTER THREE

Music, Discourse

In a talk given in Rome on 20 May 1977, subsequently published in Italian in the *Nuova rivista musicale italiana* as 'La musica, la voce, il linguaggio' (1978),[1] Barthes explains why it is not easy to talk and write about music: 'Many writers have spoken well about painting; none, I believe, has spoken well about music, not even Proust. The reason is that it is very difficult to link language, which is of the order of the general, and music, which is of the order of difference' (V, 523).[2] All writing on music – Proust's included – is unsatisfactory, he contends, because it has failed to meet the demands of a typically Nietzschean approach to the work of interpretation, which requires a positing of values (an 'évaluation' (V, 523)). In other words, for Barthes, writing about music usually consists of indifferent commentaries that ignore the value of music 'for me' ('pour moi') in favour of a generalized 'for everyone' ('pour tous' (V, 523)).[3] It is inhabited by a 'futile discourse, [a] discourse of music-in-itself or of music for everyone'[4] that ignores the constraint to evaluate and to affirm that music's force, its 'différence', places on its listeners (see V, 524). Like Proust's novel, the human voice – the focus of his essay is the operatic and concert baritone Charles Panzéra (1896–1976) – is viewed by Barthes as inexhaustible. It too, he says, is underdetermined by scientific discourse (commentary) upon it:

> there is no science (physiology, history, aesthetics, psychoanalysis) that exhausts the voice: no matter how much you classify and comment on music historically, sociologically, aesthetically, technically, there will always be a remainder, a supplement, a lapse, something non-spoken that designates itself: the voice. (V, 524)[5]

According to Barthes, in writing about the music of the human voice, we are obliged to affirm a value actively and, in so doing, to acknowledge that our relationship with that voice is necessarily erotic ('forcément amoureux' (V, 524)).[6] Furthermore, as the title of his essay partially indicates ('la langue' is both language and the part of the human anatomy that makes – normal – speech possible (the tongue)), Barthes emphasizes the relationship between the voice and the body in Panzéra's art. He goes on to assert that Panzéra's musical practice is the site of an uncommon phenomenon: the irruption of music within language. Indeed, in order for language to be made musical and amorous, there must be, he observes, 'a certain *physique* of the voice (by *physique* I mean the way the voice behaves in the body – or in which the body behaves in the voice)' (V, 527).[7] In achieving this rare feat, Barthes declares, Panzéra sings with his whole body, *'full-throatedly'* ('*à plein gosier*' (V, 527)), and his singing voice, which is a site of pronunciation rather than expressive clarity or articulation,[8] is endowed with an erotic body, or what Barthes calls an 'erected voice – a voice with an erection' ('une voix bandée – une voix qui bande' (V, 527)).

The eroticism of the voice and its relation to the body is the focus of several other celebrated texts by Barthes. In 'Le Grain de la voix' (1972), for example, he begins by lamenting the use of adjectives in critical writing about music (as we shall see later on, novelists are by no means innocent in this regard, either):

> adjectival criticism (or predicative interpretation) has assumed, down through the ages, certain institutional aspects: the musical adjective becomes somehow legal whenever an *ethos* of music is postulated, that is, whenever a regular (natural or magical) mode of signification is attributed to music. (IV, 148)[9]

Critics' deployment of adjectives reduces musical force to signification, to 'communication, [...] représentation, [...] expression' (IV, 150), and their writing is unable to account for the erotic amorousness of musical *signifiance*. While Barthes is keen to emphasize the limitations of an approach to music laden with adjectives, and indeed to 'exorcise musical commentary and [...] liberate it from a predicative fatality' ('exorciser le commentaire musical et [...] le libérer de la fatalité prédicative' (IV, 149)), this exorcism cannot be achieved merely by modifying the kind of words we use. It would be better, he argues, 'to change the musical object itself, as it presents itself to speech: to modify its level of perception or intellection: to shift the fringe of contact between music and language' (IV, 149).[10] Barthes's aim in this article, then, is to delineate the *physique* of the voice, which he now calls its 'grain'. The grain of the voice is excessive: it exceeds culture. It is, as Barthes puts it in 'La Musique, la voix, la langue', the remainder, the supplement, the lapsus, the non-spoken, inexpressive something that makes up the voice's inexhaustible, absolute difference – that makes the human voice an object to be 'evaluated' (we might prefer 'valued') and desired. As the *physique* of the singing voice, it is inextricably bound into the musician's body:

> Listen to a Russian bass [...] something is there, manifest and persistent (you hear only *that*), which is past (or previous to) the meaning of the words, of their form [...]: something which is directly the singer's body, brought by one and the same movement to your ear from the depths of the body's cavities, the muscles, the membranes, the cartilage [...] as if a single skin lined the performer's inner flesh and the music he sings. [...] That is what the 'grain' would be: the materiality of the body speaking its mother tongue: perhaps the letter; almost certainly *signifiance*. (IV, 150)[11]

Like the obtuse meaning of the stills taken from Eisenstein's *Battleship Potemkin* and *Ivan the Terrible I* (1944), grain is a 'supplement that my intellectual understanding cannot succeed in absorbing, at once persistent and fleeting, smooth and elusive',[12] and 'an emotion value, an evaluation' ('une émotion valeur, une évaluation' (III, 493)). Each of these figures (grain, obtuse or third meaning) is aligned with *signifiance*, and the *signifiance* of the voice, its grain, is of the body. As such, it is impenetrable to a form of analysis or commentary that would treat it either as communication or as something associated with the soul ('âme' (IV, 151)).[13]

Barthes identifies further problems with Proust's writing about music in 'Piano souvenir' (1980), one of the last of his texts to be published in his lifetime:

> The piano was, in my adolescence, a continuous and distant sound: I had an aunt who taught it in the provinces, in B.: from my bedroom, or better still, on returning home through the garden, I would hear musical scales, little snatches of classical pieces [...] every time I hear, from afar, someone practising the piano, my entire childhood, including our house in B. and even the light of the South West, irrupts within my sensibility; for this ascent through time, this plunge into affect, I do not require a 'little phrase' like Vinteuil's: a scale will do. (V, 898)[14]

Here, in what could certainly be described as a rewriting that does not imitate but rather operates variations on Proust's work, Barthes distances himself from the melodies of Vinteuil's little phrase whilst simultaneously reconstructing an undeniably Proustian experience.

Given Barthes's adjective allergy, it is easy to see why Proust's description of Charles Swann's first encounter with Vinteuil's 'petite phrase' (in *Du côté de chez Swann*), for example, would not have appealed:

> below the narrow ribbon of the violin-part, delicate, unyielding, substantial and governing the whole, he had suddenly perceived, where it was trying to surge upwards in a flowing tide of sound, the mass of the piano part, multiform, coherent, level, and breaking everywhere in melody like the deep blue tumult of the sea, silvered and charmed into a minor key by the moonlight. (*ALR*, I, 205)[15]

Ponderously Romantic adjectives and metaphors abound.[16] There is quite a lot more to Barthes's dismissal of the anamnestic power of Vinteuil's little phrase than this, however. In *Le Plaisir du texte*, he describes the 'langages' he hears whilst dozing on a bench in a bar in Tangiers. This external 'stéréophonie', he observes, is reproduced internally, within the listener:

> this so-called 'interior' speech was very much like the noise of the square, like that amassing of minor voices coming to me from outside: I myself was a public square, a souk; through me passed words, tiny syntagms, bits of formulae, and *no sentence formed*, as though that were the law of such a language. This speech, at once cultural and very savage, was above all lexical, sporadic; it set up in me, through its apparent flow, a definitive discontinuity: this *non-sentence* was in no way something that could not have acceded to the sentence, that might have been *before* the sentence; it was: what is eternally, splendidly, *outside the sentence*. (IV, 249–50)[17]

Like the grain of Panzéra's voice, obtuse meaning and music's differential force, the bits and pieces that Barthes remembers absorbing and speaking within himself pose problems for any form of linguistic analysis 'that only believes in the sentence and has always attributed an exorbitant dignity to predicative syntax (as the form of a logic, of a rationality)' (IV, 250).[18] The same might also be said of a musical scale. As we saw a moment ago, Barthes says that, for him, the rehearsal of a 'gamme' is more likely than the performance of a musical phrase (a melody) to bring about an affective – almost stereotypically Proustian – plunge into memory.[19] A musical phrase, however briefly or indistinctly heard, has usually been constructed so as to have some kind of aesthetic effect in itself, or otherwise to form part of a larger composition with greater powers of signification and expression. While the pleasure of the 'phrase', be it textual or musical, is entirely 'culturel' (see IV, 250), a scale has no pretensions to cultural effects: it is a metric, and even though there may be differences in the manner of its playing, it does not make meaning through a mutable or variable structure. It, too, lives outside the sentence and cultural codes: while the expressive, aesthetic effects of a little phrase, its dominant, 'obvious' meaning, attract a predicative interpretation, the measured repetitions of a scale are relatively obtuse in their *signifiance* – in their resistance to (which is not to say their outright destruction of) representation and communication.

Barthes also suggests that an alternative to thinking of the 'phrase' in terms of cultural pleasure, or as something that is completed (rather than infinitely open), is to treat it, perversely, as a body ('unless for certain perverts the sentence is a body?' (IV, 251)).[20] Such perversion is present in the work of those who succeed in shifting the membrane, the 'fringe of contact' (IV, 149), between music and language. Judging from the following observation, which is taken from 'Rasch' (1975), Barthes views Robert Schumann as precisely this kind of pervert:

> What does the body *do*, when it enunciates musically? And Schumann answers: my body strikes, my body collects itself, it explodes, it divides, it pricks, or on the contrary and without warning [...], it stretches out, it weaves [...]. And sometimes – why not? – it speaks, it declaims, it doubles its voice: *it speaks but says nothing*: for as soon as it is musical, speech – or its instrumental substitute – is no longer linguistic but corporeal; what it says is always and only this: *my body puts itself in a state of speech: quasi parlando.* (IV, 832–33)[21]

The body of the sentence becomes musical, like Michelet's, when it enunciates the force of *signifiance* and resists – corrupts – the 'tyranny' of signification (IV, 153). Given what we already know about the role of eros and *signifiance* in the 'Charlus-Discourse', and given that, in a passage on which Barthes draws in his writing on Michelet's *broutement*, Proust's narrator likens the return of a musical refrain – Vinteuil's little phrase – to intense nervous (corporeal) pain,[22] it is surprising that (even) Proust is thought not to cut the mustard as far as his writing on music is concerned. Nevertheless, what we have seen thus far suggests that, for Barthes, Proust is not much of a writer *on* music: he, like other writers before and after him, is 'condemned' to employ adjectives ('condamn[é] à l'adjectif' (IV, 149)) and to approach music in a manner that privileges representational or expressive power over affective force. However, Barthes's observations at the round table in 1972 suggest that Proust's writing is musical, or that it derives from music in some way – or, at the very least, that musical metaphors are readily and properly applicable to his work (and not just because music is a useful metaphor (see V, 528), or because 'we must always think of Writing in terms of music').[23] We might say, in other words, that while Proust's writing about music is no good, his writing itself constitutes a special kind of music, a derivation from music rather than a reflection or commentary upon it, which Barthes describes – metaphorically – as being made of variations without a theme.[24] Furthermore, we have already encountered examples of the ways in which Barthes rewrites and operates variations on Proust's text. Later, then, and in the light of our examination of the relationship between writing (language) and music as Barthes understands it, we will try to get near the bottom of his metaphors as they pertain to Proust's novel and his own engagements with it. In so doing, we will explore the musical perversions of Proust's novel and consider the extent to which Barthes can be said to make contact with – and to rewrite – the musical body of Proust's work. Before doing these things, though, we need to compare what Barthes and other critics have said about Beethoven's *Diabelli Variations* (about their significance within the history of variation form), and to examine other instances of, and variations on, the 'variations sans thème' figure in Barthes's work.

Variations and themes

Beethoven's *Diabelli Variations,* Op. 120 were produced in response to Anton Diabelli's invitation in the early part of 1819 to all composers then in the Austrian Empire to join the *Vaterländischer Künstlerverein*[25] and, as members of that society, to contribute a variation on a waltz that he (Diabelli) provided as a theme (other contributors included Czerny, Hummel, Liszt and Schubert). While, in William Kinderman's view, Diabelli's theme itself is 'trivial',[26] Beethoven's variations are, according to Diabelli himself, 'of no ordinary type'.[27] Indeed, according to André Boucourechliev (to whom Barthes refers in his discussion of the theme-less variations of Proust's work), the *Diabelli Variations* constitute a paradigm shift in the history of the variation form: 'To approach this work through traditional notions of conventional and classical musical forms, through "variation form", would be absurd [...]. As variations "on a theme by Diabelli", the work is a giant bluff'.[28] Kinderman, moreover, goes so far as to say that the received nineteenth-century view of Beethoven's late works (in which the *Diabelli*

Variations are included) as 'chaotic and formless' is 'quite literally correct'.[29] Nevertheless, Beethoven's amorphous variations should not be viewed as entirely disconnected from Diabelli's relatively impoverished theme, which Beethoven famously dismissed as a 'Schusterfleck' (a 'cobbler's patch').[30] Kinderman (again) suggests that, in his later work on the variations (i.e. in 1822–23), Beethoven parodies the waltz but leaves its 'melodic outline and supporting context' intact.[31] Similarly, Boucourechliev says that Beethoven's composition constitutes an entirely new composition in relation to Diabelli's waltz, but he also identifies the latter's 'general constants – large harmonic fields' ('constantes générales – grands champs harmoniques') in Beethoven's first variation.[32] And, finally, as we saw in the previous chapter, Barthes describes Diabelli's theme as 'more or less inexistent, an extremely vague memory' in *Comment vivre ensemble* (p. 182). To echo Barthes's words regarding the effects of obtuse *signifiance* on obvious signification, then, Beethoven's work constitutes a subversion rather than a destruction of the theme provided by Diabelli.[33] Or, to paraphrase what he says about the shadow of the text in *Le Plaisir du texte*, Beethoven's variations contain 'a bit' of theme (see IV, 238).

While Beethoven cannot be said to abandon Diabelli's theme altogether, he does, Boucourechliev argues, do away with musical hierarchies: 'He throws these elements [the musical materials he chooses to work with] into a space that he thinks of as reversible, or almost freed from contingency, where all hierarchies are swept aside'.[34] The conventional gradings that may otherwise determine relations between musical notes ('[l]ow, high, flat, sharp, long, short, thick, thin, strong, weak'),[35] for example, find themselves disrupted by a 'a pre-existing, global and ever-renewed intellectual vision of each variation, a vision to which the material must submit at all costs'.[36] For Boucourechliev, another casualty in Beethoven's de-hierarchization of conventional musical order is the notion that variations constitute the development of a theme that is their origin. Diabelli's theme, in other words, does not have a hierarchizing (or centring) function: 'the thirty-three variations are not partial elements of a developmental process and, even though they occasionally form couples or groups, they do not unfold in accordance with a necessary, ineluctable order'.[37] There is thus a clear affinity between Beethoven's *Diabelli Variations* as they are described by Boucourechliev and by Barthes, and the retroactive, thematic unity which, according to Proust's narrator, is to be found in the work of certain nineteenth-century writers and composers. In each case, the work of variation is not subordinated to the development of a theme (significantly, Proust uses the same word in *La Prisonnière*: 'développement' (see *ALR*, III, 667)). According to Boucourechliev, this non-developmental approach was the lynchpin of Beethoven's overturning of a principle that had defined 'musical poetics' ('notre poétique musicale').[38] Instead of presenting the same object in several different lights (which could be understood, Boucourechliev says, as the most general definition of the variation form), the *Diabelli Variations* present thirty-three different objects 'in the same light, which passes through them'.[39] In other words, the significance of Beethoven's work lies not in its thematic content in the canonical sense (in its varied treatment of Diabelli's theme), but in the radical mutation of the variation form that it represents and initiates: while his predecessors succeed only in producing variations that are the (often creative and imaginative, etc.) development of a theme, the theme of Beethoven's *Diabelli Variations* is no less than variation itself. Unsurprisingly, for Boucourechliev, Beethoven's work inspires a specific kind of listening that is similar to the regime of reading and criticism that, according to Barthes, *À la recherche* demands: just as the audience's 'creative listening' ('écoute créatrice'), which is anxious and open to astonishment ('inquiète, ouverte à l'étonnement'), finds itself stimulated by the asymmetric, aperiodic and discontinuous polyphonic structures of the *Diabelli Variations*,[40] the theme-less variations of Proust's work require both readers and writers to operate variations rather than to interpret them.

We might now explore the extent to which Barthes's musical metaphors are apposite as descriptions of Proust's novel and the kind of work it inspires. Before doing so, or rather in order to be able to do so, I want to look briefly at several other texts by Barthes, none of which contains references to Proust, in which these metaphors – or variations on them – appear.

As the blurb on the back cover of Richard Howard's English translation of Michel Butor's *Mobile: étude pour une représentation des États-Unis* (1962) indicates, the text is 'composed from a wide range of materials, including city names, road signs, advertising slogans, catalogue listings, newspaper accounts of the 1893 World's Fair, Native American writings, and the history of the Freedomland theme park'.[41] In an article entitled 'Littérature et discontinu' that was published in *Critique* the same year as *Mobile* appeared, Barthes emphasizes the 'wounds' inflicted by Butor's eclectic composition on the very foundations of what he calls 'the traditional nature of the Book' ('la nature traditionnelle du Livre' (II, 431)).[42] For Barthes, the author's typographical experiments, for example, constitute a violent 'shaking' or 'shuddering' (an 'ébranlement essentiel')[43] of the continuum of literary discourse, and an offence to the 'Book' understood as an object that links things together, develops, runs and flows:

> spreading words out on a page, combining italic and roman type in accordance with a project that is visibly not part of an intellectual demonstration [...], breaking the flow of the sentence with disparate paragraphs, and making a word as important as a sentence – each of these liberties contributes to the very destruction of the Book. (II, 431)[44]

Butor's attack on the conventions of literature is such that, like Beethoven's *Diabelli Variations* and Michelet's sentences, his text cannot be viewed as a smooth or sliding development.[45] Its fragmentary order is also anathema to an outmoded, reductive and overly delicate form of literary criticism:

> our criticism has gone to school, where it has been taught to discern 'schemas' ['des plans'] and to recognize those of others; but the divisions of the 'schema' [...] are the main breaks of the journey, that is all; what underlies the 'schema' is *the detail*: the detail is not a fundamental raw material, it is inessential small change; major ideas are coined into 'details' without for a moment entertaining the notion that major ideas can be generated from the mere arrangement and disposition of 'details'. Paraphrase is therefore the rational operation of a criticism which demands of the book, above all, that it be continuous: we 'caress' the book, just as we ask the book's continuous language to 'caress' life, the soul, evil, etc. (II, 432–33)[46]

Barthes's words on this occasion clearly anticipate his assertion at the round-table discussion that the role of the critic as operator of variations, in contrast to the habits of more orthodox critical modes (be they 'hermeneutic' or 'thematic'), is to bring about a 'de-structuring' ('déstructuration') – rather than a caressing – of the Proustian text, and to undermine 'the rhetorical structuring (the "schema") that has until now been prevalent in studies on Proust'.[47] For Barthes, then, neither *À la recherche* nor *Mobile* is 'reassuringly composed of a *small number of well-developed ideas*' (II, 433).[48] As such, neither work is 'immobile, panoramique', and both pose problems for 'planimetric' or 'tabular' (i.e. structural) analysis.[49] In fact, the discontinuity of Butor's text, Barthes argues, constitutes a particularly elaborate attack on an aesthetics of 'développement' (II, 438). The figure of 'variations on a theme' is not appropriate here:

> We grant, at a push, that a work can be composed of several themes [...]
> in spite of everything, the theme remains a literary object insofar as it
> submits itself to variation, that is to say, to development. Now in *Mobile*,
> there is no theme, from this point of view [...]. Whereas in the traditional
> aesthetic, all literary effort consists in disguising the theme, in giving it
> unexpected variations, in *Mobile* there is no variation, but only variety,
> and this variety is purely combinatory. (II, 438–49)[50]

In his rejection of thematic development and the textual unity it is usually
thought to guarantee, Barthes uses the same word as Proust's narrator
in his discussion of the vital and non-logical unity of certain nineteenth-
century art works: 'variété' (for Marcel, as we saw in the previous chapter,
the identification of thematic unity *après le fait* does not compromise
artistic variety or execution (see *ALR*, III, 667)). While, in the passage
above, Barthes does not promote an ulterior joining up of previously
disparate fragments, the variety he identifies in Butor's work is, arguably,
another name for – a variation on – 'variations without a theme': the
text is not the development of a theme (there is no theme, Barthes says,
not even a disguised one), and the combinatory variety of Butor's text
is not made of variations in the conventional, musical sense of the term
(i.e. of variations on a theme). There is no 'plan', no 'thematic grouping'
('groupement thématique').[51] Like Proust's novel, which, according to
Barthes, might be the 'true incarnation of the Book Mallarmé dreamed
of' ('la véritable incarnation du Livre rêvé par Mallarmé'),[52] Butor's text is
brought to life not by virtue of its internal growth and development, but
through the distribution of textual units that are characterized by their
extreme mobility. Their movement, Barthes suggests, is one of unending
transmission ('translation perpétuelle' (II, 439)). In other words, like the
particles of *À la recherche*, they are the agents of 'a sort of non-hysterical
theatricality' that is founded on a principle of spatial permutation.[53]

According to Barthes, traditional forms of criticism cannot cope
with this kind of textual shuffling. Indeed, in his preface to *Essais
critiques* (1963), he argues that critics frequently set out to still the text's
inexhaustible variations by transforming them into stagnant themes:

> The writer is a public experimenter: he varies what he recommences;
> persistent, faithless, he knows only one art: that of theme and variations.
> On the side of the variations will be found his battles, his values, his
> ideologies, his times, his desire to live, to know, to participate, to speak,
> in short his content; but on the side of the theme will be found the
> persistence of forms, the great signifying function of the imaginary,
> which is to say the very intelligence of the world. Only, contrary to

what happens in music, each of the writer's variations is itself taken for an authentic theme, whose meaning is immediate and definitive. This mistake is not a slight one; it constitutes literature itself, and more precisely that infinite dialogue between criticism and the work, so that literary time is both the time of authors who advance and the time of criticism which catches up with them. (II, 274)[54]

A brand of criticism that is well-schooled in the identification of rhetorical and thematic schemas, in mistakenly transforming mobile variations into still and definitive motifs (and in positing these as 'Literature'), cannot hope to do justice to the awkward variety of Butor's and Proust's work. Significantly, Barthes's description of the *Diabelli Variations* in 'Musica practica' (1970) suggests that they are made of similar stuff:

Beethoven's deafness designates the lack where all signification is lodged: it appeals not to a music that is abstract or interior, but one that is endowed, one might say, with sensuous intelligibility, with an intelligibility somehow perceptible to the senses. This category is specifically revolutionary, inconceivable in terms of old aesthetics; the oeuvre that submits to it cannot be received according to pure sensuality, which is always cultural, nor according to an intelligible order, which would be that of (rhetorical or thematic) development; without it, neither the modern text nor contemporary music can be accepted. As we know since Boucourechliev's analyses, this Beethoven is exemplarily the one of the *Diabelli Variations*. (III, 449–50)[55]

Beethoven's (and, as we shall see later on, Proust's) work is marked by a sensual force that is not entirely reducible to a cultural order of signification – by a symptom that outplays the aesthetic paradigm of pure sensuality and intelligibility and, in so doing, demands a certain (unconventional) critical activity:

The operation that permits us to grasp this Beethoven (and the category he inaugurates) can no longer be either execution or hearing, but reading [...] this means that [...] we must assume with regard to this music the state, or better the activity, of a performer who can displace, regroup, combine, dispose [...]. Just as the reading of the modern text (at least as we can postulate it, require it) does not consist in receiving, in knowing, or in feeling this text, but in writing it anew, in traversing its writing by a new inscription, in the same way, to read this Beethoven is to *operate* his music, to lure it (as it lends itself) into an unknown praxis. (III, 450)[56]

It is only by operating variations on Beethoven's composition and on Proust's novel, then, that we are able to get to grips with the (modern) aesthetic category their works embody – a category that requires us to be alive to variety rather than to be fixed, unproductively, upon the identification of transcendental themes and their development in works of art. We have little choice, it seems, but to engage with them as amateurs. The activity of the amateur, Barthes argues, is not necessarily defined 'by a lesser knowledge, an imperfect technique' ('par un savoir moindre, une technique imparfaite'),[57] and in a society where the reader finds him or herself removed from the world of production, the amateur 'must revalorize the productive function, which commercial circuits have reified' ('doit revaloriser la fonction productive que les circuits commerciaux ont réifiée').[58] Similarly, the task of the writer, including critics and also novelists, is to accentuate 'the pleasure of production [...] to make him or herself a producer, which is to say an amateur' ('le plaisir de la production [...] se faire soi-même un producteur, c'est-à-dire un amateur')[59] and, in so doing, to bring about what Barthes describes as a narcissistic deformation of others' work in his or her own (see *Préparation*, p. 191). The critical activity of the amateur is to be understood as an active and productive operation: the inspirational work – the work the amateur loves and desires – is not simply imitated. Instead, Barthes encourages readers and writers to engage with 'every beautiful work' ('toute belle œuvre'),[60] including Beethoven's and Proust's, intensively and adventurously – to make something new with the old (to deform and to rewrite) rather than to caress, copy and consume.

Criticism is thus not the creation of a meta-language, a synthesis (see *Préparation*, p. 177). Admittedly, Barthes does not single out Proust for special treatment in this regard (not consistently, at least): he is not allergic to synthetic meta-commentaries simply because he is also a reader of Proust. As he puts it in *Le Lexique de l'auteur* (his notes for a series of seminars that took place at the École pratique des hautes études in 1973–74), for example, 'he writes continuously in metaphors' ('il écrit continûment par métaphores'),[61] and it is the repetition of metaphors – a habit he may or may not have learned from Proust – that allows him to write 'variations without origin' ('variations sans origine').[62] Nevertheless, while Barthes may be opposed to giving works of art the meta-linguistic treatment in a general sense, 'pour des raisons "philosophiques"', he is also keen, as we have seen, to emphasize that Proust's novel and Beethoven's *Diabelli Variations* (all music, in fact), like labyrinths and other 'decentred networks' ('réseaux décentrés'), are the operators of a 'specific resistance to becoming the object of a metalinguistic synthesis' ('résistance particulière à devenir l'objet d'une synthèse métalinguistique').[63]

If we have gained some purchase on the operation of Barthes's musical metaphors, it remains to be seen, nevertheless, in what the resistance of Proust's text consists. As we proceed, therefore, we will explore the affinities between aspects of Proust's work as they are presented by Barthes and the material we have covered in this chapter so far and towards the end of the previous one: Michelet's *broutement* and interruption of *glissement*; the affective, differential force of music and its relation to the cultural 'pleasure' of the sentence, the body and the voice; the *Diabelli Variations* as they are understood by both Boucourechliev and Barthes; the significance of variations and themes (and theme-less variations) in Barthes's texts on other topics; and, finally, Barthes's injunction to readers and critics that they should aim to be productive non-professionals: amateurs.

Barthes's variety

We have already examined Barthes's analysis of the temporal nature and the relative proximity of objects as they are presented in the work of Robbe-Grillet and Cayrol, which he describes as thoroughly modern and (in the case of Robbe-Grillet's work) as un-Proustian. We have also demonstrated, however, that Barthes's own observations help us to identify ways in which Proust's treatment of objects in *À la recherche* neutralizes a paradigmatic distinction between the extreme modernity of the *nouveau roman* and the classical novel. There is, in other words, a 'variety' in Marcel's encounters with objects that serves to bring together literary regimes and conventions that Barthes tries (in the 1950s, at least) to keep separate.

Turning now to Barthes's own writing on Proust, we see that it, too, is marked by a rather messy inconsistency, and certainly by ambivalence. As we have already seen, he describes Proust's novel as infinitely plural or as the embodiment of the *texte scriptible* in 1972,[64] and he identifies Proust, in texts published in 1953 and 1954, as the creator of an 'introduction to Literature' ('introduction à la Littérature') in which a thoroughly modern 'trembling' ('tremblement' (I, 190)) of existence is to be felt. Nevertheless, his remarks concerning the temporal nature of objects in Proust's work show that this is not a view of *À la recherche*'s modernity to which he subscribes consistently. It is also undercut by observations he makes in articles published either side of the round table. For example, in 'De l'œuvre au texte' (1971), Proust is identified as a 'classic':

> There certainly exists a pleasure associated with the work (at least with certain works). I can enjoy reading and rereading Proust, Flaubert, Balzac, and even – why not? – Alexandre Dumas; but this pleasure, as keen as it may be and even if it is disengaged from all prejudice, remains partly (unless there has been an exceptional critical effort) a pleasure of consumption. If I can read those authors, I also know that I cannot rewrite them (that today, one can no longer write 'like that'); this rather depressing knowledge is enough to separate one from the production of those works at the very moment when their remoteness founds one's modernity (for what is 'being modern' but the full realization that one cannot begin to write the same works once again?). The Text, on the other hand, is linked to *jouissance*, to pleasure without separation. (II, 915)[65]

Even as he anticipates here some of the principal concerns of later works (most notably *Le Plaisir du texte*), Barthes also aligns *À la recherche* with the practices and politics of the reader as consumer: it is not, in short, a text that is linked to *jouissance*. Rereading Proust's work may have its pleasures, but *À la recherche* is now also profoundly un-writerly: like the classics of the nineteenth-century French novel, it cannot be rewritten. Thus, while in 1972 Barthes announces Proust's novel as a work that demands to be rewritten (as an ideal object of critical desire), in 1971 the act of reading – and writing about – *À la recherche* seems to be closer to a '*referendum*' ('De l'œuvre au texte', III, 122) marked by the regrettable divorce of producer and consumer. Four years on, in *Roland Barthes par Roland Barthes* (1975), the lament remains more or less the same:

> it is no longer possible to rewrite either Balzac, Zola, or Proust, or even the bad socialist-realist novels, though their descriptions are based on a social division that still applies. Realism is always timid, and there is too much *surprise* in a world which mass media and the generalization of politics have made so profuse that it is no longer possible to figure it projectively: the world which can no longer be either *Mimesis* or *Mathesis* but merely *Semiosis*, the adventure of what is impossible to language, in a word: *Text*. (IV, 694)[66]

While Barthes conceives of Proust's novel elsewhere as the writerly embodiment of infinite linguistic machinations, in this passage, its 'realism' is also seen as alien to the concerns of a modern literary enterprise. We encounter further discrepancies in Barthes's analyses of (fictional) spoken language in *Le Degré zéro de l'écriture* and 'La Division des langages' (1973). In the former, Barthes argues that it is the personal particularity of their speech that sets Proust's characters apart from their nineteenth-century ('classical') predecessors, whose words are little more than a relay for the expression of social power relations:

> Balzac, Sue, Monnier, Hugo found enjoyment in reinstating a few really aberrant forms of pronunciation and vocabulary: thieves' slang, country dialects, German jargon, or the lingo of the concierges. But this social speech, which was a kind of theatrical costume hung on to an essence, never involved the speaker as a total person; the mechanism of the passions went on functioning over and above the speech. It was perhaps necessary to wait for Proust to see the writer fuse certain men totally with their language and present his creatures only through that solid and colourful guise, their way of speaking. While Balzac's creatures, for instance, are easily reducible to the power relations of the society of which they are, so to speak, the algebraic expressions, a character of Proust materializes into the opacity of a particular language, and it is really at this level that his whole historical situation – his profession, his class, his wealth, his heredity, his bodily frame – is integrated and ordered. (I, 219)[67]

The novelty of their language notwithstanding, Barthes realigns Proust's speaking creatures with Balzac's in 'La Division des langages', published some twenty years later. Balzac possesses an acute awareness of social languages, but his apparently natural, acratic sociolects are in fact highly caricatural. They are copies of cultural copies: 'he *frames* them, a little like set pieces, rhetorically produced; he marks them with a folkloric, picturesque index' (IV, 349).[68] Similarly, while Proust's work may provide an 'encyclopédie' of language, he still produces encratic, characterized pastiches: even Proust's reported language fails to escape from a 'folklorist (one might say colonial) view of exceptional languages' ('vue folkloriste (on pourrait dire: coloniale) des langages exceptionnels' (IV, 350–51)). For Barthes, the unfortunate upshot of this culturally mimetic limitation is a Balzac-like treatment of linguistic fragments as so many idiolects, and not as a 'total and complex system of *production* of languages' ('un système total et complexe de *production* des langages' (IV, 351)).[69]

What are we to make of this disorder – of these critical shifts and dispersals? If, as Barthes suggests in what turned out to be his final stand-alone text on Proust ('"Longtemps, je me suis couché de bonne heure"'), the sleepy 'logique' of *À la recherche* is one of 'vacillation' and of 'decompartmentalization' ('[d]écloisonnement' (V, 462)), then his dialogue with Proust is arguably a reflection or echo of that logic: while it does not make sense to number Barthes among those 'full-time professional Proustians' who, in the words of Bowie, 'merely scurr[y] back and forth on the stretched skin of this immense organism [*À la recherche*]',[70] his encounters with Proust are undeniably *proustien* in their mobility and variation. To mess around with Bowie's metaphor of a stretched skin: the best we can do, perhaps, is to say that, for Barthes, the skin of *À la recherche* is a skin not always pulled tight, but one whose tension varies from breaking point to loose, baggy and folded. Or, to use Barthes's words, we could say that his writing on Proust flickers in accordance with the variable resistor – the rheostat – that controls the intermittent lighting of *À la recherche*'s erotic landscape.[71]

Remaining with Barthes's views concerning the untidy logic of Proust's text, we can now return to his suggestion at the round table that the variations of *À la recherche* are theme-less. One of the consequences of this form of variation, he says, is that 'in one sense, the metaphor […] is destroyed. Or, in any case, the origin of the metaphor is destroyed'.[72] It is thus clear that, as far as Barthes is concerned, the variations of Proust's work are not reducible to a single, transcendental origin or theme.[73] But what, precisely, is he getting at here? If we are to make sense of the figures he uses to describe both the strange music – the metaphorical operations – of Proust's work and the mode of his engagement with them, we need to look elsewhere in Barthes's writing, and to try to map what we find there onto the material we have already examined in this chapter.

Proust and variation: Barthes in Morocco

Barthes left Paris in 1969 – according to Claude Coste, the events of 1968 and their aftermath had left him feeling ill at ease ('mal à l'aise') – and took up a teaching position in Morocco.[74] Employed by the University of Rabat on a three-year contract, he ended up working there for only one, from 1 September 1969 to 31 August 1970. During this first academic *séjour* in North Africa, he encountered administrative and professional difficulties and felt that he had been 'thrown into the thankless world of causes' ('plongé dans le monde ingrat des causes').[75] Nevertheless, he was also productive as a writer and as a teacher: he prepared *S/Z* and *L'Empire des signes* for publication (both appeared in 1970) and delivered a series of seminars on Edgar Allan Poe, Proust and Jules Verne. His seminar notes from this period have not been published.[76] In his seminars concerning Proust, Barthes focuses on three well-known passages from the first part of *À l'ombre des jeunes filles en fleurs*: an elaborate description of a dress worn by Mme Swann at her 'Choufleury' (*ALR*, I, 609);[77] a scene of 'blackmail' ('chantage') between the sickly narrator and his grandmother (*ALR*, I, 486–90);[78] and the account of a dinner with M. de Norpois in the opening pages of 'Autour de Mme Swann' (*ALR*, I, 423–77).

In order to go deeper into the significance of the metaphors Barthes uses to describe Proust's work, I want to look at his analysis of the 'Proustian sentence' ('la phrase proustienne') and 'Proustian discourse' ('le discours proustien') in his notes on the long description of Odette's dress (fifteen lines in the most recent, four-volume Pléiade edition of *À la recherche*) and on the fifty or so pages of Proust's novel about the evening with Norpois (we will come back to the scene of blackmail in the next chapter). Proust's sentence reads as follows:

> Beneath the profusion of sapphire charms, enamelled four-leaf clovers, silver medals, gold medallions, turquoise amulets, ruby chains and topaz chestnuts, there would be on the dress itself some design carried out in colour that pursued across the surface of an inserted panel a preconceived existence of its own, some row of little satin buttons that buttoned nothing and could not be unbuttoned, a strip of braid that sought to please the eye with the minuteness, the discretion of a delicate reminder, and these, as well as the jewels, gave the impression – having otherwise no possible justification – of disclosing a secret intention, being a pledge of affection, keeping a secret, ministering to a superstition, commemorating a recovery from sickness, a granted wish, a love affair or a philopena. (I, 609)[79]

Barthes's principal focus in his notes on this characteristically convoluted sentence is what he calls an 'infinite Catalysis' ('Catalyse infinie') – a potentially never-ending proliferation of 'comparaisons', 'substitutions' and 'expansions'. The sentence is made, he says, of 'floors, landings, uncouplings, waterfalls' ('étages, paliers, décrochages, cascades') and is both 'wildly' substitutive ('"éperdument" substitutive') and decentred ('decentrée').[80] As Barthes suggests, Proust's writing here and elsewhere attests to a vivid imaginativeness with regard to substitutive terms rather than to a 'prudish' need to still their movement ('pudeur à les arrêter'): while his sentence is 'simple' insofar as it is made of a main clause and a single subordinate clause ('une principale et une relative'), it also contains participial phrases and is replete with noun complements, comparisons and anaphoric repetitions. Proust's cascading substitution of words also creates an inversion, Barthes says, of habitual semantic hierarchies – a decentring of the sentence's meaning. In other words, at a semantic level, the main clause is now 'the least important' ('la moins importante'). Indeed, Barthes says that it is no more than a neutral pivot ('un pivot neutre'): 'the semantic impact scatters outwards, towards the margins' ('l'impact sémantique s'éparpille vers les extrémités'). Given this 'point' technique ('[t]echnique de la pointe'),[81] and anticipating his comments at the round table in 1972, Barthes describes the Proustian sentence as a 'spherical organism, voluminous, expanding: galaxy' ('organisme sphérique, volumineuse, en expansion: galaxie').[82] He adds that we encounter 'the very play of the Signifier[:] circular chain of substitutions without origin (the first term is only first by virtue of linearity)'[83] in the 'structure métaphorique' of Proust's writing. The Proustian sentence is thus made of variations without a theme and is infinitely explorable to the extent that its metaphorical structure is made of a play of potentially infinite substitutions without origin, and because its meaning is scattered such that the semantic centre will not hold. Like the Flaubertian sentence and Mallarmé's *Un coup de dés* (1897) as they are described by Barthes in 'Flaubert et la phrase' (1967), 'la phrase proustienne' resists classical – cultural – constraints of expression and is founded on 'the infinite possibility of sentential expansion' ('l'infinie possibilité de l'expansion phrastique' (IV, 85)). In its substitutive wildness and expressive underachievement, it is more scale than sentence, more 'thing' ('chose') than a communicative, cultural unit that abides by the closure of its content (see IV, 84). Furthermore, the semantic decentring of the Proustian sentence is the textual analogue of Beethoven's disruption of musical hierarchies, by virtue of which, according to Boucourechliev, the figure of variations on a theme is replaced by the work of variation as (the only) theme. Returning to (and twisting) Genette's suggestion at the round table on Proust that there is an 'effet de variation' at work in Proust's novel, then, and paraphrasing Barthes on the 'effet de réel', Proust's variations say 'we are variation': they connote variation itself.[84]

Barthes's analysis of Proustian discourse ('le discours proustien') in the description of the 'Dîner Norpois' sheds further light on the significance of his musical comparisons.[85] He observes that the narrator's account of his *soirée* with Norpois is made of two diegetic threads (the dinner and the actress Berma's performances) and of an extraordinary number of digressions: these are classed by Barthes as extra-diegetic ('general remarks, in the present tense, of philosophical, psychological, aesthetic etc. significance: bits and books of philosophy')[86] or as related either to the narrator's desire or to 'worldliness' ('la mondanité'). His notes also contain a rudimentary graph on which the movement between these narrative variables is plotted. It strongly resembles a cardiogram, suggesting something like the pulsating *physique* of Proust's discourse. Now, in spite of the digressions and elaborate switching between diegetic threads in Proust's text, Barthes emphasizes that it remains 'Regular = readerly: logico-temporal' ('Régulier = lisible: logico-temporel'). We move, he argues, from a before to an after, from cause to effect: the 'action [...] proceeds from moment to moment, term to term, articulation to articulation, towards an end, a conclusion, a saturation, a close'.[87] Moreover, Proust's text is not 'improvised as it goes along' ('improvisé au fur et à mesure'). Instead, it evolves 'in layers' ('par marcotte'): there are 'skillfully and subtly planted seeds that will be at the heart of important episodes later on'.[88] It would appear, then, that Proust's work is resolutely un-*scriptible*. However, Barthes also notes that the narrative of *À la recherche* (its 'récit') is marked by two 'shakings' or 'shudders' ('ébranlements'): 'vacillation' and 'diffraction'. As we have seen, he employs the same terms in later texts on Proust – the former in '"Longtemps, je me suis couché de bonne heure"' to describe the logic of *À la recherche*, the latter at the round table on Proust to describe what happens to the theme as it passes through its variations.

With regard to 'vacillation' or 'vacillement', Barthes emphasizes the tenuity of the episode's diegetic threads: there are terms missing in the course of the narrator's account of the dinner, he says, and there are several narrative 'éclipses'. The chronology of the episode is also 'blurred' ('floue'). Proust's diegesis is thus only 'sketched: light, economical, allowing the interest [of the episode] to swerve off in different directions' ('esquissée: légère, économe pour laisser l'intérêt se déporter ailleurs'). While the 'figure' and the 'ordre' of the episode remain intact, its 'interest' is not located in the principal diegetic threads – its theme – but in the digressions and variations in which those threads are visible. Here, Barthes's approach to the 'variations' of Proust's work is more nuanced than at the round-table discussion, and more in line with his presentation of *À la recherche* in *Le Degré zéro de l'écriture* as a modern work in which the conventions of 'la Littérature', though suspended and never honoured, loom just over the horizon (see I, 500). His suggestion that Proust's text is simultaneously readerly (in the sense that its logico-temporal order is not hidden or obliterated) and affected by a shuddering vacillation is also more in keeping with his description of the *Diabelli Variations* in *Comment vivre ensemble*, where he says that the theme is 'more or less inexistent, an extremely vague memory flashes through the thirty variations, all of which are thus an absolute digression' (p. 182).[89] The theme of Proust's discourse exists (it remains more or less intact), but it is also made to tremble by diffractions (to which we will return in a moment), digressions, substitutions, vacillations and variations.

In light of these observations, and following Barthes's unpublished lecture notes (on which he appears to have worked during his stay in Rabat) on Freud's 'A Case of Paranoia Running Counter to the Psycho-Analytic Theory of the Disease' (1915), we might say that Proust's work is a 'mutant' text ('texte mutant') rather than a catechistic one ('catéchisme').[90] Freud's and Proust's mutant works simultaneously obey a 'classical narrative logic' ('une logique narrative classique') – they are both readerly in this sense – and are shaken by 'the irruption of a freedom, of a novelty at the level of the signifier, a blow to the signified, the defeat of stereotypes, the depletion of an internal fullness'.[91] Furthermore, Barthes's mutant Proust is close to Barthes's mad Flaubert: as we saw in Chapter Two, for Barthes, Flaubert is able to perforate narrative discourse *'without rendering it meaningless'* (*'sans le* [le discours] *rendre insensé'* (*Le Plaisir du texte*, IV, 223)). The rupturing of discourse is no longer exceptional or sporadic, and a generalized asyndeton ('asyndète')[92] takes hold of all narrative enunciation, producing a discourse that is both highly readable and *'furtively,* one of the maddest one can imagine' (*'en sous main* l'un des plus fous qu'on puisse imaginer' (IV, 223)). Like Proust, then, Flaubert is able to produce a discourse that is broken apart or decentred but never reduced to insignificant babble. Proust is not, Barthes tells his students in Rabat, 'a "chatterbox" who stops narrating, loses his thread in order to speak about something else' ('un "bavard" qui s'arrête de raconter, perd son fil pour parler d'autre chose'). In the work of both authors, readability and writerly 'madness' are permitted to coexist. Narrative discourse is deconstructed or emptied out, but this does not simply destroy the text's readability. As Barthes puts it in *Le Plaisir du texte*: 'the story remains readable nonetheless' ('l'histoire reste cependant lisible' (IV, 223)).

Proust's secret

In terms of making sense of his comparison of *À la recherche* to Beethoven's (almost) theme-less *Diabelli Variations* and of the mode of his engagement with Proust's work across his oeuvre, it is Barthes's description of the work of diffraction in Proust's novel that is the most revealing. Having identified its sentences as 'wildly' substitutive and its discourse as digressive, he adds that what counts ('[c]e qui compte') in the novel 'is not the "subject" of the digression, but the language of the enunciator' ('n'est pas le "sujet" de la digression, mais le langage de l'énonciateur'). The same subject, or what we might call a theme, is 'submitted to several languages' ('soumis à plusieurs langages') in a 'prisme' of languages, and the 'diffraction of an object' ('diffraction d'un objet') in this linguistic prism, he says, is 'the whole "secret" of Proustian discourse' ('tout le "secret" du discours proustien'). Furthermore, the linguistic diffraction of an object, he suggests, makes desire 'vacillate' ('fait vaciller le désir'). Borrowing terms from his contribution to a colloquium on Georges Bataille in 1972 (the same year as the round table on Proust), what matters in *À la recherche* is thus not 'what' ('quoi') but 'who' ('qui'): in Proust's text, we witness 'the intrusion of value into the discourse of knowledge' ('l'intrusion de la valeur dans le discours du savoir') in the form of vacillations of desire and affect.[93] In Nietzschean terms, a swimmer in the waters of *À la recherche* is not hindered unduly by considerations of *'what is valuable in itself,* or of *what is valued by everyone'* ('ce qui vaut en soi, ou de *ce qui vaut pour tous'* (see V, 523)). In other words, what matters in Proust's text is not a theme – not *what* people speak about – but the myriad diffractions of that theme in rich linguistic variations, in the prismatic mouths and in the desires of *those who speak*, rather than in any purely linear or teleological development. It is in this sense that, in Proust's writing, the theme is 'diffracted entirely' ('se diffracte entièrement') in the variations and there is no longer a varied treatment of a theme.[94] The diffractions of *À la recherche* thus bring it close not only to the non-developmental variety of Butor's *Mobile* (and, concomitantly, to the perpetual transmissions and place-changing theatricality of Mallarmé's *Livre total*), but also, once again, to Freud's case of paranoia. Each of the 'partners' ('partenaires') in Freud's text (including the paranoid young woman, the lawyer, the analyst and also the reader), Barthes suggests, is an interpreter, and instead of taking the fictional narrative the paranoid woman tells herself as their referent, the narratives that Freud deploys 'have no other referent than another narrative' ('n'ont pas d'autre référent qu'un autre récit'). In this sense, Barthes observes, Freud's text is 'up in the air, without an original' ('en l'air, sans original') and the fact ('le fait'), the original 'theme', is not the foundation of the narrative and does not authenticate the discourse ('il n'authentife pas le discours'). Given this affinity between Proust and Freud at the level of the 'play of interpretations' ('jeu d'interprétations') in which their writing consists (a structural feature they also share with Beethoven's *Diabelli Variations*, whose theme, as we saw earlier, is variation itself), we might suggest that *À la recherche* is excellent material for critical desire[95] precisely because, like Freud's text (as Barthes describes it in his lecture notes), it posits the possibility of infinite interpretation, which Barthes describes – celebrates – as 'the virtual destruction of all critique' ('l'interprétation infinie, c['est] à d[ire] la destruction virtuelle de toute critique').

The motto ('devise') of Proust's text, Barthes notes, is 'Expenditure ≠ Exchange: move outside communication towards *signifiance*' ('Dépense ≠ Échange: sortir hors de la communication vers la signifiance'). While this injunction anticipates Barthes's work on signification and *signifiance* in *Le Troisième Sens* and *Le Plaisir du texte*, for example, it also has a distinctly Bataillean ring to it. In 'La Notion de dépense' (1933), Bataille contrasts a form of human activity that is entirely reducible to processes of production and conservation with one that is represented by 'unproductive' expenditures ('les dépenses dites improductives').[96] A form of writing in which expenditure does not amount to exchange is one that finds an end in itself rather than in the expression of a given theme or origin – an obvious meaning – for which it might be ultimately exchanged: while its 'signification' has not been abandoned altogether, Proust's radically decentred and digressive discourse tends ineluctably towards a trembling and mobile *signifiance*.

We can now bring Barthes's seminars on Proust in Rabat to bear upon our understanding and appreciation of his work on Proust and say how this illuminates his comparison of *À la recherche* and the *Diabelli Variations*. So far, we have identified an affinity between Barthes's brief, frequently contradictory references to *À la recherche* and the emphasis he places, in each of his more studious engagements, on its diffractions, digressions, substitutions, vacillations and variations. Put simply, the punctual inconsistencies of his writing can be viewed as critical echoes and rewritings of the logic of Proust's text as he sees it. We have also touched on what makes Barthes's approach to *À la recherche* different from other critics of Proust's novel. We have already encountered

Genette's observations that there is an extreme 'effect of variation' at work in *À la recherche* and that 'it would be quite pleasant', therefore, 'to think that the role of the critic, like the musician, is to *interpret variations*'.[97] To cite one further example: in *Proust et le monde sensible* (1974), Jean-Pierre Richard argues that 'when one reads Proust, one is immediately struck by the extraordinary multiplication, variation, lability of both personal and sensory identities, and by the importance of the hiatuses, the gaps separating each of their situations'.[98] Nevertheless, for Richard, the apparent dislocatedness of the Proustian universe 'does not really culminate in incoherence; it allows, rather, for the discovery of another order, of a sensory organization that is perhaps more primitive'.[99] As Richard memorably puts it, 'with Proust, what is disjointed is also what is in the process of being joined up' ('chez Proust, le décousu est toujours aussi l'en-train-de-se-coudre').[100] Now, there are signs of disagreement or at least difference between these authors and Barthes. As we saw earlier, Barthes does not accept Genette's notion that the role of the critic is to interpret the text's variations (those that are 'effectivement dans le texte'), and he argues that the critic's job is 'not to execute, but to operate variations' ('non pas exécuter, mais opérer des variations').[101] Furthermore, unlike Richard, he refuses to reduce the variations of Proust's work – be they stylistic, thematic, temporal or structural – to a single, primitive (anterior) theme. In its punctual variations, Barthes's writing on Proust thus nourishes a desire to engage with Proust's novel heterogeneously and intensively, just as his work is itself driven by the very same critical desire. This is, moreover, a mode of engagement that the variations and vacillations of *À la recherche* demand.[102]

Barthes's seminars in Rabat show that there is more to his writing on Proust than this, though. Indeed, if we read those seminars alongside Robbe-Grillet's remarks about the 'sliding' ('glissement') of Barthes's writing in his *Pourquoi j'aime Barthes* (a transcription of a discussion between Robbe-Grillet, Barthes and others at Cérisy in June 1977), another possibility emerges: it is the form, the rhythm of Barthes's engagements with *À la recherche* that reveals – or even reproduces – the secret of Proustian discourse as Barthes conceives of it in his Rabat seminar notes. For Robbe-Grillet, what counts in Barthes's writing, its 'sens' (its meaning but also its direction, its movement), is located not in 'the elements between which the thought has slid' ('les éléments entre lesquels la pensée aura glissé') but in 'sliding' ('le glissement').[103] The only content of Barthes's work is its form, 'this kind of sliding that takes place' ('cette espèce de glissement qui s[e] produit'),[104] and in this, Robbe-Grillet argues, Barthes is a 'modern novelist' ('romancier moderne') rather than the author of a form of 'conceptual thought organized in the normal way' ('pensée conceptuelle normalement organisée'):

> instead of presenting a text, such as a Balzac novel, that is easy to assemble, gathered around its solid core of meaning and truth, the modern novel simply presents fragments which, to crown it all, always describe the same thing – a thing which is almost nothing. But the movement of literature is this sliding from one scene to the same scene that repeats itself in a form that is barely diverted, barely converted, barely inverted.[105]

Barthes's writing on Proust cannot be viewed as 'Balzacian' (at least as Robbe-Grillet defines this term): there is no well-formed and stable epistemic centre. Instead, it slides between fragments (or variations) in which the same thing, a theme (i.e. *À la recherche*), is described either in contradictory ways or in ways that emphasize the decompartmentalized and vacillating nature of the text on which they focus. This is not, then, a *glissement* of the Chateaubriand sort: it may slide, albeit jerkily, but we cannot – and Robbe-Grillet does not – characterize the movement of Barthes's writing as a teleological navigation or articulation towards a final euphoria. With all of this in mind, and following his own observations about Proust's novel, it might be argued cogently that what counts in Barthes's work on Proust – or one of the reasons that this work really counts – is the intrusion into critical discourse of a 'who' in favour of a 'what': what matters, then, is not the content of Barthes's various *énonciations*, not *what* he says about Proust's work, but the diffractions of Proust's writing in the 'prism' of Barthes's language (of his tongue), and the 'affectation of the subject through Writing' – the vacillations of desire, the evaluations – to which those diffractions attest.[106] Robbe-Grillet's description of his work suggests that the form of Barthes's engagements with Proust are a mark of his credentials as a writer of 'modern' novels rather than a sign that, as Bowie puts it, 'Proust was too important to be submitted to dissection or decipherment'.[107] Nevertheless, while we may be inclined to accept Robbe-Grillet's suggestion that the meaning of Barthes's work is to be found in a movement between fragments or themes which appear here and there[108] and which are 'almost nothing' ('presque rien'),[109] reading Barthes on Proust reveals that the varied and inconsistent *glissement* – we could also call it a *broutement* – of Barthes's work (on Proust or otherwise) is not just novelistic or musical: it is also Proustian. Barthes, we might say, is already in Proust.[110]

Barthes's Rabat seminar notes thus contain tools for making sense of the metaphors he uses to describe Proust's work – and the active critical treatment it demands – in 1972. In order to examine these musical comparisons even further, and to shed more light on the relationship between Proust's novel and music (both in terms of its theme-less variations and its textual 'music' more generally), we need to return to Barthes's seminars on the 'Charlus-Discourse' and to consider its affinities with some of his essays that are specifically about music, several of which we explored earlier on in this chapter.

Charlus, Charles (and Robert)

Towards the end of his final seminar on Charlus (on 30 March 1977), Barthes identifies the sense in which music is 'fondamentale' in Proust's work:

> Not in the sense of the Little-Vinteuil-phrase discourse (philosophy of memory), but the music of language, language as music. Voices are described in their mobility: subtlety and acuity in respect to how a voice rises and falls. Charlus specifically: the space of Charlus (his identity as a field of forces): his voice. (p. 218)[111]

In order to grasp how this observation (which anticipates his dismissal of the anamnestic effects of Proust's little phrase in 'Piano souvenir') and how much of the other material in Barthes's seminars on the 'Charlus-Discourse' resonates with his writing on Proust and on music, we first need to investigate the links between those seminars, which are one of Barthes's most sustained – albeit notational – engagements with *À la recherche*, and another text that has informed some of our discussion in this and previous chapters: *S/Z* (which is a meticulous reading of a short story by Balzac and is often said, as we have seen, to mark Barthes's 'rupture brutale' with structuralism).[112] While there are prominent echoes of *S/Z* in the Proust round-table discussion (*À la recherche* is triumphantly 'plural', for example), they nevertheless remain only implicit. In contrast, the relationship between the seminars on Charlus and *S/Z* is stated explicitly:

> Let's begin by doing away with one methodological illusion: Charlus's discourse is not an example, a sample. It does not represent a typical

class, that of 'holding forth'. It is caught in a difference – and, to my mind (as an erstwhile structural analyst), in a double difference: 1) with respect to 'holding forth' on the *doxa*, the stereotype, 2) with respect to an earlier analysis: *S/Z*. (p. 204)[113]

Barthes describes the first difference of the 'Charlus-Discourse' at the beginning of the session of 23 March 1977. Charlus's speech is 'sustained, dense, continuous, unbroken, browbeating the Narrator' ('tenu, dense, continu, nappé, assommé au Narrateur' (p. 203)), and thus conforms, Barthes argues, to a stereotypical (ancient) understanding of discourse and rhetoric. At the same time, it is mobile and changeable, 'like a landscape on a cloudy day' ('comme un paysage sous nuages' (p. 203)). Its aspects are restless and changing: it is 'a sort of subtle shimmer of inflections' ('sorte de moire subtile d'infléxions' (p. 203)). It repeats, furthermore, the decadence of Wagner's musical 'textile' ('tissu musical') insofar as it is a compact yet fluid mass: it is simultaneously continuous and inflective (p. 203).

Barthes prefaces his examination of Charlus's second difference with what is, in fact, a similarity between *S/Z* and the seminars on the 'Charlus-Discourse': both explore 'unique' texts. In *Comment vivre ensemble*, 'l'Unique = le Texte' (p. 204). While Charlus's discourse is atypical, it does not cast itself fully outside structuration and into the ineffable ('dans l'ineffable' (p. 204)): it is a non-negating derision of discourse. In *S/Z*, the 'unique' text 'is valid for all the texts of literature, not in that it represents them (abstracts and equalizes them), but in that literature itself is never anything but a single text' (III, 128).[114] It is thus one entry point among many in a rhizomatic intertextual network ('réseau à mille entrées'), granting access to 'a perspective (of fragments, of voices from other texts, other codes), whose vanishing point is nonetheless ceaselessly pushed back, mysteriously open' (III, 128).[115] Later on in *Comment vivre ensemble*, Barthes identifies both a further similarity and a difference between Proust's and Balzac's unique texts: 'Charlus: cultural code (style of the seats, for example) + an affective, emotive, enunciative supplement' (p. 204).[116] In other words, the 'Charlus-Discourse' is both like and unlike *Sarrasine*. The 'voice' of cultural codes is easily discernible in both texts. For example, in *Sarrasine*, Balzac refers to 'Germans who accepted as fact these clever witticisms of Parisian scandal-mongering' (III, 153),[117] eliciting the following observation in *S/Z*: 'Ethnic Psychology: a paradigm of the period: the naïve German, the witty Parisian' (III, 153).[118] In the

'Charlus-Discourse', 'the passage about the young man from Berlin; he, at least, has heard of Wagner and the *Walküre*' (p. 205),[119] for example, is the off-stage voice ('voix-*off*' (III, 135)) of a musical 'code culturel' (see p. 205). Both texts thus refer to 'numerous codes of knowledge or wisdom' ('[de] très nombreux codes de savoir ou de sagesse') and appear to take a 'scientific or moral authority' ('autorité scientifique ou morale' (III, 133)) as their basis. So far, so analogous.

In *S/Z*, Barthes suggests that each of the aforementioned codes is 'one of the forces that can take hold of the text (of which the text is the network), one of the Voices out of which the text is woven' (III, 135).[120] They are described in *Comment vivre ensemble* as the principal focus of 'structural analysis, that is to say the locating of units, morphemes of discourse' (p. 205).[121] And here we encounter the important difference: where, in *Comment vivre ensemble*, Barthes refers to 'the appearance of the notion of force in analysis' ('l'apparition de la notion de force dans le champ de l'analyse' (p. 205)), he does so in order to interrogate the less known ('le moins connu' (p. 205)) rather than to regurgitate what is already familiar to readers of *S/Z*. While, in *Sarrasine*, culture is a 'référence', in the 'Charlus-Discourse', it is also a place of enunciation: 'the cultural code allows him [Charlus] to position himself in the eyes of the other, to enter into a reciprocal play of images, of positions' (p. 204).[122] Charlus's affective shimmering ('moire affective' (p. 209)) is thus a supplement in the full Derridean sense: it is, as Derek Attridge puts it, 'a little extra ingredient beyond the mass of culturally coded material' and, as such, it is 'the one thing that the work could not do without'.[123] For Barthes, it is what makes Charlus's discourse tick (or, rather, tic, since it is both the motor that ensures its progression and the guarantor of its *rhuthmos*). Moreover, in suggesting that, in addition to 'Chance', 'Enthymeme' and 'Layering' ('Hasard', 'Enthymème' and 'Marcotte' (p. 206)),[124] for example, the force of Charlus's marks of affect is one of the principal 'opérateur[s]' (p. 208) of his discourse, Barthes illuminates the forces of linguistic *production* – rather than mere caricature – at work in Proust's text.

Shimmering (*moire*) is central to Barthes's analysis of enunciation in both *Sarrasine* and *À la recherche*. Commenting on Balzac's presentative phrase 'It was a man' ('C'était un homme' (III, 152)), Barthes writes:

> Who is speaking? [...] Here is it is impossible to attribute an origin, a point of view, to the statement. Now, this impossibility is one of the ways in which the plural nature of the text can be appreciated. The more

indeterminate the origin of the statement, the more plural the text. In modern texts, the voices are so treated that any reference is impossible: the discourse, or better, the language, speaks: nothing more. By contrast, in the classical text the majority of the utterances are assigned to an origin, we can identify their father and owner [...] however, it may happen that in the classical text, always haunted by the appropriation of speech, the voice gets lost, as though it had leaked out through a hole in the discourse. The best way to conceive the classical plural is then to listen to the text as an iridescent exchange carried on by multiple voices, on different wavelengths and subject from time to time to a sudden *dissolve*, leaving a gap which enables the utterance to shift from one point of view to another, without warning: writing is set up across this tonal instability (which in the modern text becomes atonality), which makes it a shimmering texture of ephemeral origins. (III, 152)[125]

How does this bear upon our understanding of the plurality of Charlus's affective *moire*? Does Barthes's insistence in *Comment vivre ensemble* on the importance of our taking enunciation into account, of a 'consideration of the position occupied by subjects in discourse' ('prise en considération de la place des sujets dans le discours' (p. 219)), suggest that Proust's text is not as immodestly plural as Barthes might have thought – that the origin of enunciation is in fact fully determinate? We know who is speaking, don't we? And after all, doesn't Barthes say that his analysis of the 'Charlus-Discourse' belongs to a 'philology of the *who* and not of the *what*' ('philologie du *qui* et non du *quoi*' (p. 220))? Is Proust's disorigination of enunciation in the 'Charlus-Discourse' even more restricted than Balzac's on this occasion – discernible only in the convergence of coded voices by virtue of which the origin 'gets lost' ('se perd') amongst the *'already-written'* ('déjà-écrit' (III, 135))?

While we know that it is Charlus who addresses the narrator, it is difficult to attribute his out-of-whack utterance, his affective shimmers, to a stable origin or enunciating subject. Charlus, as we have already seen, is an 'enormous flickering sign': his erotic discourse is a 'field, a play of forces, of mobile intensities' ('champ, un jeu de forces, d'intensités mobiles' (p. 216)). The 'Charlus-Discourse' not only proceeds, according to Barthes, in accordance with a series of direct triggers ('déclencheurs directs'), but it is also pushed along by 'inflectors' of discourse ('infléchisseurs' or 'inflexèmes' (p. 214)) and by explosions of affect ('explosèmes' (p. 217)), none of which can be accommodated comfortably within the realm of the Logos. There is a radical instability of tone in the erratic modulations of Charlus's voice. While the 'Charlus-Discourse' may be haunted by 'the appropriation of speech' ('l'appropriation de la parole' (III, 152)), the intensity of its variegations is such that enunciation can migrate in the manner described by Barthes in the passage on *Sarrasine* above ('from one point of view to another, without warning'), or, as he puts it in the seminar notes on Charlus, 'in an absolutely unexpected way' ('d'une façon absolument inattendue' (p. 209)). Thus, while there is shimmering in both *Sarrasine* and *À la recherche*, there is a notable difference between the enunciative disoriginations they enact: while the music of *Sarrasine* leaves us unsure as to 'qui parle?', the enigmatic variations of the 'Charlus-Discourse' are driven and inhabited by 'the forces, the intensities, the excesses and the deflations, the flushes and blanches *of the person who is speaking*' (p. 219).[126]

Barthes draws analogies between text and music in both *S/Z* and *Comment vivre ensemble*. In the long quotation from *S/Z* we have just examined, he tells us that we must listen to the exchange between multiple voices in the classical text if we are to appreciate its plurality. The space of the readerly text, he argues, is comparable to a (classical) musical score (see III, 141). The classical is 'tonal':

> tonal unity is basically dependent on two sequential codes: the revelation of truth and the coordination of the actions represented: there is the same constraint in the gradual order of melody and in the equally gradual order of the narrative sequence. *Now, it is precisely this constraint which reduces the plural of the classical text.* The five codes mentioned, frequently heard simultaneously, in fact endow the text with a kind of plural quality (the text is actually polyphonic), but of the five codes, only three establish permutable, reversible connections, outside the constraint of time (the semic, cultural, and symbolic codes); the other two impose their terms according to an irreversible order (the hermeneutic and proairetic codes). The classical text, therefore, is actually tabular (and not linear), but its tabularity is vectorized, it follows a logico-temporal order. It is a multivalent but incompletely reversible system. What blocks its reversibility is just what limits the plural of the classical text. (III, 142–43)[127]

In *Comment vivre ensemble*, Barthes contends that, in *S/Z*, he underestimated the methodological challenges posed by the polyphonic triggering of codes (see p. 205). This seems unduly pessimistic: polyphony is integral to the plurality of both the 'Charlus-Discourse' and the classical text. In spite of this affinity, the music of the 'Charlus-Discourse' is not the same as *Sarrasine*'s. First, a polyphony of cultural codes is supplemented by the musical blasts of Charlus's voice, in which 'everything seems transcended – or annulled – by a melodic differential of intensities' ('tout semble transcendé – ou annulé – par un différentiel mélodique des intensités' (p. 218)). Charlus's place, his 'identité' (p. 218), is thus one of forces understood in the Nietzschean sense: as the engendering of difference. Secondly, as we have already seen, his *rhuthmotic* judders cannot be interpreted according to the movement and development of a 'hermeneutic' space (p. 218). They are not fully amenable to a 'truth-oriented project' ('projet aléthique' (III, 918)) or to structural analysis. While the music of his discourse may not be entirely atonal – there may be reference in the melodic differential of Charlus's voice to a scale or tonic – the affective *moire* of the 'Charlus-Discourse' is nevertheless a paradigm example in Proust's text of a reversible (musical) form: variation without a theme. Indeed, the description of the *Diabelli Variations* in what Barthes calls Boucourechliev's 'little book' ('petit livre')[128] on Beethoven is perfectly substitutable as a description of the reversibility of Charlus's affective variations. As we saw earlier on, Boucourechliev argues that Beethoven 'throws these elements [the musical materials he chooses to work with] into a space that he thinks of as reversible, or almost freed from contingency, where all hierarchies are swept aside'.[129] He continues:

> Low, high, flat, sharp, long, short, thick, thin, strong, weak – there are so many states and positions of the raw material of music dictated by a sort of pre-existing, global, and ever-renewed intellectual vision of each variation [...]. Thirty-three constellations of the imagination, none of which can be said more or less to resemble an initial 'model' or to be more or less close to one. We cannot think of these constellations in straight lines, as coming one after the other, but as existing in a circle of metamorphoses without beginning or end, or better still, as a galaxy in which each star is of the same 'size' and equidistant from all the others.[130]

Charlus's song is multivalent and reversible: a mobile constellation in what is for Barthes – at times, at least – an infinitely expansive, writerly galaxy. Both the 'Charlus-Discourse' and *Sarrasine*, then, are 'comparable at every point to a (classical) musical score' ('en tout point comparable à une partition musicale (classique)' (III, 141)). However, Charlus's explosions are a far cry from the logically and temporally ordered partitions that we find in *Sarrasine*. If the supplements of affect in the 'Charlus-Discourse' recall the metamorphoses of the *Diabelli Variations*, the polyphonic music of *Sarrasine* is arguably closer to the *Kreuzer Sonata* (1803), the variations of which, according to

Boucourechliev, are always characterized by a 'resemblance to the initial model, which is preserved throughout the movement' ('ressemblance au modèle initial, préservée tout au long du mouvement').[131]

It may come as little surprise that Proust's 'man-woman' ('homme-femme' (*ALR*, III, 23)) should list '*Sarrazine [sic]*' (*ALR*, III, 438) among Balzac's great works.[132] As Leo Bersani has observed, in his attempts to read and interpret the mysterious signs of Charlus's sexual tastes, Marcel is confronted by an 'incessant crossing over from one sex to the other' that 'wreaks havoc with the boundaries that usually keep each [sexual] category in place'.[133] Spying on the entomological pickup scene between Charlus and Jupien at the beginning of *Sodome et Gomorrhe*, Marcel sees his earlier suspicions concerning the usually hyper-virile baron's effeminacy confirmed: 'I now understood how, earlier in the day, when I had seen him coming away from Mme de Villeparisis's, I had managed to arrive at the conclusion that M. de Charlus looked like a woman: he was one!' (*ALR*, III, 16).[134] In his subsequent musings on 'inverts' ('les invertis'), Marcel imagines that their origins go all the way back to an original human hermaphroditism. The baron is, in other words, neither simply male nor female, but both at once.

Besides linking the baron to the complex destabilization of sexual categories that Balzac's castrato embodies, how are we to interpret the unmissable (especially after *S/Z*) error in Proust's orthography – the substitution, in keeping with the spelling of the male version of the name, of a 'z' for the second 's' in the title of Balzac's novella?[135] What does Proust's mistake tell us about his notorious baron? Famously, for Barthes, 'Z' is the 'sharp' letter of 'mutilation':

> Z stings like a chastising lash, an avenging insect; graphically, cast slantwise by the hand across the blank regularity of the page, amid the curves of the alphabet, like an oblique and illicit blade, it cuts, slashes, zebras; from a Balzacian viewpoint, this Z (which appears in Balzac's name) is the letter of deviation [...]; finally, Z is here the first letter of La Zambinella, the initial of castration, so that by this orthographical error committed in the middle of his name, in the centre of his body, Sarrasine receives the Zambinellian Z in its true sense – the wound of lack. Further, S and Z are in a relation of graphological inversion: the same letter seen from the other side of the mirror: Sarrasine contemplates in La Zambinella his own castration. (III, 207)[136]

The onomastic mistake in Balzac's text pierces Sarrasine's name with the 'true sense' of castration as lack, and marks the '"difference *within*" which prevents any subject from coinciding with itself'.[137] While

Sarrasine may 'read' Zambinella as a 'perfectly readable, motivated sign [...], as full and transparent Logos', she is 'the very image of the empty and arbitrary sign'.[138] In the language of *Le Plaisir du texte*, which can produce a rather creepy impression, Sarrasine believes that Zambinella is a product to be devoured ('Sarrasine dévorait des yeux la statue de Pygmalion' (see III, 318)),[139] but the soprano can, in fact, only be grazed upon. It may be possible, Barbara Johnson argues, to 'read Balzac's opposition between the ideal woman and the castrato as metaphorically assimilable to Barthes's opposition between the readerly and the writerly'.[140] Nevertheless, for Johnson, the difference is to be found not '*between* the readerly and the writerly, but *within* the very ideals of the readerly'.[141] The name of Balzac's artist, spelled with an 's', also embodies a 'deconstruction of the readerly ideal':[142] it, too, marks the limits and blindness of – or within – the readerly. Indeed, while we may identify a difference 'between' Sarrasine's ideal and Zambinella (and, by metaphorical extension, between the readerly and the writerly), there is already a spectral trace of this difference within Sarrasine's name itself.

Things are a little different in Proust's work. In fact, the 'Charlus-Discourse' is marked by a quadruple rather than a double difference: 1) 'with respect to "holding forth" on the *doxa*, the stereotype'; 2) 'with respect to an earlier analysis: S/Z';[143] 3) with respect to, or rather 'within', itself – Charlus's discourse is inhabited by the irreducible difference of 'variations without a theme'; and 4) with respect to the name of Balzac's novella and its protagonist. Charlus speaks the name of Balzac's work and its eponymous artist, and Proust permits the sting of the *punctum*-like 'Z' to appear both in Charlus's erroneous naming of the novella and in the zig-zagging divagations of his discourse. Proust writes that which haunts *Sarrasine*: the Z of Zambinella that is 'thematized in the very name of Sarrasine, of the sculptor, but as a lack' ('thématisé dans le nom même de Sarrasine, du sculpteur, mais par *manque*')[144] is inscribed within Charlus's discourse. Charlus's '*Sarrazine*' is thus a mark that shows *À la recherche* to be close to Balzac even as it is distant from him. In other words, *À la recherche* says what *Sarrasine* will not: the force of 'Z', the letter of deviation, is now not so much *received* as the wound of lack as it is *voiced* by Charlus as he names *Sarrasine* incorrectly and sings the variations of an affective shimmering that supplements the rhythmical music of his discourse's cultural codes.

Returning now to the language of Barthes's writing on music, we can say that structural analysis and commentary cannot hear (all of) the music of the 'Charlus-Discourse' and that the differential force of the latter brings with it a constraint to evaluate and to affirm.[145] It is made of culturally coded 'phrases', of what Proust (in relation to Michelet) calls a scholar's precaution, but it is also the site of a melodic differential of intensities – of a musician's cadence (see *ALR*, I, 306). Thus, like Beethoven's *Diabelli Variations* as they are described by Barthes in 'Musica practica', the 'Charlus-Discourse' cannot be 'received according to pure sensuality, which is always cultural, nor according to an intelligible order which would be that of (rhetorical or thematic) development' (III, 449–50).[146] This resonance also suggests that readers of the baron's discourse are required to *operate* it, to 'write it anew' ('l'écrire de nouveau' (III, 450)). Moreover, and borrowing terms from one of Barthes's essays on music to which we have not so far referred ('Écoute' (1977)), Charlus's speech, like the work of a 'modern' composer (Barthes's example is John Cage), requires a form of reading and listening that is alive not (or not only) to 'the advent of a signified, object of a recognition or of a deciphering', but (also) to 'the very dispersion, the glimmerings of signifiers' – to an unending activity that seeks to produce new glimmerings from old ones, 'without ever arresting their meaning' (V, 351).[147] Charlus's voice is an 'object of a semiotics of forces, of active philology' ('objet de la sémiotique des forces, de la philologie active' (*Comment vivre ensemble*, p. 218)). As such, like Charles Panzéra's, it is made, at least in part, of 'declamation and *pronunciatio*' ('la déclamation, la *pronunciatio*' (p. 218)). The voices of Charles and Charlus are thus both endowed with a certain *physique*, by virtue of which music, perversely, enters into – and eroticizes – (their) language.

Barthes describes the relationship between Charlus's language and his body in the following terms: 'the "Charlus-Discourse" = a Text, spoken by a voice, a body, and what a body! Charlus's body is very present, very figured, in all of the *Recherche du temps perdu*' (*Comment vivre ensemble*, p. 204).[148] Charlus's voice, then, has 'grain': it is inhabited by a supplementary force that exceeds culture. It also constitutes an unusual combination of what Barthes refers to in 'Le Grain de la voix' as the 'pheno-song' ('*phéno-chant*'), a relatively un-grainy form that encapsulates 'everything which, in the performance, is at the service of communication, of representation, of expression: what is usually spoken of, what forms the tissue of cultural values' (IV, 150),[149] and the voluptuous 'geno-song' ('*géno-chant*'), which is connected to the volume of the singing and speaking voice and to 'a signifying game alien to communication, to representation (of feelings), to expression'

(IV, 150–51).[150] In allowing pheno- and geno-song to touch, the effects of the 'Charlus-Discourse' come close to the perversions of Schumann's *Kreisleriana* as they are described by Barthes in 'Rasch':

> In Schumann's *Kreisleriana*, I actually hear no note, no theme, no contour, no grammar, no meaning, nothing which would permit me to reconstruct an intelligible structure of the work. No, what I hear are blows: I hear what beats the body, or better: I hear this body that beats. Here is how I hear Schumann's body (indeed, he had a body, and what a body! [...]). (IV, 827)[151]

Both Charlus's (virtual) body and Schumann's (real) body-made-virtual-in-the-music are quite something, then ('quel corps!'), and their physical presence determines the significance (or rather *signifiance*) of the music they produce: just as Charlus's erotic song brings together cultural codes of knowledge and the enunciating subject's forces of affect, Schumannian 'beating' ('battement'), Barthes suggests, is 'panic, but it is also coded (by rhythm and tonality) [...] the panic of the blows apparently remains within the limits of a docile language' (IV, 829).[152] Furthermore, where Charlus's discourse is marked by affective 'explosèmes', Schumann's music is similarly non-developmental: '[it] *does not follow* (by contrasts or amplification), it explodes: it is a continuous *big-bang*' (IV, 828).[153] The bodies of both Schumann's *intermezzi* (see IV, 828) and Charlus's speech are 'riddled with losses' ('troué[s] de pertes' (IV, 834)), but their loss does not mean, as we have seen on several occasions in this and the previous chapter, that they are dispossessed of all cultural – obvious – signification.

While Barthes may appear to give priority to the writerly, to the third meaning or *signifiance*, to *jouissance* and to Charlus's singular intensities, none of them is entirely independent of the coded operations (Balzacian, classical, or otherwise) they supplement and subvert. *À la recherche* thus performs 'today's task' as Barthes describes it: the disassociation of subversion and destruction. As we have seen, for Barthes, signification (the obvious) and *signifiance* (the obtuse) are in conversation with each other: they are related dialogically. To borrow a term from Derrida (with its own aptly musical connotations), the forces of the 'Charlus-Discourse' 'composent' with a polyphonic triggering of cultural codes.[154] Barthes marks their composition with a '+' symbol. The music of the 'outside code' ('hors code') and the 'always coded' ('toujours codé')[155] is one in which regular cadence and *rythmos* are upset or lost (in the speleological sense of the word) rather than simply destroyed. Or, as Lyotard puts it in *Discours, figure*, 'closed signification' ('la signification fermée') can be inhabited by 'la force'.[156] Similarly, taken in synchronic isolation, Barthes's references to Proust between the 1950s and the end of his life might be understood as an attempt to remain within the realm of 'pertinence' and thus to resist the effacement or blurring of what he calls the 'slash' of opposition ('la barre de l'opposition' (III, 173)): while bits of *À la recherche* may provide paradigmatic examples of an absolute, writerly plurality, others remain resolutely classical, realist, readerly. However, reading across Barthes's oeuvre, a more unstable and vacillating logic emerges: the network of echoes, affinities and contradictions in Barthes's engagements with Proust, coupled with the logic of supplementarity that informs his understanding of the relationship between the 'Charlus-Discourse' and *Sarrasine*, for example, suggest that the stuff of which *À la recherche* is made is not hygienically antithetical. Neither *À la recherche* nor Barthes's engagements with it obey the strictures of a metronomic or mathematical *rythmos*: the rhythm of Barthes's Proust variations must admit of 'one more or one less, an imperfection, a supplement, a lack' ('un plus ou un moins, une imperfection, un supplément, un manque') as he rubs against – as he integrates and covers – the subtle swing, the 'supple, open, mobile rhythm; momentary form' ('rythme souple, disponible, mobile; forme passagère')[157] of *À la recherche* itself.[158] Proust's novel constitutes, then, a disturbance in classification – a lifting (or at least a trembling) of the dividing line, the paradigmatic slash mark that permits meaning to function pertinently. *À la recherche*, in other words, is profoundly neutral, a degree zero that disrupts the relentless binarism of the paradigm.[159] It is to this – and other forms of – neutrality that we now turn.

Notes

1 The text of the lecture was published in French – under the title 'La Musique, la voix, la langue' – in *L'Obvie et l'obtus* (1982).

2 'Il est [...] très difficile de parler de la musique. Beaucoup d'écrivains ont bien parlé de la peinture; aucun, je crois, n'a bien parlé de la musique, pas même Proust. La raison est qu'il est très difficile de conjoindre le langage, qui est de l'ordre du général, et la musique, qui est de l'ordre de la différence'. I have taken – and occasionally modified – translations of this work from the following edition: Roland Barthes, 'Music, Voice, Language', in *The Responsibility of*

Forms: Critical Essays on Music, Art and Representation, trans. Richard Howard (Oxford: Blackwell, 1986), pp. 278–85.

3 Barthes refers to Nietzsche – or rather, as is frequently the case, to Deleuze on Nietzsche – explicitly on this occasion. He writes: 'either out of idealism or out of scientism, we disguise the founding evaluation: we swim in "the *indifferent* waters [= without difference] of *what is valuable in itself, of what is valued by everyone*" (Nietzsche, Deleuze)' ('soit par idéalisme, soit par scientisme, nous travestissons l'évaluation fondatrice: nous nageons dans "l'élément *indifférent* [= sans différence] *de ce qui vaut en soi*, ou de *ce qui vaut pour tous*" (Nietzsche, Deleuze)' (V, 523)). For Deleuze's discussion of Nietzsche on evaluation, see, for example, *Nietzsche et la philosophie*, pp. 86–88 (the section entitled 'La Formule de la question chez Nietzsche').

4 'le discours vain, le discours de la musique en soi ou de la musique pour tous'.

5 'il n'est aucune science (physiologie, histoire, esthétique, psychanalyse) qui épuise la voix: classez, commentez historiquement, sociologiquement, esthétiquement, techniquement la musique, il y aura toujours un reste, un supplément, un lapsus, un non dit qui se désigne lui-même: la voix'.

6 There is, Barthes asserts, 'no human voice that is not the object of desire – or of repulsion' ('aucune voix humaine au monde qui ne soit objet de désir – ou de répulsion' (V, 524)). Barthes's essay was first delivered as a talk in Rome on 20 May 1977, the year *Fragments d'un discours amoureux* was published. For a discussion of Proust's novel in the light of a number of Barthes's texts on the voice as an object of love and desire (and in particular his work in *Fragments d'un discours amoureux* on Marcel's grandmother's voice over the telephone and on the *fading* of the other), see Patrick ffrench, 'Barthes and the Voice: The Acousmatic and Beyond', *What's So Great About Roland Barthes?*, ed. Thomas Baldwin, Katja Haustein and Lucy O'Meara, *L'Esprit Créateur* (Special Issue), 55/4 (Winter 2015), pp. 56–69.

7 'une certaine *physique* de la voix (j'entends par *physique* la façon dont la voix se tient dans le corps – ou dont le corps se tient dans la voix)'.

8 For Barthes, to articulate is to 'weigh meaning down with a parasitic clarity' ('encombrer le sens d'une clarté parasite' (V, 527)). In Panzéra's art, by contrast, it is through 'prononciation' that 'music enters into language' ('la musique [...] vient dans la langue' (V, 527)).

9 'la critique adjective (ou l'interprétation prédicative) a pris, le long des siècles, certains aspects institutionnels: l'adjectif musical devient en effet légal, chaque fois qu'on postule un *ethos* de la musique, c'est-à-dire chaque fois qu'on lui attribue un mode régulier (naturel ou magique) de signification'. I have taken – and occasionally modified – translations of this work from the following edition: Roland Barthes, 'The Grain of the Voice', in *The Responsibility of Forms: Critical Essays on Music, Art and Representation*, trans. Richard Howard (Oxford: Blackwell, 1986), pp. 267–77.

10 'il vaudrait mieux changer l'objet musical lui même, tel qu'il s'offre à la parole: modifier son niveau de perception ou d'intellection: déplacer la frange de contact de la musique et du langage'.

11 'Écoutez une basse russe [...] quelque chose est là, manifeste et têtu (on n'entend que *ça*), qui est au-delà (ou en-deça) du sens des paroles, de leur forme [...]: quelque chose qui est directement le corps du chantre, amené d'un même mouvement, à votre oreille, du fond des cavernes, des muscles, des muqueuses, des cartilèges [...] comme si une même peau tapissait la chair intérieure de l'exécutant et la musique qu'il chante. [...] Le "grain", ce serait cela: la matérialité du corps parlant sa langue maternelle: peut-être la lettre; presque sûrement la signifiance'.

12 'supplément que mon intellection ne parvient pas bien à absorber, à la fois têtu et fuyant, lisse et échappé' (III, 488).

13 See IV, 151: 'this [the pheno-song, in which there is very little, if any, 'grain'] is an excessively expressive art [...]: here it is the soul that accompanies the song, not the body (c'est un art excessivement expressif [...]: c'est ici l'âme qui accompagne le chant, ce n'est pas le corps'). We hear clear echoes of these words in 'Rasch' (1975), where Barthes describes what he hears in Schumann's *Kreisleriana*, Op. 16 (1838) in the following terms: 'no note, no theme, no contour, no grammar, no meaning, nothing which would permit me to reconstruct an intelligible structure of the work. No, what I hear are blows: I hear what beats the body, or better: I hear this body that beats' ('aucune note, aucun thème, aucun dessin, aucune grammaire, aucun sens, rien de ce qui permettrait de reconstituer quelque structure intelligible de l'œuvre. Non, ce que j'entends, ce sont des coups: j'entends ce qui bat dans le corps, ce qui bat le corps, ou mieux: ce corps qui bat' (IV, 827)). We will examine both Barthes's distinction between the pheno-song and the geno-song and the significance (or *signifiance*) of 'blows' later on in this chapter, when we look more closely at Barthes's seminars on the 'Charlus-Discourse' in the light of his writing on music.

14 'Le piano fut, dans mon adolescence, un son continu et lointain; j'avais une tante qui l'enseignait, en province, à B.: de ma chambre, ou mieux, rentrant à la maison à travers le jardin, j'entendais des gammes, des bribes de morceaux classiques [...] chaque fois que j'entends de loin un piano qu'on travaille, c'est toute mon enfance, notre maison de B. et jusqu'à la lumière du Sud-Ouest qui font irruption dans ma sensibilité; pour cette remontée dans le temps, cette plongée dans l'affect, je n'ai pas besoin d'une "petite phrase", comme celle de Vinteuil: une gamme y suffit'.

15 'au-dessous de la petite ligne du violon, mince, résistante, dense et directrice, il avait vu tout d'un coup chercher à s'élever en un clapotement liquide, la masse de la partie de piano, multiforme, indivise, plane et entrechoquée comme la mauve agitation des flots que charme et bémolise le clair de lune'.

16 For a discussion of Barthes's dismissal (in 'Piano souvenir') of the 'little phrase' as a source of what is, nevertheless, a typically Proustian experience,

see Éric Marty, 'Barthes et la musique, avec et contre Proust', <https://vimeo.com/129974841> [accessed 1 June 2019].

17 'cette parole dite "intérieure" ressemblait beaucoup au bruit de la place, à cet échelonnement de petites voix qui me venaient de l'extérieur: j'étais moi-même un lieu public, un souk; en moi passaient les mots, les menus syntagmes, les bouts de formules, et *aucune phrase ne se formait*, comme si c'eût été la loi de ce langage-là. Cette parole à la fois très culturelle et très sauvage était surtout lexicale, sporadique; elle consitutait en moi, à travers son flux apparent, un discontinu définitif: cette *non-phrase* n'était pas du tout quelque chose qui n'aurait pas eu la puissance d'accéder à la phrase, qui aurait été avant la phrase; c'était: ce qui est éternellement, superbement, *hors de la phrase*'.

18 'qui ne croit qu'à la phrase et a toujours attribué une dignité exorbitante à la syntaxe prédicative (comme forme d'une logique, d'une rationalité)'.

19 There is also something decidedly Proustian about Barthes's suggestion that he becomes the things around him (their 'langages') in the square in Tangiers. Consider, for example, the third line of Proust's novel: 'it seemed to me as if I myself had become the subject of my book: a church, a quartet, the rivalry between François I and Charles V' ('il me semblait que j'étais moi-même ce dont parlait l'ouvrage: une église, un quatuor, la rivalité de François Ier et de Charles Quint' (*ALR*, I, 3)).

20 '[à] moins que, pour certains pervers, la phrase ne soit un corps?'.

21 'Qu'est-ce que le corps *fait*, lorsqu'il énonce musicalement? Et Schumann répond: mon corps frappe, mon corps se ramasse, il explose, il se coupe, il pique, ou au contraire et sans prévenir […], il s'étire, il tisse légèrement […]. Et parfois même – pourquoi pas? – il parle, il déclame, il dédouble sa voix: *il parle mais ne dit rien*: car dès lors qu'elle est musicale, la parole – ou son substitut instrumental – n'est plus linguistique, mais corporelle; elle ne dit jamais que ceci, et rien d'autre: *mon corps se met en état de parole: quasi parlando*'. I have taken – and occasionally modified – translations of this work from the following edition: Roland Barthes, 'Rasch', in *The Responsibility of Forms: Critical Essays on Music, Art and Representation*, trans. Richard Howard (Oxford: Blackwell, 1986), pp. 299–312.

22 The description is repeated almost word for word later on in *La Prisonnière*, where the narrator describes the coming and going of themes in Vinteuil's septet: 'A phrase of a plaintive kind rose in opposition to it, but so profound, so vague, so internal, almost so organic and visceral that one could not tell at each of its repetitions whether they were those of a theme or of an attack of neuralgia' ('Une phrase d'un caractère douloureux s'opposa à lui, mais si profonde, si vague, si interne, presque si organique et viscérale qu'on ne savait pas, à chacune de ses reprises, si c'était celles d'un thème ou d'une névralgie' (*ALR*, III, 764)).

23 'il faut toujours penser l'Écriture en termes de musique' (*Préparation*, p. 321).

24 Several critics have discussed the role of sound and music in Proust's work. For two recent examples, see Cécile Leblanc's *Proust écrivain de la musique: l'allégresse du compositeur* (Turnhout: Brepols, 2017) and Joseph Acquisto's *Proust, Music, and Meaning: Theories and Practices of Listening in the Recherche* (London: Palgrave Macmillan, 2017). For Acquisto, the way the narrator listens to and otherwise experiences music provides a model for our reading of *À la recherche*: reading Proust's novel, like the narrator's listening, is an insecure, sceptical activity that does not foreclose 'meaning by capturing it in a truth perceived with certainty' (p. 107) – that does not seek, in other (Barthes's) words, to reduce variations to a fixed, overarching theme.

25 *Vaterländischer Künstlerverein* has various translations, including 'Patriotic Artists' Association', 'Art Association of the Fatherland', 'Patriotic Culture Club', 'Fatherland's Society of Artists', 'National Artists' Association', 'Native Artist's Association' and 'Native Society of Artists'.

26 William Kinderman, *Beethoven's Diabelli Variations* (Oxford: Oxford University Press, 1989), p. 67.

27 Quoted in Donald Francis Tovey, *Essays in Musical Analysis: Chamber Music* (Oxford: Oxford University Press, 1972), p. 124.

28 'L'approche de cette œuvre à travers les notions traditionnelles de formes musicales connues et classiques, à travers la "forme variations", s'avère absurde [...]. En tant que variations "sur un thème de Diabelli", l'œuvre est un formidable bluff' (Boucourechliev, *Beethoven*, p. 83).

29 Kinderman, *Beethoven's Diabelli Variations*, p. 67.

30 See Oscar George Sonneck, 'Beethoven to Diabelli: A Letter and a Protest', *The Musical Quarterly*, 13/2 (April 1927), pp. 294–316 (p. 296).

31 Kinderman, *Beethoven's Diabelli Variations*, p. 71.

32 Boucourechliev, *Beethoven*, p. 85.

33 See III, 502: 'the *contemporary* problem is not to destroy the narrative but to subvert it; today's task is to dissociate subversion from destruction' ('le problème *actuel* n'est pas de détruire le récit, mais de le subvertir: dissocier la subversion de la destruction, telle serait aujourd'hui la tâche').

34 'il jette ces éléments dans un espace qu'il considère comme réversible, voire comme presque libéré de toute contingence, où toutes les hiérarchies sont balayées' (Boucourechliev, *Beethoven*, p. 86).

35 'Bas, haut, grave, aigu, long, bref, épais, mince, fort, faible' (Boucourechliev, *Beethoven*, p. 86).

36 'vision intellectuelle préalable et globale, toujours nouvelle, de chaque variation, vision à laquelle la matière doit se plier coûte que coûte' (Boucourechliev, *Beethoven*, p. 86).

37 'Les trente-trois variations ne sont pas les éléments partiels d'un processus en développement et, quoiqu'elles forment parfois des couples ou des groupes, elles ne se déroulent pas selon un ordre nécessaire, inéluctable' (Boucourechliev, *Beethoven*, p. 87).

38 Boucourechliev, *Beethoven*, p. 90.

39 'dans la même lumière, qui les traverse' (Boucourechliev, *Beethoven*, p. 91). As we have already seen, Barthes also uses light-related metaphors to describe the mobility of Proust's work. The lights controlled by the variable shifts of a rheostat, understood as the embodiment of the shuffling combinations and divagations of Mallarmé's *Livre total*, are the luminous equivalents of a Beethoven-like musical variation (see Barthes, 'Table ronde sur Proust', p. 29), and the theme in Proust's work is 'diffracted' entirely in variations.

40 See Boucourechliev, *Beethoven*, p. 90.

41 See Michel Butor, *Mobile*, trans. Richard Howard (Champaign: Dalkey Archive Press, 2004).

42 Barthes writes: 'Behind every collective rejection of a book by our stock criticism we must look for *what has been wounded*' ('Derrière tout refus collectif de la critique régulière à l'égard d'un livre, il faut chercher *ce qui a été blessé*' (II, 430)).

43 As we shall see in due course, Barthes also uses the term 'ébranlement' in relation to the digressive narrative of Proust's novel.

44 'échelonner des mots isolés sur une page, mêler l'italique, le romain et le capitale selon un projet qui n'est visiblement pas celui de la démonstration intellectuelle [...], rompre matériellement le fil de la phrase par des alinéas disparates, égaler en importance un mot et une phrase, toutes ces libertés concourent en somme à la déstruction même du Livre'.

45 Butor himself was no stranger to the unconventional variations of Beethoven's Op. 120, of course. His *Dialogue avec 33 variations de Ludwig van Beethoven sur une valse de Diabelli* was published nine years after *Mobile*, in 1971. Later on, Marguerite Duras replaces the direct sound of the road with the music of the *Diabelli Variations* and her own voice-over in *Le Camion* (1977).

46 'notre critique a bien été à l'école, où on lui a enseigné à faire des "plans" et à retrouver le plan des autres; mais les divisions du "plan" [...] sont les grosses étapes du chemin, c'est tout; ce qui est au-dessous du plan, c'est le *détail*: le détail n'est pas un matériau fondamental, c'est une monnaie inessentielle: on monnaye les grosses idées en "détails", sans pouvoir imaginer un instant que les grosses idées puissent naître du seul agencement des "détails". La paraphrase est donc l'opération raisonnable d'une critique qui exige du livre, avant tout, qu'il soit continu: on "caresse" le livre, tout comme on demande au livre de "caresser" de sa parole continue la vie, l'âme, le mal, etc.'.

47 'la structuration rhétorique (le "plan") qui a prévalu jusqu'ici dans les études sur Proust' ('Table ronde sur Proust', p. 48). We will discuss Barthes's criticism of the 'schema' ('le plan') (and, in particular, its relation to the 'Book' and to the 'Album') in *La Préparation du roman* in more detail in the next chapter.

48 'composé[s] d'une façon fort rassurante, d'un *petit nombre d'idées bien développées*'. It remains to be seen, of course, how this can be said to apply to

Proust's work. Barthes echoes the title of Butor's text when he calls Proust's novel a 'true "mobile"' ('véritable "mobile"') at the start of the round-table discussion in 1972 (Barthes, 'Table ronde sur Proust', p. 29).

49 See *Comment vivre ensemble*, p. 205: 'Structural analysis (of the narrative) [...]. That preliminary analysis takes the form of a table. Tabular = immobile, panoramic, planimetric nature of the text as object' ('Analyse structural (du récit) [...]. Caractère tabulaire de cette première analyse. Tabulaire = caractère immobile, panoramique, planimétrique du texte comme objet').

50 'Qu'une œuvre soit en effet composée de quelques thèmes, c'est ce que l'on admet à la rigueur [...]: malgré tout, le thème reste un objet littéraire dans la mesure où il s'offre, par statut, à la variation, c'est-à-dire au développement. Or, dans *Mobile*, il n'y a, de ce point de vue, aucun thème [...]. Alors que dans l'esthétique traditionnelle, tout l'effort littéraire consiste à déguiser le thème, à lui donner des variations inattendues, dans *Mobile*, il n'y a pas variation, mais seulement variété, et cette variété est purement combinatoire'.

51 This is Barthes's definition of 'le plan' in *Le Neutre. Notes de cours au Collège de France 1977–1978*, ed. Thomas Clerc (Paris: Seuil/IMEC, 2002), p. 37.

52 Barthes, 'Table ronde sur Proust, p. 29.

53 'une sorte de théâtralité non hystérique [...], fondée sur des permutations de places' (Barthes, 'Table ronde sur Proust', p. 40). For further discussion of the relationship between *À la recherche* and the permutations of Mallarmé's *Livre total* as it is presented in *La Préparation du roman*, see Chapter Four.

54 'L'écrivain est un expérimentateur public: il varie ce qu'il recommence; obstiné et fidèle, il ne connaît qu'un art: celui du thème et des variations. Aux variations, les combats, les valeurs, les idéologies, le temps, l'avidité de vivre, de connaître, de participer, de parler, bref les contenus: mais au thème l'obstination des formes, la grande fonction signifiante de l'imaginaire, c'est-à-dire l'intelligence même du monde. Seulement, à l'opposé de ce qui se passe en musique, chacune des variations de l'écrivain est prise elle-même pour un thème solide, dont le sens serait immédiat et définitif. Cette méprise n'est pas légère, elle constitue la littérature même, et plus précisément ce dialogue infini de la critique et de l'œuvre, qui fait que le temps littéraire est à la fois le temps des auteurs qui avancent et le temps de la critique qui les reprend'. The translation of this passage is taken from the following edition: Roland Barthes, 'Preface', in *Critical Essays*, trans. Richard Howard (Evanston: Northwestern University Press, 1972), pp. xi–xxi.

55 'La surdité de Beethoven désigne le manque où loge toute signification: elle en appelle à une musique non pas abstraite ou intérieure, mais douée, si l'on peut dire, d'un intelligible sensible, de l'intelligible comme sensible. Cette catégorie est proprement révolutionnaire, on ne peut la penser dans les termes de l'esthétique ancienne; l'œuvre qui s'y soumet ne peut être reçue selon la pure

sensualité, qui est toujours culturelle, ni selon un ordre intelligible qui serait celui du développement (rhétorique, thématique); sans elle, ni le texte moderne, ni la musique contemporaine ne peuvent être acceptés. On le sait depuis les analyses de Boucourechliev, ce Beethoven est exemplairement celui des *Variations Diabelli*'. I have taken – and occasionally modified – translations of this work from the following edition: Roland Barthes, 'Musica Practica', in *The Responsibility of Forms: Critical Essays on Music, Art and Representation*, trans. Richard Howard (Oxford: Blackwell, 1986), pp. 261–66.

56 'L'opération qui permet de saisir ce Beethoven (et la catégorie qu'il inaugure) ne peut plus être ni l'exécution ni l'audition, mais la lecture [...] ceci veut dire que [...] il faut se mettre à l'égard de cette musique dans l'état, ou mieux dans l'activité, d'un performateur, qui sait déplacer, grouper, combiner, agencer [...]. De même que la lecture du texte moderne [...] ne consiste pas à recevoir, à connaître ou à ressentir, mais à l'écrire de nouveau, à traverser son écriture d'une nouvelle inscription, de même, lire ce Beethoven, c'est *opérer* sa musique, l'attirer (elle s'y prête) dans une praxis inconnue'.

57 'Réquichot et son corps', IV, 396.

58 'Littérature/enseignement', IV, 885.

59 'Le Jeu du kaléidoscope', IV, 849.

60 *Préparation*, p. 189.

61 Roland Barthes, *Le Lexique de l'auteur. Séminaire à l'École pratique des hautes études 1973–1974*, ed. Anne Herschberg Pierrot (Paris: Seuil, 2010), p. 319.

62 *Le Lexique de l'auteur*, p. 319.

63 *Préparation*, pp. 165 and 177.

64 There is one significant difference between the writerly text as it is described in *S/Z* and *À la recherche* as Barthes envisages it at the beginning of the round table with Deleuze et al.: while there is 'perhaps nothing to say' ('peut-être rien à dire' (III, 122)) as far as writerly texts are concerned, there is 'an infinite amount to say' ('infiniment à dire') about Proust's work (Barthes, 'Table ronde sur Proust', p. 30)). What is the difference between the infinite and nothing? For Barthes, they are fairly close. Indeed, they could be said to live together: to 'rewrite' the writerly text, about which there may be nothing to say, is to effect its dissemination and dispersal 'in the field of infinite difference' ('dans le champ de la différence infinie' (III, 122)).

65 'Certes, il existe un plaisir de l'œuvre (de certaines œuvres); je puis m'enchanter à lire et à relire Proust, Flaubert, Balzac, et même, pourquoi pas, Alexandre Dumas; mais ce plaisir, si vif soit-il, et quand bien même il se serait dégagé de tout préjugé, reste partiellement (sauf un effort critique exceptionnel) un plaisir de consommation; car, si je puis lire ces auteurs, je sais aussi que je ne puis les ré-écrire (qu'on ne peut aujourd'hui écrire "comme ça"); et ce savoir assez triste suffit à me séparer de la production de ces œuvres, dans le moment même où leur éloignement fonde ma modernité (être moderne, n'est-ce pas

connaître vraiment ce qu'on ne peut pas recommencer?). Le Texte, lui, est lié à la jouissance, c'est-à-dire au plaisir sans séparation'.

66 'il n'est plus possible de réécrire ni Balzac, ni Zola, ni Proust, ni même les mauvais romans socialistes, bien que leurs descriptions se fondent sur une division sociale qui a encore cours. Le réalisme est toujours timide, et il y a trop de *surprise* dans un monde que l'information de masse et la généralisation de la politique ont rendu si profus qu'il n'est plus possible de figurer projectivement: le monde, comme objet littéraire, échappe; le savoir déserte la littérature qui ne peut plus être ni Mimésis, ni *Mathésis*, mais seulement *Sémiosis*: aventure de l'impossible langagier, en un mot: *Texte*'.

67 'Balzac, Sue, Monnier, Hugo se plurent à restituer quelques formes bien aberrantes de la prononciation et du vocabulaire; argot des voleurs, patois paysan, jargon allemand, langage concierge. Mais ce langage social, sorte de vêtement théâtral accroché à une essence, n'engageait jamais la totalité de celui qui le parlait; les passions continuaient de fonctionner au-dessus de la parole. Il fallut peut-être attendre Proust pour que l'écrivain confondît entièrement certains hommes avec leur langage, et ne donnât ses créatures que sous les pures espèces, sous le volume dense et coloré de leur parole. Alors que les créatures balzaciennes, par exemple, se réduisent facilement aux rapports de force de la société dont elles forment comme les relais algébriques, un personnage proustien, lui, se condense dans l'opacité d'un langage particulier, et, c'est à ce niveau que s'intègre et s'ordonne réellement toute sa situation historique: sa profession, sa classe, sa fortune, son hérédité, sa biologie'.

68 'il les *encadre*, un peu comme des morceaux de bravoure, des pièces emphatiquement rapportées; il les marque d'un indice pittoresque, folklorique'.

69 As we shall see later on, Barthes's work on the 'Charlus-Discourse' in *Comment vivre ensemble* suggests that his exposition of reported speech in Proust – at least in 'La Division des langages' – is itself quite caricatural.

70 Bowie, 'Barthes on Proust', pp. 514, 518.

71 See Barthes, 'Table ronde sur Proust', p. 29.

72 'en un sens la métaphore [...] est détruite. Ou, en tout cas, l'origine de la métaphore est détruite; c'est une métaphore, mais sans origine' (Barthes, 'Table ronde sur Proust', pp. 42–43).

73 This passage supplies a counterexample to Lucy O'Meara's suggestion that, although 'Barthes *suggests* the metaphoric potency of [Romantic] music, he never actually uses it metaphorically' ('Atonality and Tonality: Musical Analogies in Roland Barthes's Lectures at the Collège de France', *Paragraph*, 31/1 (2008), p. 20). On this occasion (and perhaps only on this occasion), Barthes uses the workings of Romantic music both metaphorically and to describe a 'destruction' of metaphor.

74 See Coste, 'Notes de cours pour le Maroc', p. 9.

75 'On échoue toujours à parler de ce qu'on aime', V, 909. For further discussion of Barthes's reasons for going to and leaving Rabat, see Coste,

'Notes de cours pour le Maroc', pp. 10–11 and Louis-Jean Calvet's *Roland Barthes* (Paris: Flammarion, 1990), pp. 212–13.

76 Barthes's teaching notes from this year form part of the 'Fonds Roland Barthes' held at the Bibliothèque nationale de France, Paris. They are contained within folder BRT2. A3. 03 'Rabat (1969–70)'. I am grateful to Claude Coste, Marie-Odile Germain and Éric Marty for their assistance in locating the relevant documents, and to Michel Salzedo for permission to consult and to quote from them.

77 M. *Choufleury restera chez lui le 24 janvier* (1861) is the title of an operetta by Jacques Offenbach and the Duc de Morny (under the pseudonym 'M. de St Rémy'). Choufleury is a snob who invites members of Parisian high society to private parties and musical *soirées* in his drawing room.

78 In his 'Notes de cours pour le Maroc', Coste confuses this passage with another that occurs in *Le Côté de Guermantes*, in which the narrator's grandmother is taken ill during one of their frequent outings to the Champs-Elysées (see *ALR*, II, 605–08). In the passage from *À l'ombre des jeunes filles en fleurs* on which Barthes focuses, it is the narrator, rather than his grandmother, who is unwell (see *ALR*, I, 486–87). Here, the grandmother is a victim of her grandson's blackmail ('chantage' (see I, 487–88)). Coste's disorientation is arguably an effect of the variations and repetitions that Proust creates.

79 'Sous la profusion des porte-bonheur en saphir, des trèfles à quatre feuilles d'émail, des médailles d'argent, des médaillons d'or, des amulettes de turquoise, des chaînettes de rubis, des châtaignes de topaze, il y avait dans la robe elle-même tel dessin colorié poursuivant sur un empiècement rapporté son existence antérieure, telle rangée de petits boutons de satin qui ne bouton-naient rien et ne pouvaient pas se déboutonner, une soutache cherchant à faire plaisir avec la minutie, la discrétion d'un rappel délicat, lesquels, tout autant que les bijoux, avaient l'air – n'ayant sans cela aucune justification possible – de déceler une intention, d'être un gage de tendresse, de retenir une confidence, de répondre à une superstition, de garder le souvenir d'une guérison, d'un vu, d'un amour ou d'une philippine'. According to the *OED*, a 'philopena' is a 'game or custom, originating in Germany, in which a gift or forfeit may be claimed by the first of two people who have shared a nut with two kernels to say "philopena" at their next meeting; an occasion on which this is done; a gift or forfeit claimed in this way. Also: a nut with a double kernel, or a kernel from such a nut'.

80 There are clear affinities between Barthes's observations concerning the Proustian sentence and Leo Spitzer's analysis of 'Le Rythme de la phrase' in *Études de style* (first published in 1970). Barthes's remarks concerning 'floors', for example, echo Spitzer's discussion of Proust's 'arrangement of levels' ('[l]a disposition des niveaux' (*Études de style*, p. 402)) and the superimposed 'planes' ('plans' (p. 401)) of which his sentences are made. Nevertheless, there is also an important difference between their analyses. While Barthes speaks

of both 'saturation' and of infinite catalysis, Spitzer emphasizes only the sealing and locking of Proust's sentences ('le scellement, le verrouillage de la phrase') – their 'resolute progression' ('la progression résolue') towards an end (p. 407).

81 Readers of Barthes's 1961 preface to La Rochefoucauld's *Réflexions ou sentences et maximes* (1665) will hear an echo here of his discussion of antithesis as 'a *point*, which is to say, the very spectacle of meaning' ('une *pointe*, c'est-à-dire le spectacle même du sens' (IV, 33)) in that text.

82 As we saw in the Introduction, Barthes also refers to *À la recherche* as 'a sort of galaxy open to infinite exploration because the particles move about and change places' ('une sorte de galaxie qui est infiniment explorable parce que les particules en changent de place et permutent entre elles' ('Table ronde sur Proust', p. 29)).

83 'le jeu même du Sa [le signifiant][:] chaîne circulaire de substitutions sans origine (le 1er terme n'est premier que par linéarité)'.

84 See 'L'Effet de réel', III, 32: 'Flaubert's barometer, Michelet's little door finally say nothing but this: *we are the real*; it is the category of the "real" (and not its contingent contents) which is then signified' ('le baromètre de Flaubert, la petite porte de Michelet ne disent finalement rien d'autre que ceci: *nous sommes le réel*; c'est la catégorie du "réel" (et non ses contenus contingents) qui est alors signifiée').

85 While Barthes aligns Michelet's 'discours' with 'style' (see I, 306), and while Charlus's 'discours' is his speech (or the way he addresses Marcel), Barthes tells his students in Rabat that the 'discours' of Proust's text operates at 'the level of the "narrative", a fragment of narrative, an episode' ('à l'échelle du "récit", d'un fragment de récit, d'un épisode') and constitutes 'the level of organization above the sentence' ('le niveau d'organisation supérieur à la phrase'). For further discussion of discourse as 'groups of words superior to the sentence' ('ensembles de mots supérieurs à la phrase') and as units and combinatory rules ('unités et [...] règles générales de combinaison' (II, 1250)), see 'Le Discours de l'histoire' (II, 1250–62)).

86 'remarques générales, au présent, de portée philosophique, psychologique, esthétique etc.: morceaux et livres de philosophie'.

87 'action [...] va de moments en moments, de termes en termes, d'articulation en articulation, vers une fin, une conclusion, une saturation, une fermeture'.

88 'des germes savamment et subtilement deposés comme en passant, qui donneront plus tard le noyau d'épisodes très importants'. In his seminar notes on the 'Charlus-Discourse', Barthes writes: '*Marcottage*, or layering. A principle of Russian formalism: if a nail is hammered in at the beginning it is so that the hero can hang himself on it at the end' ('Marcottage, ou surgeon. Principe des formalistes russes: si un clou [est] planté au début, c'est pour que le héros s'y pende à la fin' (*Comment vivre ensemble*, p. 206)).

89 'à peu près inexistant, un très vague souvenir en traverse par éclairs les trente-deux variations, dont chacune est ainsi une digression absolue'.

90 Barthes's notes for a lecture entitled 'Analyse d'un texte de Freud' are contained within folder BRT2. A3. 01 'Freud (1969–70)' at the Bibliothèque nationale de France, Paris. Once again, I am indebted to Claude Coste, Marie-Odile Germain and Éric Marty for their assistance in locating the relevant documents, and to Michel Salzedo for permission to consult and to quote from them. It is unclear whether Barthes ever delivered the lecture (in Rabat or anywhere else). It has not, to my knowledge, been published. Folder BRT2. A3. 01 'Freud (1969–70)' also contains seminar notes on another text by Freud, 'The Psychogenesis of a Case of Homosexuality in a Woman' (1920). According to Claude Coste, this seminar 'was not delivered in Morocco, even if it was no doubt planned there' ('n'a pas été donné au Maroc, même s'il y a sans doute été conçu' ('Notes de cours pour le Maroc', p. 11)).

91 'l'irruption d'une liberté, d'une nouveauté du signifiant, atteinte portée au signifié, défaite des stéréotypes, déplétion du plein intérieur'.

92 Asyndeton is a figure of speech in which one or several conjunctions are omitted from a series of related clauses. It is what Aristotle describes in his *Rhetoric* as 'strings of unconnected words, and constant repetition of words and phrases' (Aristotle, *Rhetoric*, ed. Jenny Bak and trans. W. Rhys Roberts (New York: Dover Publications, 2004), Book III, Chapter XII, p. 142).

93 Roland Barthes, 'Les Sorties du texte', in *Bataille*, ed. Philippe Sollers (Paris: Union générale d'éditions, 1973), pp. 59–60.

94 See Barthes, 'Table ronde sur Proust', p. 42.

95 See Barthes, 'Table ronde sur Proust', p. 30.

96 For example, see Georges Bataille, 'La Notion de dépense', in *La Part maudite* (Paris: Minuit, 1967), p. 28: 'luxury, mourning, wars, cults, the construction of sumptuary monuments, games, spectacles, arts, perverse sexual activity [...] represent activities which [...] have no end beyond themselves' ('le luxe, les deuils, les guerres, les cultes, les constructions de monuments somptuaires, les jeux, les spectacles, les arts, l'activité sexuelle perverse [...] représentent autant d'activités qui [...] ont leur fin en elles-mêmes').

97 'il serait assez agréable de penser que le rôle du critique, comme du musicien, est *d'interpréter des variations*' (Genette, 'Table ronde sur Proust', p. 35).

98 'À lire Proust, on est immédiatement sensible à l'extraordinaire multiplication, variation, labilité des identités, tant personelles que sensibles, et à l'importance des hiatus, des trous séparant chacune de leurs stations' (Jean-Pierre Richard, *Proust et le monde sensible* (Paris: Seuil, 1974), p. 240).

99 'n'aboutit pas vraiment à une incohérence; elle permet plutôt la découverte d'un autre ordre, d'une organisation sensible peut-être plus primitive' (Richard, *Proust et le monde sensible*, p. 243).

100 Richard, *Proust et le monde sensible*, p. 243.

101   Barthes, 'Table ronde sur Proust', p. 49.

102   We will return to the differences between Barthes's approach and that of Proust specialists ('Proustians') in the next chapter and in the Afterword.

103   Robbe-Grillet, *Pourquoi j'aime Barthes*, p. 32.

104   Robbe-Grillet, *Pourquoi j'aime Barthes*, p. 31.

105   'au lieu de présenter un texte, comme le roman balzacien, bien rassemblable, tout rond autour de son noyau solide de sens et de vérité, le roman moderne ne fait que présenter des fragments qui, par-dessus le marché, décrivent toujours la même chose et cette même chose n'etant presque rien. Mais le mouvement de la littérature est ce glissement d'une scène à la même scène qui se répète sous une forme à peine détournée, à peine contournée, à peine retournée' (Robbe-Grillet, *Pourquoi j'aime Barthes*, p. 32).

106   'l'affectation du sujet par l'Écrire' (*Préparation*, p. 207).

107   Bowie, 'Barthes on Proust', p. 518.

108   Robbe-Grillet, *Pourquoi j'aime Barthes*, p. 31.

109   Robbe-Grillet, *Pourquoi j'aime Barthes*, p. 32.

110   See *Le Plaisir du texte*: IV, 230: 'today comes from yesterday, Robbe-Grillet is already in Flaubert, Sollers in Rabelais, and all of Nicolas de Staël is in two square centimetres of Cézanne' ('aujourd'hui sort d'hier, Robbe-Grillet est déjà dans Flaubert, Sollers dans Rabelais, tout Nicolas de Staël dans deux centimètres carrés de Cézanne').

111   'Non point au plan du discours Petite-Phrase-Vinteuil (philosophie de la mémoire), mais au plan de la musique de la langue, la langue comme musique. [...] Description des voix dans leur mobilité: finesse et acuité des hauts et des bas de la voix. Charlus précisément: le lieu de Charlus (son identité de forces): sa voix'.

112   Marty, *Roland Barthes: le métier d'écrire*, p. 144.

113   'Auparavant éliminer un leurre méthodologique: le discours de Charlus n'est pas un exemple, un échantillon. Il ne représente pas une masse typique, qui serait celle des "discours tenus". Il est pris dans une différence – et pour moi (ancien analyste structural) dans une double différence: 1) par rapport au "tenir discours" de la *doxa*, du stéréotype, 2) par rapport à une analyse antérieure: *S/Z*'.

114   'vaut pour tous les textes de la littérature, non en ce qu'il les représente (les abstrait et les égalise), mais en ce que la littérature elle-même n'est jamais qu'un seul texte'.

115   'une perspective (de bribes, de voix venues d'autres textes, d'autres codes), dont cependant le point de fuite est sans cesse reporté, mystérieusement ouvert'.

116   'Charlus: code culturel (style des sièges, par exemple) + un supplément affectif, émotif, énonciatif'.

117   'des Allemands qui prenaient pour des réalités ces railleries ingénieuses de la médisance parisienne'.

118 'Psychologie ethnique: paradigme d'époque: l'Allemand naïf/le Parisien railleur'.

119 'passage du jeune Berlinois qui lui, au moins, connaît Wagner et la *Walkyrie*'.

120 'l'une des forces qui peuvent s'emparer du texte (dont le texte est le réseau), l'une des Voix dont est tissé le texte'.

121 'l'analyse structurale, c'est-à-dire le repérage d'unités, de morphèmes du discours'.

122 'le code culturel lui [Charlus] sert à se placer face à l'autre, à entrer dans un jeu réciproque d'images'.

123 Attridge, 'Roland Barthes's Obtuse, Sharp Meaning', p. 84.

124 As Barthes puts it: 'For all of this, see *S/Z*' ('Pour tout cela, voir *S/Z*' (*Comment vivre ensemble*, p. 207)).

125 'Qui parle? [...] Impossible, ici, d'attribuer à l'énonciation une origine, un point de vue. Or cette impossibilité est l'une des mesures qui permettent d'apprécier le pluriel d'un texte. Plus l'origine de l'énonciation est irrepérable, plus le texte est pluriel. Dans le texte moderne, les voix sont traitées jusqu'au déni de tout repère: le discours, ou mieux encore, le langage parle, c'est tout. Dans le texte classique, au contraire, la plupart des énoncés sont originés, on peut identifier leur père et propriétaire [...] mais il arrive que dans ce texte classique, toujours hanté par l'appropriation de la parole, la voix se perde, comme si elle disparaissait dans un trou du discours. La meilleure façon d'imaginer le pluriel classique est alors d'écouter le texte comme un échange chatoyant de voix multiples, posées sur des ondes différentes et saisies par moments d'un *fading* brusque, dont la trouée permet à l'énonciation de migrer d'un point de vue à l'autre, sans prévenir: l'écriture s'établit à travers cette instabilité tonale (dans le texte moderne elle atteint l'atonalité), qui fait d'elle une moire brillante d'origines éphémères'.

126 'des forces, des intensités, des excès et des déflations, des empourprements et des pâleurs *de qui parle*'. Barthes refers to the encounter between Charlus and the narrator as a 'discours-scène' (*Comment vivre ensemble*, p. 210). This conveys not only its theatricality, but also, in an echo of Barthes's definition of the 'scène' in *Fragments d'un discours amoureux* (published in 1977, the year the seminars on Charlus took place), suggests the modernity of Proust's text (or part of it, at least). In the passage from *S/Z* cited above, Barthes identifies the 'modern' text as one in which 'language speaks' ('le langage parle' (III, 152)). The 'scène', for Barthes, is 'interminable, like language: it is language itself, grasped in its infinity' ('interminable, comme le langage: elle est le langage lui-même, saisi dans son infini' (V, 256)). I have taken – and occasionally modified – translations of this work from the following edition: Roland Barthes, *A Lover's Discourse: Fragments*, trans. Richard Howard (New York: Hill and Wang, 1978).

127 'l'unité tonale [...] dépend essentiellement de deux codes séquentiels:

la marche de la vérité et la coordination des gestes représentés: il y a même contrainte dans l'ordre progressif, de la mélodie et dans celui, tout aussi progressif, de la séquence narrative. *Or c'est précisément cette contrainte qui réduit le pluriel du texte classique.* Les cinq codes repérés, entendus souvent simultanément, assurent en effet au texte une certaine qualité plurielle (le texte est bien polyphonique), mais sur les cinq codes, trois seulement proposent des traits permutables, réversibles, insoumis à la contrainte du temps (les codes sémique, culturel, symbolique); les deux autres imposent leurs termes selon un ordre irréversible (les codes herméneutique et proaïrétique). Le texte classique est donc bien tabulaire (et non pas linéaire), mais sa tabularité est vectorisée, elle suit un ordre logico-temporel. Il s'agit d'un système multivalent mais incomplètement réversible. Ce qui bloque la réversibilité, voilà ce qui limite le pluriel du texte classique'.

128 Barthes, 'Table ronde sur Proust', p. 42.

129 'jette ces éléments [...] dans un espace qu'il considère comme réversible, voire comme presque libéré de toute contingence, où toutes les hiérarchies sont balayées' (Boucourechliev, *Beethoven*, p. 86).

130 'Bas, haut, grave, aigu, long, bref, épais, mince, fort, faible – autant d'états et de positions de la matière musicale commandés par une sorte de vision intellectuelle préalable et globale, toujours nouvelle, de chaque variation [...]. Trente trois constellations de l'imagination dont aucune ne peut être dite plus ou moins ressemblante, plus ou moins proche d'un "modèle" initial, on pourrait les penser non en ligne droite, à la suite les unes des autres, mais comme en un cercle de métamorphoses, sans commencement ni fin, ou mieux encore, comme une galaxie ou chaque étoile, de même "grandeur", est équidistante de toutes les autres' (Boucourechliev, *Beethoven*, pp. 86–7).

131 Boucourechliev, *Beethoven*, p. 77.

132 While Barthes cites Bataille on '*Sarrazine [sic]*' on the final page of *S/Z* (III, 341), he does not refer to Charlus's literary preferences (either in *S/Z* or elsewhere).

133 Leo Bersani, *Homos* (Cambridge, MA: Harvard University Press, 1995), p. 137.

134 'je comprenais maintenant pourquoi tout à l'heure, quand je l'avais vu sortir de chez Mme de Villeparisis, j'avais pu trouver que M. de Charlus avait l'air d'une femme: c'en était une!'

135 This is a misspelling, as the quotation on the final page of *S/Z* demonstrates, that also appears in Georges Bataille's *Le Bleu du ciel* (1935).

136 'Z est cinglant à la façon d'un fouet châtieur, d'un insecte érinnyque; graphiquement, jeté par la main, en écharpe, à travers la blancheur égale de la page, parmi les rondeurs de l'alphabet, comme un tranchant unique et illégal, il coupe, il barre, il zèbre; d'un point de vue balzacien, ce Z (qui est dans le nom de Balzac) est la lettre de la déviance [...]; enfin, ici même, Z est la lettre

inaugurale de la Zambinella, l'initiale de la castration, en sorte que par cette faute d'ortographe, installée au cœur de son nom, au centre de son corps, Sarrasine reçoit le Z zambinellien selon sa véritable nature, qui est la blessure du manque. De plus, S et Z sont dans un rapport d'inversion graphique: c'est la même lettre, vue de l'autre coté du miroir: Sarrasine contemple en Zambinella sa propre castration'.

137   Barbara Johnson, 'The Critical Difference', in *Critical Essays on Roland Barthes*, ed. Diana Knight (New York: G. K. Hall & Co., 2000), p. 181.

138   Johnson, 'The Critical Difference', p. 181.

139   'With his eyes, Sarrasine devoured Pygmalion's statue'.

140   Johnson, 'The Critical Difference', p. 182.

141   Johnson, 'The Critical Difference', p. 178.

142   Johnson, 'The Critical Difference', p. 181.

143   'par rapport au "tenir discours" de la *doxa*, du stéréotype, 2) par rapport à une analyse antérieure: S/Z' (*Comment vivre ensemble*, p. 204).

144   Roland Barthes, '*Sarrasine*' de Balzac. *Séminaires à l'École des hautes études 1967–1968 et 1968–1969*, ed. Claude Coste and Andy Stafford (Paris: Seuil, 2011), p. 108.

145   See 'La Musique, la voix, la langue', V, 524.

146   'reç[u] selon la pure sensualité, qui est toujours culturelle, ni selon un ordre intelligible qui serait celui du développement (rhétorique, thématique)'.

147   Barthes writes: 'ce qui est écouté ici et là [...], ce n'est pas la venue d'un signifié, objet d'une reconnaissance ou d'un déchiffrement, c'est la dispersion même, le miroitement des signifiants, sans cesse remis dans la course d'une écoute qui en produit sans cesse des nouveaux, sans jamais arrêter le sens' (V, 351). I have taken – and occasionally modified – translations of this work from the following edition: Roland Barthes, 'Listening', in *The Responsibility of Forms: Critical Essays on Music, Art and Representation*, trans. Richard Howard (Oxford: Blackwell, 1986), pp. 245–60.

148   'Le "Discours-Charlus" = un Texte, dit par une voix, un corps, et quel corps! Celui de Charlus est très présent, très figuré, dans toute la *Recherche du temps perdu*'.

149   'tout ce qui, dans l'exécution, est au service de la communication, de la représentation, de l'expression: ce dont on parle ordinairement, ce qui forme le tissu des valeurs culturelles'.

150   'un jeu signifiant étranger à la communication, à la représentation (des sentiments), à l'expression'.

151   'Dans les *Kreisleriana* de Schumann, je n'entends à vrai dire aucune note, aucun thème, aucun dessin, aucune grammaire, aucun sens, rien de ce qui permettrait de reconstituer quelque structure intelligible de l'œuvre. Non, ce que j'entends, ce sont des coups: j'attends ce qui bat dans le corps, ce qui bat le corps, ou mieux, ce corps qui bat. Voici comment j'entends le corps de Schumann (celui-là, à coup-sûr, avait un corps, et quel corps! [...])'.

152 'est affolé, mais il est aussi codé (par le rhythme et la tonalité) [...]
l'affolement des coups se tient apparemment dans les limites d'une langue
sage'. There is an ontological distinction to be made between the two bodies,
of course. While Charlus's is a fictional body experienced through the text,
Schumann had a real body: Barthes may not 'hear' his 'real' body at all, but a
virtual body experienced through the music – a body he calls 'Schumann's'.

153 '[Il] *ne suit pas* (par contrastes ou amplification), il explose: c'est un
big-bang continu'.

154 Jacques Derrida, 'Les Morts de Roland Barthes', in *Psyché: inventions
de l'autre* (Paris: Galilée, 1987), p. 279.

155 Derrida, 'Les Morts de Roland Barthes', p. 280.

156 See Lyotard, *Discours, figure*, p. 15.

157 Barthes, *Comment vivre ensemble*, p. 69.

158 It is in this sense that Barthes is in tune with the 'music' of Proust's novel
– that he reproduces 'in his own language, according to "*a precise spiritual
mise en scène*", the symbolic conditions of the work' ('dans son propre langage,
selon "*quelque mise en scène spirituelle exacte*", les conditions symboliques de
l'œuvre' (*Critique et vérité*, II, 797)).

159 See *Le Neutre*, p. 31: 'I call neutral everything that outplays the
paradigm' ('j'appelle neutre tout ce qui déjoue le paradigme').

CHAPTER FOUR

Neutral, Nuance

Proust's mature novel may have contributed to a process of linguistic solidification that began towards the middle of the nineteenth century and established literary language as an opaque and weighty substance, as the stuff of a 'Littérature-Objet',[1] but it was Albert Camus's *L'Étranger* (1942), Barthes argues, that inaugurated a 'new' writing that is neutral.[2] In Camus's work, *écriture* (which, for Barthes, is a formal reality chosen by writers that is positioned between their language and their style, neither of which they are able to choose)[3] has acquired the silence of a pure equation and is no thicker than an 'algebra'.[4] Camus's thin and colourless — strictly speaking, white — writing (*écriture blanche*) is analogous to a linguistic third or neutral term, a zero element, because it is freed from all bondage to ordering hierarchies of usage (Camus famously avoids using the past historic tense in his first novel).[5] It is also 'indicative', 'amodale' (I, 217) and robustly non-committal: while it may position itself among the emotive judgements and blurtings of journalism, for example, it is able to do so, Barthes suggests, without fully attaching itself to any of them.[6]

It does not follow from this, of course, that Barthes sees nothing of the neutral in *À la recherche* (or, indeed, that Barthes's work invites us to do the same), or that the neutrality of Proust's work is to be entirely disconnected from Camus's bleached, degree-zero production. As we have seen, Barthes's writing on Proust suggests that the neutral twinklings[7] of *À la recherche* are located not within a writerly purity, a Camusian innocence or style of absence that is 'almost an ideal absence of style',[8] but in its capacity to thwart a variety of paradigms that are made — by Barthes — of an opposition between the classical and the modern.[9] For example, Marcel's proxemic ordeals reveal a classical distance at the heart of an extreme, modern closeness; the occulting eroticism of the 'Charlus-Discourse', its unstable rhythm and supplementary logic, is such that structural analysis, which comprehends the classical work's cultural codes, cannot be separated cleanly from a (non-structural) mode of critical attention that considers the role of affective forces and the position of subjects within discourse (and which, as we shall see later on, resonates with, but is by no means identical to, what Barthes calls 'pathetic criticism');[10] and the musical *signifiance*, the third meaning of Proust's discourse, is made of both classical (logico-temporal) order and the diffraction of themes in tireless variations.

While Proust's and Camus's regimes of neutrality may be quite different, Barthes's observations in '"Longtemps, je me suis couché de bonne heure"', the text of a lecture he delivered on 19 October 1978 at the Collège de France (and redelivered in part as the first lecture in the *Préparation du roman* series), suggest an affinity between the third-term colourlessness of Camus's writing and the original, generic particularities of *À la recherche*. In its combination of both speculative and narrative fragments, Proust's work is shielded, Barthes contends, from the 'ancestral law of Narrative or of Rationality' ('la loi ancestrale du Récit ou du Raisonnement' (V, 463)). *À la recherche*, in other words, is a 'third form' ('*tierce forme*' (V, 463)) – it is neither novel nor essay, or both at once.[11] In line with the metaphor selected by Proust's narrator as he endeavours to describe the architecture of the work he intends to write[12] and, less explicitly, with his own previous deployment of musical metaphors in relation to Proust's text, Barthes characterizes its structure as 'rhapsodic, i.e. (etymologically) *stitched together*' ('rhapsodique, c'est-à-dire (étymologiquement) *cousue*' (V, 463)). It is made like a dress: 'pieces, fragments are subject to criss-crossings, to arrangements, to reappearances: a dress is not a *patchwork*, any more than is *La Recherche*'.[13] *À la recherche* is thus rhapsodic – dress-like – not because it is fashioned out of miscellaneous bits and pieces sewn together (relatively) arbitrarily, but because the individual fragments of which it is made (disparate though they may seem) are stitched into a form with a certain structural logic.

Barthes returns to the rhapsody of Proust's neutral *tierce forme* in the first and second parts of *La Préparation du roman* (in 1978–79 and 1979–80 respectively), as he outlines the content and the form of what is, for him, a new form of writing – of what he calls the 'fantasized novel' ('le Roman fantasmé' (p. 45)). While the novels he loves are 'novels of Memory' and are made out of 'material (of "memories") *recalled* from childhood, from the life of the writing subject' (p. 42),[14] the work he fantasizes about writing will not be made of the same fabric, because his 'affective link' ('lien affectif' (p. 45)), he tells his audience, is with his present rather than his past. He is unable, he says, to produce anything other than disassociated, novelistic fragments – a patchwork – with anamnestic (Proustian) material of this sort:

> I probably do experience a few memory-flashes, flashes of memory, but they do not proliferate, they are not associative ('torrential') ≠ Proust. They are instantly exhausted by the short form (cf. the *Anamneses* in *Roland Barthes*), which explains the 'novelistic' impression they can create, but which is also, precisely, what separates them from the Novel. (p. 43)[15]

Such formal and affective differences notwithstanding, Barthes also acknowledges that Proust's fragmented and sutured text provides an answer to a question that is central to his own fantasies as a writer:

> how to pass from Notation, and so from the Note, to the Novel, from the discontinuous to the flowing (to the continuous, the smooth)? [...] a *third form* should always be considered. Figure: something that seems impossible at first may turn out to be possible after all. In this case: possible to conceive of a *Novel through fragments*, a *Novel-Fragment*. Such novels probably exist – or some that come close to it: [...] I am thinking of the *cryptofragmentary* aspect of Flaubert (*blanks*) and of *Aziyadé*. There have to be many other examples – and on a deeper, less formal level: there is of course Proustian discontinuity, the *Rhapsodic*. (pp. 46–47)[16]

The rhapsodic structure of Proust's work – its careful arrangement and rearrangement of pieces and fragments, which Barthes also calls 'marcottage' (p. 251) – is thus neutral to the extent that it suggests the possibility of a third form that outplays – forms a 'passage' (p. 47) between – the terms of an oppositional logic: between the discontinuous and the continuous, the fragment (the novelistic, the *romanesque*) and the whole (the novel), the short and the long form.[17]

Later in this chapter, we will consider how the rhapsodic neutrality of Proust's text can be brought to bear upon another conceptual opposition – between the 'Book' and the 'Album' – that informs Barthes's discussion in *L'Œuvre comme volonté*, the second part of *La Préparation du roman*. We will also use this discussion to identify affinities between the figures of rhapsody and variations without a theme. Before doing these things, however, I would like to examine the relationship between Proust's long, convoluted text and what Barthes describes in the first part of his lecture series as an 'ultrashort' form and as an 'exemplary form of the Notation of the Present' ('forme exemplaire de la Notation du Présent' (p. 53)): the haiku.

Proust vs haiku

During the session of 16 December 1978, Barthes explains how the first part of his course (entitled *De la vie à l'œuvre*) will be organized:

> Two pivots – seemingly disparate → eccentric articulation – of a certain circumvolution of the Novel to be written, of the fantasized Novel: the Haiku/Proust (and I mean *Proust*, not *La Recherche du temps perdu*). I am convinced of the validity of this opposition but was nevertheless afraid that you would find it a little abrupt, a little elliptical, a little casual – or farfetched. (p. 48)[18]

While the written version of this statement is difficult to decipher (mostly due to the arrow and pair of dashes), Barthes unpacks it as he delivers the lecture:[19] he converts the arrow into 'forming' ('formant') and changes 'of a certain circumvolution' into 'a certain circumvolution' ('une certaine circonvolution'). 'Eccentric articulation' refers, then, to the decentred focus of Barthes's approach. He will coil around the fantasized novel rather than approach it head-on, and in order to achieve this oscillating indirectness, he will make what appear to be two very different (indeed, opposed) entities – a writer (rather than his novel) and a traditional, very short form of Japanese poetry – the organizing pivots of his deliberations.[20]

The significance of 'Proust' remains unclear, however. Does it refer to 'the civil name of an author filed away in the histories of literature', for example, or to 'Marcel', whom Barthes describes elsewhere as 'a singular being, at once child and adult, *puer senilis*, impassioned yet wise, victim of eccentric manias and the site of a reflection on the world, love, art, time, death' (and with whom, as we shall see later on, Barthes identifies)?[21] The subsequent discussion of a quotation from Proust's 'Vacances de Pâcques', an article that appeared in *Le Figaro* on 25 March 1913, provides little by way of clarification on this matter. If he were to write a novel, Proust says, he would try to 'distinguish between the differing music of each successive day' ('différencier les musiques successives des jours'), and music of this sort, Barthes contends, is exactly what the haiku is made of ('= le haïku même' (p. 48)). Now, while, for Barthes, there may be important distinctions to be made between

Proust (rather than *À la recherche*) and the haiku, his commentary on the quotation from Proust's *Figaro* article does not help us to see what they may be like. Rather than reinforce the validity of an opposition, in fact, it suggests an affinity between its terms – between the music of short-form poetry and of the novel Proust would have liked to write (or which he had begun to write and publish: *Du côté de chez Swann* appeared in November of the same year).

In fact, much of what Barthes has to say in *La Préparation du roman* about the relationship between the haiku and 'Proust' pertains less to an individual (*Scriptor, Scribens* or otherwise)[22] than to well-known examples – figures, episodes – taken from *À la recherche*. He opposes the temporal fulgurations of the haiku to the re-findings – the analeptic creations – of involuntary memory:

> On the one hand, it is clear that the haiku is not an act of writing in the Proustian manner, i.e. one that is destined to find (lost) Time again *later, afterwards* (shut up in the cork-lined bedroom), through the sovereign agency of involuntary memory. On the contrary: *find* (and not *find again*) Time immediately, straight away; Time is saved immediately. (p. 85)[23]

A haiku is thus an instantaneous '*fruition* of the sensible and of writing' ('*fruition* immédiate du sensible et de l'écriture' (p. 86)). As a new and paradoxical category of remembrance, it is able to transform events into memories on the spot:

> 'Immediate memory', as if *Notatio* (the fact of noting) allowed us to remember straight away (≠ Proust's involuntary memory: immediate memory does not proliferate, it is not metonymic). (p. 86)[24]

We are reminded here of Barthes's observation concerning the un-Proustian memory of the photograph in *La Chambre claire*:

> The photograph does not call up the past (nothing Proustian in a photograph). The effect it produces on me is not to restore what has been abolished (by time, distance), but to attest that what I see has indeed existed. (V, 855)[25]

If the haiku is a hologrammatic flash of contingency that is without duration, and if a photograph is a pure emanation of the real, of the 'that-has been' ('ça-a-été' (V, 853)), it is unsurprising that Barthes should distinguish both of them from the rituals of anamnestic lingering triggered by Proust's plump little cake. As he puts it in *La Préparation du roman*:

> The whole of *La Recherche du temps perdu* unfurls from the Madeleine like a Japanese paper flower in water: development, drawers opening, infinite *unfolding*. In a haiku, the flower is still compact, a Japanese flower without the water: it remains a *bud*. The word (the hologram of the haiku) is like a stone in water that amounts to nothing: we do not stick around to watch the ripples: we register the sound (the *plop*), that is all. (p. 74)[26]

This opposition may make sense (whereas the madeleine triggers an infinite expansion, the haiku is experienced as a sudden fulguration), but its pertinence as a description of Proust's work more generally – or of the act of writing in the Proustian manner – is quite limited. In other words, Barthes's attempts to separate *À la recherche* from the haiku (or from the photograph, for that matter) depend on a familiar metonymic reduction – on the selection of a point of view in relation to Proust's novel that comprises only the madeleine episode and the effects of involuntary memory. While it may not be entirely far-fetched, then, Barthes's opposition is certainly a little abrupt, elliptical and casual. Indeed, if we read his work on the haiku in the first half of *La Préparation du roman* alongside his Rabat seminar notes, or if we compare that work to the analysis of the 'Charlus-Discourse' in *Comment vivre ensemble* (in which neither the madeleine episode nor the effects of *la mémoire involontaire* are discussed), we will obtain further evidence in support of his assertion regarding the vitality and multidirectional diffuseness of *À la recherche* (which are further signs of its neutrality).[27] We will also see that Proust's novel and the haiku are anything but disparate.

Weather in Proust

Barthes begins his discussion of the relationship between the haiku and 'the Weather' ('le Temps qu'il fait' (p. 66)) by identifying both a similarity and a difference between *À la recherche* and a haiku by Shido Yaha (1663–1740).[28] Yaha's poem 'captures' – the play on words is no accident –[29] the intensity of summer as it is experienced indoors:

> The summer *captured* in the bedroom is more intense: it is captured as an absence, captured outside. It is indoors, precisely where it has been driven out that summer is most powerful: it triumphs outside and intensifies → its intensity: intensity of the Indirect, which shows that the Indirect is the very path of communication, of manifestation of the Essence. (p. 67)[30]

Barthes likens Yaha's vivid evocation of the 'Essence' of summer to what 'Proust, from the starting point of the hotel room in Balbec, says about the summer in those one or two densely written pages' (p. 67).[31] However, while Proust's narrator speaks at length about the view from the windows of Balbec's Grand-Hôtel (see *ALR*, II, 160–64, for example), on this occasion Barthes appears to have confused seaside and countryside. It is likely that the passage he has in mind occurs in *Du côté de chez Swann*, where the narrator describes the sound of flies buzzing in his dark and yet fresh room (in Combray) whilst he is reading. Along with the obscure freshness of the room, he says, the flies afford him a fuller sense of the essence of summer than observing the world outside ever could (see *ALR*, I, 82).[32] In spite of this minor slip, Barthes's point is clear: the effects they produce may be similar, but the haikist's three lines and seventeen syllables are able to capture a summery 'Essence' in a fraction of the space used by Proust (just over half a page in the most recent Pléiade edition).

This quantitative discrepancy notwithstanding, Barthes's subsequent observation that the haiku is not '*finite, closed*' ('*fini, fermé*' (p. 67)) suggests that the short form and *À la recherche* cannot be made into the terms of a full, paradigmatic opposition. We should not be misled, he insists, by the haiku's tenuity, since the words of the poem mark, in fact, the beginning of an 'infinite speech' ('parole infinie') that can 'unfold the summer by *taking the path of an Indirect that* [...] *has no structural reason to come to an end*' (p. 67).[33] The indirect language of the spatially limited haiku thus suggests the same virtual infinity as the wildly substitutive – the endlessly catalytic and infamously long – Proustian sentence as Barthes describes it in Rabat. In their different ways, then, the haiku and 'la phrase proustienne' resist the structural and existential logic of the typically Chateaubriandish sentence that proceeds, uninterrupted, towards a euphoric death. In so doing, both imply what Barthes (in his Rabat seminar notes) calls an openness to the 'infinite fabric of the world: there is always something to say about the world, infinitely'.[34]

Talk about the weather, Barthes says, exemplifies a form of language used for general purposes of social interaction, rather than to convey information or to ask questions: in linguistic terms, it is phatic. Moreover, since our relationship with 'l'atmosphère' involves a 'force of individuation, of difference, of nuance, of shimmering existentiality' (p. 71),[35] the climatic-phatic is also inhabited by an affective intensity (a 'charge existentielle' (p. 72)) by virtue of which a subject's '*feeling-being, the* pure and mysterious sensation of life' (p. 71) can be felt.[36] It constitutes a language that serves as a means of communication, of speaking and making sense to others, and of instituting 'the subject – of creation' ('un appareil d'institution du sujet – de création' (p. 72)). Barthes uses the following notation to express the workings of this creative combination:

> (1) a code (a law): the Season + (2) a performance (speech, discourse) that enacts the code: *the* Weather = the code *spoken* by the moment, the day, the hour, the individuation of existence, which is to say, by what enacts, or what baffles […]: in France, which is a country of subtle, complex *variability*, you sometimes (often) see a season being disputed by the weather (winter in summer, etc.) while still being enacted, confirmed by its products (flowers, fruit, etc.). (pp. 72–73)[37]

Even as they dispute, outplay or baffle it, the performative variations of the weather (its *moire*, its 'differential of intensities')[38] continue to enact and to speak – to compose with – the seasonal code they supplement. The haiku that captures the weather, moreover, is an 'intense individuation, with no concessions to generality – *despite and while making use of the code of the seasons*' (p. 74).[39] In relaying a lived instant that is caught within a seasonal code, the speaking subject of the haiku transforms natural units ('les unités naturelles') into particular 'subject-effects, effects of language' ('des effets de sujet, des effets de langage' (p. 74)).

The structural similarities between the climatic haiku and the 'Charlus-Discourse' are plain to see.[40] Barthes distinguishes between Balzac's reference to cultural codes and the supplementation of codes with forces of affect in *À la recherche* as follows:

> If Balzac refers to a cultural code (allusions to art, for instance): dull units are denoted (as it were), it is the being-there, the naturalness of culture that is presented: a use of the code, but without connotation. ≠ Charlus: cultural code (style of seats, for example) + an affective, emotive, enunciative supplement […] 'Charlus-Discourse': a banal interweaving of codes (*cf. Sarrasine*) + some supplements. Culture, for instance, is not simply a reference, an origin (Balzac), it is a space of enunciation. (*Comment vivre ensemble*, pp. 204–05)[41]

The haiku is '*in* the code' ('*dans* le code' (p. 76)), and Charlus 'places himself in the cultural unit' ('[l]e sujet Charlus se place dans l'unité culturelle' (*Comment vivre ensemble*, p. 204)). To put it another way: in both cases, natural codes (or cultural codes that have acquired a certain naturalness) are made into the particular, mobile effects of an enunciating subject, and discourse does a certain performative violence to – but does not destroy – the language (the *langue*) that is its raw material, its law.[42] Just as the haiku, for Barthes, confirms a Nietzschean image of subjectivity as mobile, as a discontinuous mutation rather than a 'river, even an ever-changing one'[43] (it is 'a plurality of person-like forces, in which now this one, now that one stands in the foreground and assumes the aspect of the ego'),[44] the 'Charlus-Discourse' is a subtle *moire* of inflections, a 'play of forces, of mobile intensities' (*Comment vivre ensemble*, p. 203) in which a subject who speaks also makes use of cultural codes in order to position himself 'in the eyes of the other, to enter into a reciprocal play of images, of positions'.[45] Charlus may not know Japanese, then, but he does occasionally speak in something like haikus.

Given what we know about the relationship between music, the body and the 'Charlus-Discourse', it is unsurprising that Barthes should refer to the haiku as a moment of exclamatory affect in which we witness a 'forgetting of the thetic [...], a brief sob or sigh (as in music)' (p. 105),[46] or as a bodily protestation of emotion, an 'I-body' ('*Je*-corps' (p. 106)) that requires readerly 'discrétion' and evaluation rather than the grasping 'will-to-possess' ('vouloir-saisir' (p. 111)) of commentary and interpretation. However, in spite of the potential for a 'passage' between notational fragments and *À la recherche* that these affinities suggest, there is also an important difference between Barthes's analysis of the haiku (and other moments in *À la recherche*, in fact) and of the 'Charlus-Discourse': they cannot be related to what he calls 'pathetic criticism' in the same way.

Pathetic reading and writing

A good haiku, Barthes says, '*sets a bell ringing*' ('fait *tilt*' (p. 123)). It triggers a neutral, anti-interpretative deictic – a confirmatory '*C'est ça!*' – that serves as an introduction ('une sorte de propédeutique' (p. 203)) to the impact of what he calls 'moments of truth'. He provides two examples of such moments, both of which are taken from the 'novels of Memory' mentioned earlier in the series: the episodes of the death of the narrator's grandmother in *À la recherche*, and the death of Prince Bolkonsky in Tolstoy's *War and Peace*.[47] The 'moment de vérité', Barthes says, is a phenomenon of reading, not of writing, in which literature suddenly coincides with an emotional event for the reader who suffers:

'Moment of truth' = [...] [m]oment of a story, of a description, of an enunciation, a sudden knot in the path of reading that assumes an exceptional character: conjunction of an overwhelming emotion (to the point of distress) and a self-evident truth giving rise, within us, to the certainty that what we are reading is the truth (has been the truth). Moment of truth: that which, in my reading, happens to *me*, a subject in the first order sense.[48]

While pathos is scorned by a prevailing preference for 'laws, generalities, for the Reducible, exquisite pleasure taken in *equalizing* all phenomena rather than registering their extreme difference' (p. 87),[49] one could, Barthes claims, theorize a '[c]ritique pathétique' (p. 160) – an account of the novel which, in contrast to structural analysis, would take affective elements rather than logical units ('unités logiques' (p. 160)) as its starting point. To engage with the novel in this way, he argues, is to 'devalue it, to disrespect the Whole, to do away with parts of it, to *ruin* it → in order to make it live' (p. 161).[50] Barthes's account of this non-structural, atomizing critical approach in *La Préparation du roman* recalls his suggestion in *Comment vivre ensemble* that structural analysis does not recognize the mobile, affective forces that inhabit the 'Charlus-Discourse', and his insistence in 1972 on the need for critics and readers to de-structure and rewrite Proust's work. As we saw in the previous chapter, Barthes's engagements with Proust have something 'pathetic' about them: they constitute a pathos-driven, partial and life-giving writing, whose theme is the affective variations, the intensive *moire* of a desiring *who* (Barthes as a reading and writing subject) rather than the identification of an interpretative or logical *what*. Be this as it may, Barthes's work on the 'Charlus-Discourse' also promotes another brand of pathetic criticism – one that may be closer to what he describes, fleetingly, as a moment of truth on the level of writing ('au plan de l'écriture') that embodies 'solidarity, compactness, concision of affect and writing' ('solidarité, compacité, fermeté de l'affect et de l'écriture' (p. 159)). Indeed, he does not discuss the 'Charlus-Discourse' explicitly in terms of its moments of truth (i.e. in terms of what happens to him – Barthes – as a first-order, reading and suffering subject). The pathetic moments of the 'Charlus-Discourse' are thus unlike those triggered by the haiku and by the death of the narrator's grandmother (or by the photographic *punctum*): they are the affective fluctuations of a second-order subject, a fictional creation for whom culture is a place of enunciation and not a point of reference, an origin. As such, they are identified and scrutinized by Barthes as a phenomenon of writing – as supplements of enunciation in writing – rather than of reading.

In his analysis of Proust's work in *Comment vivre ensemble* and *La Préparation du roman*, then, Barthes delineates two pathetic modes – two paths that might be taken by a form of criticism that is alive to both cultural coding and differentials of narrative intensity. He also demonstrates that, in their different ways, these critical approaches reach beyond the conventions of structural analysis. In doing these things, Barthes reveals not only that the typologies on which his arguments depend are 'disposable', as Jonathan Culler puts it,[51] but also that the intense mobility of *À la recherche* is such that Proust's work cannot be made to sit comfortably within the paradigms it is used to construct.

Rhapsody in Proust

Another typology: not long into his first lecture in 1980 (5 January), Barthes suggests that an individual who fantasizes about writing a work in the future necessarily has artistic (practical or physical) rather than hieratic considerations in mind. He observes:

> We could widen the scope of the question [concerning what an individual who desires to write fantasizes about in the work to be written] by going back to the grand Nietzschean typology: *Priest/Artist*; there is no way around it: the problems of 'content', of 'subject matter', are on the side of the priest, while we who are on the side of producing [...] are on the side of the artist. (*Préparation*, p. 239)[52]

The writer as producer and artist does not dwell on the future novel's content, its theme:[53] these are 'meta' rather than 'poetic' categories, of interest only to priests, critics, professors and theoreticians.[54] Instead, he or she focuses on how it will be assembled.[55] Accordingly, in the second part of his lecture course, Barthes organizes the discussion of the fantasized work's *physique* around two new pivots, which he takes from Mallarmé: the 'Book' and the 'Album'.

Borrowing heavily from Jacques Scherer's *Le 'Livre' de Mallarmé: premières recherches sur des documents inédits* (1957), Barthes describes the incomplete state and the projected form of Mallarmé's 'Book' as follows:

> What remains is a manuscript of two hundred pages: not *the Book* but thoughts on the Book; as I said, we do not know very much about

the content, only the ritual: public readings, an admission fee (a whole financial plan of theatre and publishing), permutable verses or lines, the combinations varying with each performance, multiplying the dissemination of the book → Features of this total book: objective (impersonal), not circumstantial (= the totality of living things, the sum of essences), organized in accordance with a structure (≠ album). (*La Préparation du roman*, p. 247)[56]

Like Barthes, Mallarmé attempts to give expression to a writing fantasy that revolves predominantly around questions of form. These efforts are situated, as Barthes puts it, in relation to the 'continuousness/discontinuousness of discourse' ('par rapport au continu/discontinu du discours' (p. 246)). The *Livre total* that Mallarmé envisages is paradoxical, Barthes suggests, insofar as it is at once metaphysical – a 'pure' work that is the '"hyperbole" of all existing books'[57] – and a physical mechanism for the operation of infinite disseminations and permutations.[58] As an object, then, it is limitless, but it is also 'architectural and premeditated' ('architectural et prémédité' (p. 246)): it is on the side of the continuous in this sense. The Album is the Book's paradigmatic other: it is a discontinuous, anthological scattering of fragments and is exemplified, according to Mallarmé, by his own *Divagations* (1897), a collection of 'poèmes critiques' that he presents as a mixture of, or as something between, critical essays and prose poems (another third form, perhaps). While Mallarmé disparages the fragmented Album in favour of the structured Book, other artists (Barthes's examples are Baudelaire, Poe and Schumann) celebrate the Album as the Book's equal. Barthes asserts that the veneration of the Album in this way constitutes an 'ardent – and often revolutionary – defence of the *Rhapsodic*' ('la défense ardente – et souvent révolutionnaire – du *Rhapsodique*'), a term which he aligns on this occasion with the 'Idea of the *Stitched, Tacked together, Patch-work*' ('Idée du *Cousu, Apiécé, Patch-Work*' (p. 251)). Now, if Albums promote rhapsody, then *À la recherche* is unmistakably of their kind.[59] On the next page of his lecture notes, however, Barthes indicates quite clearly that this is not the case. While he does not reiterate his suggestion that *À la recherche* may be the 'true incarnation of the Book Mallarmé dreamed of',[60] he nevertheless includes Proust's work in a list that exemplifies a form of rhythmical structuring that is characteristic of the Book: 'Book: there is a *cadence* (think of the books referred to: *The Divine Comedy, La Recherche du temps perdu, Monsieur Teste*)'.[61]

If *À la recherche* is on the side of both the Book and the Album, the hygienic opposition of Mallarmé's paradigm is under threat. Indeed, while Proust's 'indécision' (p. 258) led to the production of a *tierce forme*, an interweaving of both essay and novel, Barthes lives with his own hesitation in relation to Proust's work by describing it as a complex structure whose fragments are not 'necessarily on the side of the Album' ('nécessairement du côté de l'Album' (p. 251)):

> Last year, a member of the audience pointed out to me, quite rightly, that *La Recherche du temps perdu* is actually an interweaving of fragments. There is an architecture (in the musical sense), which is not of the order of the schema ['le plan'] but rather of a return, a *marcottage*: a return *foreseen* by Proust ('the book, architectural and *premeditated*'). (p. 251)[62]

As O'Meara has shown, Barthes emphasizes the 'superior strength' of the non-hierarchical, scattered Album in relation to the Book's 'monistic universe' in *L'Œuvre comme volonté*.[63] Nevertheless, what he says about Proust's rhapsodic text also suggests that it is possible to produce something like a Book that is made out of fragments (that is Album-like) without also producing something entirely discontinuous (think of the dress analogy earlier). In other words, what Barthes calls 'Proustian discontinuity' ('le discontinu proustien' (p. 47)) is in fact possessed of a certain continuity, a rhythm (which is more *rhuthmos* than *rythmos*): it is made of a tension, a 'passage', between the continuous and the broken. It is neither Book nor Album, in fact, or both at once. The structure of *À la recherche* constitutes a third or neutral form – and destabilizes Mallarmé's paradigm – because it is rhapsodic in a special sense.[64] While the definitions of the term that Barthes takes from Poe and Baudelaire suggest that it refers to little more than unstructured patchwork,[65] the rhapsody of *À la recherche* is built with fragments, which we could also call its variations, that are not arranged haphazardly. At the same time, it is not diary-like. If it were, it would be more patchwork than rhapsody: its variations do not amount to a linear, 'chronological, unstructured [...] *continuation*' ('un *suivi* [...] chronologique, sans construction' (p. 251)) or to an 'As it comes' ('Comme cela vient' (p. 255)), but to a complex architecture. They are a structured, rhythmical body, a transversal unity whose considered arrangements and rearrangements across the pages of *À la recherche* constitute what Barthes identifies (via Deleuze, again) as a Nietzschean superimposition of constructions,[66] and whose productive principle, which becomes discernible only at the end ('à la fin' (p. 252)), is the unstable, fertile rhythm of continuous variation – of variety – rather than the stable development of a theme (of a 'plan'). It is the tailoring or dress-like structure of Proust's great *tierce forme*, then, that invites us to conceive of 'to write' as an intransitive verb that refers to a personal and intimate tendency: while Camus's writing may be neutral because it is colourless, *À la recherche* outplays paradigms because it is a motley, *poikilos*[67] rhapsody, and the rhapsodic, Barthes suggests, 'distances the Object, magnifies the Tendency, the *Writing*' ('éloigne l'Objet, magnifie la Tendance, l'*Écrire*' (p. 203)). If Proust's novel is an item of clothing, it is also something possessed of an insecure and unstable completeness. The process of its making can be unimaginably complex, a process of fitting and refitting, adding and taking away, revising and recutting. The garment is to be seen only when the last stitch has been observed, and even then we cannot know the final shape of the garment for sure.

Our reading of Barthes's writing on Proust in (or across) *Comment vivre ensemble*, '"Longtemps, je me suis couché de bonne heure"' and *La Préparation du roman* has revealed that *À la recherche* destabilizes the very oppositions it is used (by Barthes) to build and to articulate. We could continue in a similar vein and locate further rhapsodic figures and formations – more fragments and stitching – in Proust's work as Barthes conceives of it, both in these late texts and elsewhere. His discussion of *À la recherche* – with reference to George D. Painter's two-volume biography of Proust[68] – in the '"Longtemps"' lecture and in *L'Œuvre comme volonté* as a 'biographie symbolique',[69] for example, which Nathalie Léger aligns with the work on 'biographèmes' in *Sade, Fourier, Loyola* (1971),[70] has been subject to some critical commentary. It suggests that Proust's work is a third form that marks neither a full, Sainte-Beuveian return of the author nor an outright (structuralist) erasure of biographical elements (Barthes's 1966 article on Painter's biography[71] rejects 'the idea of a one-way reading of literary work and biography in favour of a *parallel* reading in which both reciprocally illuminate each other',[72] and it can be read as an early move towards an engagement with Proust as a writerly figure and creative subject).[73] It also reveals why *À la recherche* should be able to breed what the author of 'La Mort de l'auteur' (1968) now calls a 'special interest' ('intérêt spécial' (V, 463)) in the life of Marcel Proust: a 'Marcellisme' (*Préparation*, p. 278) that identifies not with Proust as a social image – as the author of a monumental, canonical work of literature – but with Marcel, an 'absolutely personal subject' ('un sujet absolument personnel'), a tormented *Scribens* who returns to his life (as a *Persona*) 'not as to a curriculum vitae, but as to a constellation of circumstances and figures' (V, 464),[74] and for whom the novel is not a finite, complete, past entity

but what Hill calls an 'infinite, incomplete, futural prospect'.[75] Barthes's
'Marcellisme' is also at the heart of a provocative 'Scienza Nuova' (V,
470) of the intimate predicated on the view that, in Proust's words,
it is 'at the very pinnacle of the particular that the general blossoms'
(this phrase from a letter written by Proust to Daniel Halévy in 1919 is
partly quoted by Barthes in '"Longtemps, je me suis couché de bonne
heure"' and is glossed at greater length in the sixth lecture in the
Préparation du roman I series (20 January 1979)).[76] For Barthes, then,
'Marcel' is 'the proper name of an *effect* of reading and of a *desire* to
write'[77] that embodies an intimate conjoining of the utterly individual
and the universal. In the wake of his mother's death in 1977, Barthes's
personal investment and quasi-biographical interest in the compositional dilemmas, the practice, of the writer 'Marcel' informs his belief,
as O'Meara has demonstrated, that a focus on the particular 'is required
in a climate that figures such retrenchment into the self as shameful or
irresponsible',[78] and that an abandonment to the personal, to a 'pour
moi', far from being scandalously egotistical, is in fact the 'expression
of a generous, even a desperate, longing to do justice to other, beloved
people'.[79] Nevertheless, rather than dwell any further on the variety of
selves that Barthes's engagements with Proust invite us to encounter,[80]
or on the neutrality of 'Marcel' and of *À la recherche* more generally,
the concluding section of this chapter will focus on the variations that
Barthes operates upon the nuanced fabric of Proust's work.

Neutral variation

In the 'Préliminaires' to his lecture course entitled *Le Neutre*, Barthes
suggests that his fragmentary exposition of figures 'in which [...] there is
some neutral'[81] may be a consequence of his own inability to construct
a 'développement' (p. 35). He also blames it on the subject matter:
'[t]he inorganized sequence of figures required by the Neutral itself,
inasmuch as it embodies the refusal to dogmatize: the exposition of the
non-dogmatic cannot itself be dogmatic. Inorganization = inconclusion'
(p. 36).[82] Significantly, Barthes connects this inconclusive neutrality of
exposition to another figure with which we have become familiar. He
writes:

> The sequence of fragments: it would put 'something' (the subject, the
> Neutral?) in a state of continuous variation (instead of articulating it with
> a view to a final meaning): relation to contemporary music, where the

'content' of forms matters less than their circulation, and also perhaps to Deleuze's current research. (p. 35)[83]

The organizing principle of – or what matters in – Barthes's discontinuous, neutral lecture fragments is not the varied development or articulation of a theme towards logical resolution, but an unending, rhizomatic form of variation.[84] The figure of 'variations without a theme' (whose presence is to be felt far beyond contemporary music, of course) is thus one in which there is 'some neutral'. Later in the same session (of 18 February 1978), Barthes qualifies his previous point about the relationship between the neutral and the dogmatic:

> There is a passion of the Neutral, but [...] this passion is not that of a will-to-possess → I sometimes recognize this passion in myself through the calm with which I witness the display of 'wills-to-possess', of dogmatisms. But this is discontinuous, erratic, as desire always is: this is not about a wisdom but about a desire. (p. 39)[85]

Here, an itinerant (sceptical) dogmatism reflects variations of desire: a provisional taking-hold that lets go and moves onto other things.[86] It invites us to conceive of teaching (and of criticism) as a dynamic and desire-oriented activity involving (a lot) more than the identification of logical units or fixed, stable themes. Indeed, anticipating (inadvertently, no doubt) his comments in 'Un homme, une ville' concerning the inexhaustibility – the kaleidoscopic diffuseness, etc. – of Proust's work and the critical approach it demands (the interview was broadcast on *France culture* later the same year (1978)), Barthes defines the neutral as 'the shimmer: that whose aspect, perhaps whose meaning, is subtly modified according to the angle of the subject's gaze'.[87] Furthermore, the unmarked colour of the neutral's moire, he argues, suggests a principle of organization that has little to do with the rigid oppositional logic of the paradigm:

> Now, the monochrome (the Neutral) substitutes for the idea of opposition that of the slight difference, of the onset, of the effort towards difference, in other words, of nuance: nuance becomes a principle of total organization (which covers the whole surface, as in the landscape or the triptych) that in a way skips the paradigm: this integrally and almost exhaustively nuanced space is the shimmer. (p. 83)[88]

Neither Barthes's lecture series on the neutral nor his writing on *À la recherche* should be understood as 'the presentation of the current state of a thought' ('l'état d'une pensée'), but rather as a neutral 'moire d'individuation' (*Le Neutre*, p. 79). Indeed, what we have seen in this and previous chapters demonstrates that Barthes's work on *À la recherche* is a space of variation, of modulation and erratic dogmatism, that draws attention to and reproduces the novel's own shimmers and shades. Barthes's engagements with Proust, in other words, meet the requirements imposed upon them by *À la recherche*'s variations: they are neutral in each of the senses Barthes gives to the term.

We can shed further light on Barthes's own efforts towards difference by examining – and by appending nuances to – Claude Coste's observations in '"J'ai toujours eu envie d'*argumenter* mes humeurs": savoir et subjectivité dans *La Chambre claire* et *Sur Racine*' (2015). In his article, Coste suggests that several of the passages in *Le Discours amoureux* and *Fragments d'un discours amoureux* that are dedicated to 'affective blackmail' ('chantage affectif'),[89] and in particular the fragment in the latter on 'Les Lunettes noires' (V, 71–74),[90] rework and develop ('reprennent et développent')[91] the argument of the section entitled 'Techniques d'agression' in *Sur Racine* (1963). While he does not explain in what this diachronic reworking and development consists, the connections between the texts Coste mentions are easy to identify. In 'Techniques d'agression', for example, Barthes argues that the principal weapons wielded by Racine's battling couples (composed of a 'maître' and a 'sujet') are, respectively, 'frustration' and 'blackmail' ('chantage' (II, 83)). The various disappointments and cancellations inflicted upon the subject by a tyrannical master suggest a form of sadism (II, 81), and the subject's threat of suicide is always a form of blackmail or punishment designed to trigger feelings of guilt in the torturer ('le bourreau' (II, 84)). In 'Les Lunettes noires', Barthes describes the conundrum, the 'double discours' in which the amorous subject is caught. He or she wonders to what degree the turbulences of his or her passion should be concealed from the other:

> On the one hand, I tell myself: what if the other, by some arrangement of his or her own structure, needed my demand [*ma demande*]? Then would I not be justified in abandoning myself to the literal expression, the lyrical utterance of my 'passion'? Are not excess and madness my truth, my strength? And if this truth, this strength ultimately prevailed? But on the other hand, I tell myself: the signs of this passion run the risk of smothering the other. Then should I not, *precisely because of my love*, hide from the other how much I love him or her? I see the other with a double vision: sometimes as object, sometimes as subject; I hesitate between tyranny and oblation. I thus doom myself to blackmail: if I love

the other, I am forced to seek his or her happiness; but then I can only do myself harm: a trap: I am condemned to be a saint or a monster: unable to be the one, unwilling to be the other: hence I procrastinate: I show my passion *a little*. (V, 72)[92]

In each of the texts to which Coste refers, Barthes describes the relationship between the subject and the other as a careful and manipulative negotiation – as a hesitation between revelation and concealment, tyrannical domination and self-sacrifice. In the fragment on 'Les Lunettes noires' (the subject wears dark glasses both to conceal swollen eyes and to reveal that he or she is hiding something), Barthes nuances – reworks and develops – the argument of the earlier text through the addition of references to the Lacanian notion of 'demande' and to 'oblation', both of which figure prominently in *Le Discours amoureux*.[93]

Barthes's use of these terms in 'Les Lunettes noires' suggests, in fact, that it is as much a nuancing of his work on Racine in 1963 as of his Rabat seminar notes on Proust from 1969–70, where he discusses an episode – Barthes calls it 'Un chantage' – in which the young and sickly narrator manipulates, or rather 'blackmails' his grandmother (see *ALR*, I, 486–90).[94] He identifies the scene as an example of 'Proust's "sadism" (or at least the Narrator's)' ('le "sadisme" de Proust (ou du moins du N[arrateur]')) and of 'hurting those we love' ('faire du mal à qui l'on aime'). Desperate to join Gilberte for a game of tag in the Champs-Elysées gardens, the narrator conceals his nausea and a high fever from his family. The ruse works, but after their outing, Françoise reveals that the narrator has been 'indisposed' ('que je m'étais "trouvé indisposé"' (*ALR*, I, 487)).[95] At this point, we learn that he has been prescribed caffeine and alcohol for choking fits, and that his grandmother, who sees her grandson already dying a drunkard's death ('déjà mourant alcoolique' (*ALR*, I, 487)), fiercely disapproves of the prescription – so much so, in fact, that the narrator is 'often obliged, so that my grandmother should allow them to give it to me, instead of dissembling, almost to make a display of my state of suffocation' (*ALR*, I, 487).[96] The ensuing game of showing and hiding is a complex (almost farcical) one:

> as soon as I felt an attack coming, never being quite certain what proportions it would assume, I would grow distressed at the thought of my grandmother's anxiety, of which I was far more afraid than of my own sufferings. But at the same time my body [...] gave me the need to warn my grandmother of my attacks with a punctiliousness into which I finally put a sort of physiological scruple. If I perceived in myself a

disturbing symptom that I had not previously observed, my body was in distress so long as I had not communicated it to my grandmother. If she pretended to pay no attention, it made me insist. Sometimes I went too far; and that dear face, which was no longer able always to control its emotion as in the past, would allow an expression of pity to appear, a painful contraction. Then my heart was wrung by the sight of her grief; as if my kisses had had power to expel that grief, as if my affection could give my grandmother as much joy as my recovery, I flung myself into her arms. And its scruples being at the same time calmed by the certainty that she now knew the discomfort that I felt, my body offered no opposition to my reassuring her. I protested that this discomfort had been nothing, that I was in no sense to be pitied, that she might be quite sure that I was now happy; my body had wished to secure exactly the amount of pity that it deserved [...]. One evening, after my grandmother had left me comparatively well, she returned to my room very late and, seeing me struggling for breath, 'Oh, my poor boy', she exclaimed, her face quivering with sympathy, 'you are in dreadful pain'. She left me at once; I heard the outer gate open, and in a little while she came back with some brandy which she had gone out to buy, since there was none in the house. Presently I began to feel better. My grandmother, who was rather flushed, seemed put out about something, and her eyes had a look of weariness and dejection. 'I shall leave you alone now, and let you get the good of this improvement', she said, rising suddenly to go. I detained her, however, for a kiss, and could feel on her cold cheek something moist, but did not know whether it was the dampness of the night air through which she had just passed. Next day, she did not come to my room until the evening, having had, she told me, to go out. I considered that this showed a surprising indifference to my welfare, and I had to restrain myself so as not to reproach her with it. (*ALR*, I, 487–88)[97]

The twists and turns of this long and complicated passage (Barthes says that it is made of an extreme 'permutation' and 'complexisation' of messages) reveal a narrator who is prone to something like the hesitations outlined in 'Les Lunettes noires' – a subject who conceals his suffocations from the other (from his grandmother) for fear of distressing her; whose body nevertheless feels a punctilious need to reveal its pain to her whenever she feigns ignorance; who, at the sight of the grief his own suffering causes her, and also because he feels that his discomfort has been sufficiently acknowledged, cannot help but throw himself into her arms and reassure her that there is nothing wrong. This sequence of maskings and unmaskings, in which the narrator hesitates between masochistic sanctity and sadistic monstrousness (he dooms himself to blackmail, as Barthes puts it), is followed by a moment in which the grandmother capitulates and provides the treatment whose deleterious effects she fears. Like her grandson, the grandmother is unable to keep her body quiet: she cannot hold back the tears that the spectacle of his suffering causes her to shed. What she hides with her language, her body still utters (the passage above suggests that the narrator's body, by contrast, is particularly verbose and indiscrete). Or as Barthes puts it in 'Les Lunettes noires', she is required to 'divide the economy of [her] signs' ('diviser l'économie de [ses] signes' (p. 73)), even if the young narrator is unable to read the distress signals that her body transmits (and that he sees). Subsequently, the narrator interprets an act of self-sacrifice, of oblation (Barthes calls it an 'oblation maternelle' in his notes), as a sign of indifference (as tyranny), and he struggles to conceal the anger that this perceived coldness and lack of consideration – and his grandmother's eventual absence – cause him to feel. According to Barthes, the grandmother makes herself scarce, not because she wishes more pain upon her grandson, but 'par oblation, pour ne pas faire de la peine en montrant sa peine' – because she fears that the sight of her own grief will cause him to suffer (we know that she is right). She chooses not to return, Barthes says, 'not only in order not to see, but so that [the] N[arrator] does not see her seeing' ('non seulement pour ne pas voir, mais pour que [le] N[arrateur] ne la voit pas voir').

In their different ways, then, grandmother and grandson find themselves in the position of the amorous subject described in 'Les Lunettes noires': while the narrator is aggressively manipulative in a way that his grandmother is not (she is not a monster, and treats her grandson as a feeling subject), both subjects encounter – see – the other in an atmosphere of love accompanied by anxious tension and fear. The difference between the narrator and the grandmother, perhaps, is that she is less calculating than her 'wily' ('retors' (V, 73)) grandson: unlike him, she does not point at the oblative mask she has placed over her suffering (he, in contrast, is reassured by the certainty that she is aware of the discomfort he feels, even as he reassures her that he feels none).[98] To put it another way: instead of wearing dark glasses in order (hypocritically) both to show and to hide her distress, she simply leaves him alone.

Barthes mentions Racine (Phèdre and her fury) in 'Les Lunettes noires' (see V, 71, for example), but he does not refer explicitly to Proust or to the blackmail episode. As Marty has shown, Barthes works with and against Proust in a later work, *La Chambre claire*: while Barthes refers in that text to several passages in *À la recherche* that are linked to photography in significant ways (the moment the narrator takes off his boots and confronts the irreversible permanence of his grandmother's death, for example), he also leaves out the sadism and feelings of guilt that figure so prominently in them.[99] Barthes thus protects photography from Proust: Proust is present in sanitized, edified form. The operation he performs in 'Les Lunettes noires' is quite different. He poaches an economy, a regime of blackmail from *À la recherche*, but instead of cleaning up its perversions or quelling its sadistic violence, he simply leaves Proust out of the equation: he prevents the narrator and his grandmother, in other words, from being touched explicitly by the incestuous torture that the rhizomatic contact between 'Les Lunettes noires' and the Rabat seminar notes implies. To return to the vocabulary of *Critique et vérité* with which we worked in Chapter One, Barthes rubs against the language of *À la recherche* (and his own analysis of it) and also rubs it out (or at least covers it): on this occasion, Proust's perversion figures only indirectly, in the form of a transversal trace.

In his notes, Barthes summarizes the mechanics of Proust's blackmail scene with the following statement: 'the finality of blackmail (to obtain) is surpassed to the benefit of the demand (in the Lacanian sense)'.[100] According to Malcolm Bowie, 'la demande' is a demand for love – it is an appeal to the other not only to satisfy needs but also to 'pay the compliment of an unconditional *yes*'.[101] The other to whom this appeal is addressed, however, cannot answer it completely: 'his *yes*, however loudly it is proclaimed, can only ever be a *maybe*, or a *to some extent*, in disguise'.[102] In *Écrits* (1966), Lacan emphasizes the difference between need and the demand. The effect of the demand, he writes, is to 'annul [...] the particularity of everything that can be granted, by transmuting it into a proof of love'.[103] Barthes echoes Lacan's words in *Le Discours amoureux*: 'the good response to the demand is not satisfaction [...] but the message of presence: the sign of the presence of the other comes to dominate over the satisfactions that this presence brings'.[104] Barthes's elliptical summary in Rabat suggests the following (this is the best I can do with it, and with Lacan): what begins as an affective blackmail – 'un chantage' – designed to satisfy particular needs (to obtain something in particular) gives way to a 'demande' for love – to an appeal for the sign of an absolute presence that neither the grandmother, irrespective of her physical presence or absence, nor anyone (or anything) else can answer unconditionally. As Bowie puts it, 'something else is always going on in dealings between the need-driven subject and the other who may or may not provide satisfaction. A demand for love is being made'.[105]

However we interpret Barthes's statement, one thing is clear: the fragment concerned with 'Les Lunettes noires' in *Fragments d'un discours amoureux* is a nuancing of 'Techniques d'agression', of Proust's blackmail scene, and of Barthes's notes on it. It is also connected to the discussion of Andromaque and Charlus in *Comment vivre ensemble*: the former's speech is designed to obtain something from the other ('vise à obtenir quelque chose' (p. 211)) through flattery and without suffering; the latter seeks to obtain something (to take hold of the narrator), but his tactics are obscure and enigmatic, even unconscious ('peut-être non déterminée par le sujet lui-même' (pp. 213–14)). These intertextual tintings, touchings-up and rewritings are the stuff of what Barthes calls a 'déformation narcissique' (*Préparation*, p. 191) – of a critical eclecticism that constitutes a composite self-portrait of the writer as a creator of difference rather than a straightforward piler-up or developer of theories. Indeed, Coste argues that by adding, subtracting and joining up 'fragments of thought' ('des fragments de pensée') across his work, Barthes teaches us that 'it is the gaze that counts; or rather, what counts is the spectacle insofar as it reveals a particular observer whose coherence we follow from book to book'.[106] Instead of exhausting *À la recherche* and parading its corpse, Barthes builds pieces of its rhapsodic material into a shifting (living) body of nuances that constitutes a rewriting not because it reproduces or resuscitates Proustian themes, but because it is *poikilos*: like Proust's novel, it is a neutral space of intense individuation, of difference and variation. Proust's strangely continuous and discontinuous (neutral) Book has variations operated upon it in a ruinous but vital, life-giving theatre of circulation and partial citation – in a repeated nuancing or testing out of forms, a building of differences in a variety of critical contexts that, while it may be more erratic and desire-oriented than it is premeditated, refuses to be treated as a logical reworking towards possession and redemption.

Notes

1 *Le Degré zero de l'écriture*, I, 173. According to Barthes, a mid-century ('vers 1850') tearing apart of bourgeois consciousness resulted in the disintegration of classical writing ('[l]'écriture classique a donc éclaté') and brought about the transformation of 'the whole of Literature, from Flaubert to the present day' into a 'problematics of language' ('la Littérature entière, de Flaubert à nos jours, est devenue une problématique du langage' (I, 172)). Flaubert's first novel, *Madame Bovary*, was published in 1856.

2 See I, 217.

3 See I, 179: 'between language and style, there is room for another formal reality: writing. Within any literary form, there is a general choice of tone, of ethos, if you like, and this is precisely where the writer shows himself clearly as an individual because this is where he commits himself' ('entre la langue et le style, il y a place pour une autre réalité formelle: l'écriture. Dans n'importe quelle forme littéraire, il y a le choix général d'un ton, d'un éthos, si l'on veut, et c'est ici précisément que l'écrivain s'individualise clairement parce que c'est ici qu'il s'engage'). For Barthes, language is *langue* in a broadly Saussurean sense – a 'body of prescriptions and habits common to all the writers of a given period' ('un corps de prescriptions et d'habitudes, commun à tous les écrivains d'une époque' (see I, 177)) – and style springs from the body and the past of the writer. Unlike language, its frame of reference is biological or biographical ('[s]es références sont au niveau d'une biologie ou d'un passé, non d'une Histoire' (I, 178)).

4 'une équation pure, n'ayant pas plus d'épaisseur qu'une algèbre' (I, 218). As we saw in Chapter One, Malcolm Bowie observes that, for Barthes, criticism should move towards 'the silence and the expressionless neutrality of an equation' (Bowie, 'Barthes on Proust', p. 516). This implies that the language of criticism should be neutral in much the same way as the language of *L'Étranger*. We will explore the neutrality of Barthes's writing on Proust later in this chapter.

5 See I, 217: 'A simile borrowed from linguistics will perhaps give a fairly accurate idea of this new phenomenon; we know that some linguists establish between the two terms of a polar opposition (such as singular-plural, preterite-present) the existence of a third term, called a neutral or zero element' ('Une comparaison empruntée à la linguistique rendra peut-être assez bien compte de ce fait nouveau: on sait que certains linguistes établissent entre les deux termes d'une polarité (singulier-pluriel, prétérit-présent), l'existence d'un troisième terme, terme neutre ou terme zéro').

6 See I, 217: 'The new neutral writing takes its place in the midst of all those ejaculations and judgments, without becoming involved in any of them' ('La nouvelle écriture neutre se place au milieu de ces cris et de ces jugements, sans participer à aucun d'eux').

7 In *Le Neutre*, Barthes examines the figure of the neutral as it is revealed in 'brief images, twinklings, the list of which is neither logically conducted nor exhaustive' ('images brèves, scintillations, dont la liste n'est ni conduite logiquement, ni exhaustive' (p. 117)).

8 'un style de l'absence qui est presque une absence idéale du style' (I, 217–18).

9 As the translators of *Le Neutre* point out, Richard Howard translates 'déjouer' as 'to baffle' (in *The Rustle of Language*, trans. Richard Howard (New York: Hill and Wang, 1986), p. 242). They also note that, '[s]ince the

word relates to the field of play, he also uses "fake", as in "fake out"', and that
'"[o]utwit", "thwart" or "outplay" also work' (Roland Barthes, *The Neutral.
Lecture Course at the Collège de France (1977–1978)*, trans. Rosalind E. Kraus
and Denis Hollier (New York: Columbia University Press, 2005), p. 213, n. 8).

10 See *Comment vivre ensemble*, p. 219: 'From the moment an analysis takes
enunciation into account it is no longer planimetrical, tabular. Enunciation:
consideration of the positions occupied by subjects in the discourse' ('Dès
qu'il y a – dans l'analyse – considération de l'énonciation, l'analyse n'est plus
planimétrique, tabulaire. Énonciation: prise en considération de la place des
sujets dans le discours').

11 See V, 461: 'roman? essai? Aucun des deux ou les deux à la fois'.

12 See *ALR*, IV, 610: 'I should build my book, I don't dare say, ambitiously,
as if it were a cathedral, but simply as if it were a dress I was making' ('je
bâtirais mon livre, je n'ose pas dire ambitieusement comme une cathédrale,
mais tout simplement comme une robe'). Luc Fraisse discusses the significance
of Proust's architectural and sartorial metaphors in *L'Œuvre cathédrale: Proust
et l'architecture médiévale* (Paris: Corti, 1990) and *Le Processus de la création
chez Marcel Proust: le fragment expérimental* (Paris: Corti, 1988).

13 'une robe [...] des pièces, des morceaux sont soumis à des croisements,
des arrangements, des rappels: une robe n'est pas un *patchwork*, pas plus que
n'est *La Recherche*' (V, 463). As Barthes indicates, the etymology of 'rhapsodie'
is the Greek *rhapsōidia* (from *rhaptein*, 'to stitch', and *ōidē*, 'song, ode').

14 'romans de la Mémoire = faits avec des matériaux (des "souvenirs")
rappelés de l'enfance, de la vie du sujet qui écrit'. Barthes's examples are *À la
recherche* and Tolstoy's *War and Peace* (1869).

15 'Sans doute ai-je quelques souvenirs-éclairs, des flashes de mémoire,
mais ils ne prolifèrent pas, ils ne sont pas associatifs ("torrentueux") ≠ Proust.
Ils sont immédiatement épuisés par la forme brève (cf. les *Anamnèses*, dans le
Roland Barthes), d'où l'impression de "romanesque" qu'on peut avoir, mais
aussi, précisément, ce qui le sépare du Roman'.

16 'comment passer de la Notation, donc de la Note, au Roman, du
discontinu au flux (au nappé)? [...] il ne faut pas exclure une *tierce forme*.
Figure: ce qui apparaît d'abord impossible, finalement est peut-être possible.
En l'occurrence: possible de concevoir un *Roman par fragments*, un
Roman-Fragment. Sans doute en existe-t-il – ou qui approchent: [...] Je pense
à l'aspect *crypto-fragmentaire* de Flaubert (*blancs*) et à Aziyadé. Sûrement
bien d'autres exemples – et à un niveau plus profond, moins formel: bien sûr
le discontinu proustien, le *Rhapsodique*'. As the editors of *La Préparation du
roman* observe, one of Barthes's *Nouveaux essais critiques* focuses on the
typographical presentation of – the blank spaces in – Pierre Loti's *Aziyadé* (see
'Pierre Loti: *Aziyadé*', IV, 107–20).

17 Marielle Macé explores the variations in Barthes's approach to the
notion of the *romanesque*, the novel and the essay form – from *Système de*

la mode (1967) to the *Vita nova* plans (1979) – in 'Barthes romanesque', in *Barthes, au lieu du roman*, ed. Marielle Macé and Alexandre Gefen (Paris: Éditions Desjonquères/Nota Bene, 2002), pp. 173–88.

18 'deux pivots – apparemment disparates → articulation excentrique – d'une certaine circonvolution autour du Roman à faire, du Roman fantasmé: le *Haïku/Proust* (je dis bien *Proust* – et non *La Recherche du temps perdu*). Je suis persuadé de la validité de cette opposition, mais je craignais tout de même qu'elle ne vous paraisse un peu abrupte, un peu elliptique, un peu désinvolte – ou "tirée par les cheveux"'.

19 Recordings of the majority of Barthes's Collège de France lectures are available here: <http://www.ubu.com/sound/barthes.html> [accessed 1 June 2019].

20 Readers of Barthes's notes might also interpret 'eccentric articulation' as a qualification of 'seemingly disparate' – as an indication that, while the organizing pivots of Barthes's lectures may appear to be entirely different in kind, they can also be brought together (articulated) in unusual or paradoxical ways. During the session of 3 February 1979, Barthes makes precisely this point: 'this is not, this will not be the first time that, by way of a paradox that structures this course, Proust and the haiku intersect: the shortest and the longest form' ('ce n'est pas, ce ne sera pas la première fois que par un paradoxe qui articule ce cours, Proust et le haïku se croisent: la forme la plus brève et la forme la plus longue' (p. 99)).

21 See '"Longtemps, je me suis couché de bonne heure"', V, 464: 'De plus en plus nous nous prenons à aimer non "Proust" (nom civil d'un auteur fiché dans les Histoires de la littérature), mais "Marcel", être singulier, à la fois enfant et adulte, *puer senilis*, passionné et sage, proie de manies excentriques et lieu d'une réflexion souveraine sur le monde, l'amour, l'art, le temps, la mort'.

22 Barthes defines the '*Scriptor*' as 'the writer as social image, the one who is talked about, who is discussed, who is classified according to school, or genre, in manuals, etc.' ('l'écrivain comme image sociale, celui dont on parle, que l'on commente, que l'on classe dans une école, un genre, des manuels, etc.'). '*Scribens*' is 'the *I* who is engaged in the practice of writing, who is in the process of writing, who lives writing everyday' ('le *je* qui est dans la pratique d'écriture, qui est en train d'écrire, qui vit quotidiennement l'écriture' (*Préparation*, p. 280)).

23 'D'un côté, il est évident que le haïku n'est pas un acte d'écriture à la Proust, c'est-à-dire destiné à "retrouver" le Temps (perdu) *ensuite, après coup* (enfermé dans la chambre de liège), par l'action souveraine de la mémoire involontaire, mais au contraire: *trouver* (et non *retrouver*) le Temps *tout de suite, sur-le-champ*; le Temps est sauvé *tout de suite*'.

24 'la "mémoire immédiate" comme si la *Notatio* (le fait de noter) permettait de se souvenir *sur-le-champ* (≠ mémoire involontaire de Proust: la mémoire immédiate ça ne prolifère pas, ce n'est pas métonymique)'.

25 'La photographie ne remémore pas le passé (rien de proustien dans une photo). L'effet qu'elle produit sur moi n'est pas de restituer ce qui est aboli (par le temps, la distance), mais d'attester que cela que je vois, a bien été'. I have taken – and occasionally modified – translations of this work from the following edition: Roland Barthes, *Camera Lucida: Reflections on Photography*, trans. Richard Howard (New York: Hill and Wang, 1981).

26 'toute *La Recherche du temps perdu* sortie de la Madeleine, comme la fleur japonaise dans l'eau: développement, tiroirs, *dépli* infini. Dans le haïku, la fleur n'est pas dépliée, c'est la fleur japonaise sans eau: elle reste bouton. Le mot (l'hologramme du haïku), comme une pierre dans l'eau, mais pour rien: on ne reste pas à regarder les ondes, on reçoit le bruit (le *ploc*), c'est tout'.

27 See 'Un homme, une ville', III, 13:20–45.

28 Yaha's haiku reads as follows: 'Lying down / I watch the clouds go by / Summer bedroom' ('Couché / Je vois passer des nuages / Chambre d'été' (*Préparation*, p. 67)).

29 'Capturer une photo': to take a photo.

30 'L'été *capturé* dans la chambre est plus intense: il est capturé comme absence, capturé dehors. C'est dans l'intérieur, là d'où il est repoussé que l'été est le plus fort: il triomphe dehors et presse → son intensité: Intensité de l'Indirect; comme quoi l'Indirect est la voie même de communication, de manifestation de l'Essence'.

31 'à peu près la même chose que Proust disant en une ou deux pages serrées l'été à partir de la chambre d'hôtel de Balbec'.

32 Paul de Man discusses this passage in 'Reading (Proust)', in *Allegories of Reading: Figural Language in Rousseau, Nietzsche, Rilke and Proust* (New Haven and London: Yale University Press, 1979), pp. 57–78. For De Man, the passage 'valorizes metaphor as being the "right" literary figure', but also, paradoxically, 'constitute[s] itself by means of the epistemologically incompatible figure of metonymy' (p. 18).

33 'une parole infinie qui peut déplier l'été, *par la voie d'un Indirect qui, structurellement, n'a aucune raison de finir*'.

34 'le tissu infini du monde: sur le monde, il y a toujours à dire, infiniment'.

35 'force d'individuation, de différence, de nuance, de moire d'existentialité'.

36 'le *sentir-être* du sujet, la pure et mystérieuse sensation de la vie'.

37 '1) un code (une loi): la Saison + 2) une performance (une parole, un discours) qui accomplit le code: *le Temps qu'il fait* = code parlé par le moment, le jour, l'heure, l'individuation de l'existence, c'est-à-dire qui accomplit, ou qui déjoue [...]: parfois (souvent?) on voit en France, pays d'un *variable* subtil, complexe, une saison démentie par le temps qu'il fait (hiver en été, etc.), et cependant accomplie, confirmée par les productions (fleurs, fruits, etc.)'.

38 See *Préparation*, p. 75: 'il y a une Moire, un différentiel des Intensités (du temps qu'il fait)'.

39 'une individuation intense, sans compromission avec la généralité – *malgré et en se servant du code des saisons'*.

40 While Barthes discusses the relationship between the haiku and the photograph in *La Chambre claire* (see V, 828, for example), and while several critics have discussed the role and significance of Barthes's references to Proust in that work, neither they nor Barthes consider the affinities between the haiku (or the photograph) and the 'Charlus-Discourse'.

41 'Si Balzac recourt à un code culturel (allusions à l'art, par exemple): unités mates, et comme dénotées, c'est l'être-là, la naturalité de la culture qui est donnée: code manié sans connotation. ≠ Charlus: code culturel (style des sièges, par exemple) + un supplément affectif, émotif, énonciatif [...] "Discours-Charlus": un tissu banal de codes (*cf. Sarrasine*) + des suppléments. La culture, par exemple, n'est pas seulement une référence, une origine (Balzac), mais une place d'énonciation'.

42 In *Le Neutre*, Barthes observes that discourse nuances its law, which is language (p. 74), and in *La Préparation du roman*, he discusses the 'remunerative', 'compensatory' and 'rectifying' function of discourse in relation to language (see p. 73).

43 See *Préparation*, p. 79: 'la subjectivité non comme un fleuve, même changeant'.

44 'Le moi est une pluralité de forces quasi personnifiées dont tantôt l'une, tantôt l'autre se situe à l'avant-scène et prend l'aspect du moi' (*Préparation*, p. 79).

45 See *Comment vivre ensemble*, p. 204: 'Le code culturel lui sert à se placer face à l'autre, à entrer dans un jeu réciproque d'images, de places'.

46 'un oubli du thétique [...], un bref sanglot ou soupir (comme en musique)'.

47 See *Préparation*, p. 157, and '"Longtemps, je me suis couché de bonne heure"', V, 467–68.

48 '"Moment de vérité" = [...] [m]oment d'une histoire, d'une description, d'une énonciation, nœud brusque du cursus de lecture, qui prend un caractère exceptionnel: conjonction d'une émotion qui submerge (jusqu'aux larmes, jusqu'au trouble) et d'une évidence qui imprime en nous la certitude que ce que nous lisons est la vérité (a été la vérité). Moment de vérité: ce qui, dans une lecture, m'arrive *à moi*, sujet au premier degré'.

49 'des lois, des généralités, goût du Réductible, volupté à égaliser les phénomènes au lieu de les différencier à l'extrême'.

50 'déprécier l'œuvre, [...] ne pas en respecter le Tout, [...] abolir des parts de cette œuvre, [...] la *ruiner* → pour la faire vivre'. For an example of 'pathetic criticism' in action, see Kate Briggs's *Exercise in Pathetic Criticism* (York: information as material, 2011).

51 See Jonathan Culler, 'Preparing the Novel: Spiralling Back', *Roland Barthes Retroactively: Reading the Collège de France Lectures*, ed. Jürgen Pieters and Kris Pint, *Paragraph* (Special Issue), 31/1 (2008), pp. 109–20 (p. 110).

52 'On pourrait élargir le problème en retrouvant la grande typologie nietzschéenne: *Prêtre/Artiste*; rien à faire: les problèmes de "contenu", de "sujet", sont du côté du prêtre, mais nous qui sommes du côté du faire [...] nous sommes du côté de l'artiste'.

53 Barthes writes: 'At first, it is not a content or a theme that I fantasize and "visualize"' ('Ce n'est donc aucun contenu, aucun thème qu'au départ je fantasme et "visionne"' (*Préparation*, p. 240)).

54 See *Préparation*, p. 239, where Barthes says that content is a 'catégorie de critiques, de professeurs, de théoriciens'.

55 As we have already seen, Barthes is more priestly in the first part of his lecture series: he does have something to say about the (present-oriented) content of the work he would like to write (as well as the notational form that corresponds to it).

56 'Reste un manuscrit de 200 feuillets: non pas *le Livre*, mais pensées sur le Livre; je l'ai dit, on ne sait pas grand-chose sur le contenu, mais seulement sur le rituel: lecture au cours de séances payantes (tout un plan financier de théâtre et d'édition), de vers ou versets permutables, la combinatoire variant selon les séances, multipliant la dissémination du livre → Caractères de ce livre total: objectif (non personnel), non circonstanciel (= totalité des choses existantes, somme d'essences), ordonné selon une structure (≠ album)'.

57 Jacques Scherer, *Le 'Livre' de Mallarmé: premières recherches sur des documents inédits* (Paris: Gallimard, 1954), p. 23. Barthes misquotes Scherer here and does not bother with quotation marks. He writes 'l'"hyperbole" de tous les livres excellents' (*Préparation*, p. 247) instead of 'l'"hyperbole" de tous les livres existants' (Scherer's words).

58 For a detailed analysis of the permutative complexity of Mallarmé's *Livre*, see Scherer, *Le 'Livre' de Mallarmé*, especially 'Les Séances' (pp. 75–107). Mallarmé envisages the *Livre total* as four books that can be ordered as two pairs. Each book is subdivided into five volumes. He envisions an elaborate mixing and exchange of the volumes of one book with those of another. Each volume of each book is made up of three groups of eight pages (twenty-four pages in all). Each page is discrete and may be further broken down, since it contains eighteen twelve-word lines. This disposition of words, lines, pages, page groups, volumes, and books may be shuffled into new combinations, offering a multitude of possible readings. Furthermore, Mallarmé proposes that each page be read not only in the normal horizontal way (within the page's verticality), but backwards, or vertically, or in a selective order of omissions or diagonally. He also imagines the five volumes as a block in which pagination is three-dimensional: the reader looks through the pages and reads according to depth. Each line of each page thus forms a new vertical page.

59 In spite of his use of a comma after '*Apiécé*', we can assume, I think, that Barthes's description of the idea of the rhapsodic implies that it is stitched or tacked together, and that it is *not* a patchwork.

60 Barthes, 'Table ronde sur Proust', p. 29.

61 'Livre: il y a une *cadence* (penser aux livres cités: *La Divine Comédie, La Recherche du temps perdu, Monsieur Teste*)'.

62 'L'année dernière, un auditeur m'a fait justement remarquer que *La Recherche du temps perdu* était en fait un tissu de fragments, mais il y a une architecture (au sens musical), qui n'est pas de l'ordre du plan, mais de l'ordre du retour, du marcottage: retour prévu par Proust ("le livre, architectural et *prémédité*")'.

63 O'Meara, *Roland Barthes at the Collège de France*, p. 187.

64 The neutral thwarting of the Book/Album opposition is also accomplished, Barthes argues, by a dialectic of the Book and the Album. The dialectic works as follows: either the fragments of an *Album* are collected together with a *Book* in view (an *Album* foresees a *Book* and is thus already a *Book* in a virtual sense), or the *Book* becomes an *Album*: '[w]hat remains of the Book is the *quotation* [...]: the fragment, the remainder that is transported elsewhere' ('[c]e qui reste du Livre, c'est la *citation* [...]: le fragment, le relief qui est transporté ailleurs' (*Préparation*, p. 257)).

65 See *Préparation*, p. 251. Poe: 'a magnificent and multi-coloured procession of disorganized thoughts' ('une procession magnifique et bigarée de pensées désordonnés'). Baudelaire: 'a train of thought suggested and ordered by the external world and the chance of circumstance' ('un train de pensées suggéré et commandé par le monde extérieur et le hasard des circonstances'). Barthes's understanding of the rhapsodic as a structured and fragmented unity depends on the etymology of the word in a way that more conventional definitions do not. According to the *OED*, rhapsody refers to an 'epic poem, or a part of one, of a suitable length for recitation at one time', a 'free musical composition, usually emotional or exuberant in character and in one extended movement', and (obsoletely) a 'literary work consisting of miscellaneous or disconnected pieces; a written composition having no fixed form or plan'.

66 See *Préparation*, p. 251: 'Nietzsche: writing in fragments (his paragraphs), and yet (see Deleuze), complex superimposition of constructions' ('Nietzsche: écriture par fragments (ses paragraphes), et cependant (voir Deleuze), superposition complexe de constructions').

67 Barthes gives *poikilos* as the Greek word for 'bariolé, tacheté, moucheté' ('multi-coloured, spotted, mottled' (*Préparation*, p. 203)). For a discussion of Barthes's 'Roman *poikilos*' (*Préparation*, p. 203) in relation to the Jena Romantics' ideal of literature as it is described in Philippe Lacoue-Labarthe's and Jean-Luc Nancy's *L'Absolu littéraire* (1978), including an approach to the desire to write as intransitive and – via Novalis – to the 'Fragment as Novel' ('Fragment comme Roman' (*Préparation*, p. 202)), see O'Meara, *Roland Barthes at the Collège de France*, pp. 175–82.

68 See George D. Painter, *Marcel Proust 1871–1922*, 2 vols (Paris: Mercure de France, 1966). Painter's work was first published in English in 1959.

69 See V, 464 and *Préparation*, p. 278.

70 See *Préparation*, p. 279, n. 8.

71 Barthes's article, entitled 'Les Vies parallèles', appeared in *La Quinzaine littéraire* in March 1966 (see II, 811–13).

72 Yacavone, 'Reading through Photography', p. 104.

73 Indeed, there are clear affinities between Barthes's observation in 'Les Vies parallèles' that 'it is not Proust's life that we find in his work, *but his work that we find in Proust's life*' ('ce n'est pas la vie de Proust que nous retrouvons dans son œuvre, *c'est son œuvre que nous retrouvons dans la vie de Proust*' (II, 812)) and the fantasy – as Barthes describes it in *La Préparation du roman* – of a new work and a new subjecthood, a *vita nova*, according to which the work and the writing subject are in a 'symbiotic relationship' (O'Meara, *Roland Barthes at the Collège de France*, p. 180).

74 'non comme à un *curriculum vitae*, mais comme à un étoilement de circonstances et de figures'. Barthes defines the *Persona* as 'the everyday, empirical, private individual who "lives", without writing' ('la personne civile, quotidienne, privée, qui "vit", sans écrire' (*Préparation*, p. 279)).

75 Hill, 'Roland Barthes', p. 145. In *Le Lexique de l'auteur*, Barthes describes his own divided subjecthood in terms of a similar duality: 'divide myself into RB I (the one who has written) and RB II (the one who is going to write)' ('me diviser en RB I (celui qui a écrit) et RB II (celui qui va écrire)' (p. 93)).

76 'à la cime même du particulier qu'éclot le général' (Marcel Proust, letter to Daniel Halévy (19 July 1919), in *Choix de lettres*, ed. Philip Kolb (Paris: Plon, 1965), p. 216).

77 'le nom propre d'un *effet* de lecture et d'un désir d'écriture' (Simon, 'Le Moi idéal (Barthes)', p. 167).

78 O'Meara, *Roland Barthes at the Collège de France*, p. 79.

79 O'Meara, *Roland Barthes at the Collège de France*, p. 77.

80 As Hill suggests, just as 'another Proust', by the name of 'Marcel', emerges in the course of the '"Longtemps"' lecture, so too the author of the lecture, Barthes himself, 'undergoes a transformation' and 'becomes in turn [...] *another* Barthes, who, confronted with the actuality of death, also desires some kind of resurrection [...], and to that end seeks an intimation of a new life or *vita nova* to redeem the fatal torpor' (Hill, 'Roland Barthes', p. 146).

81 See *Le Neutre*, p. 35: 'fragment non pas sur le neutre, mais dans lequel [...] il y a du neutre'.

82 'Suite inorganisée de figures demandée par le Neutre lui-même, en tant qu'il est le refus de dogmatiser: l'exposition du non-dogmatique ne pourrait elle-même être dogmatique. Inorganisation = inconclusion'.

83 'La suite de fragments: ce serait mettre "quelque chose" (le sujet, le Neutre) en état de variation continue (et non plus l'articuler en vue d'un sens final): rapport avec la musique contemporaine, où le "contenu" des formes

importe moins que leur translation, et aussi peut-être avec les recherches actuelles de Deleuze'.

84 In light of Barthes's reference to Deleuze, Nathalie Léger (see *Le Neutre*, p. 35, n. 28) points readers of *Le Neutre* in the direction of two chapters in Deleuze and Guattari's *Mille plateaux*: 'Devenir-vitesse, devenir-animal, devenir imperceptible, devenir-musique' (pp. 284–380) and 'De la ritournelle' (pp. 381–433). While Barthes refers only to Deleuze's research, and while the authors of *Mille plateaux* have a lot to say about 'continuous variation' in Proust's novel and elsewhere, Guattari's extended (107-page) study of 'Les Ritournelles du temps perdu' in *L'Inconscient machinique* is also significant in this regard. For a reading of Guattari's text alongside Barthes's comments on theme-less variation during the round-table discussion on Proust, Deleuze's observations concerning transversals in *Proust et les signes*, and Deleuze and Guattari's work on ritornellos in *Mille plateaux*, see Thomas Baldwin, 'Félix Guattari's *Swann*', *Swann at 100/Swann à 100 ans*, ed. Adam Watt, *Marcel Proust Aujourd-hui*, 12 (October 2015), pp. 35–49.

85 'il y a une passion du Neutre, mais [...] cette passion n'est pas celle d'un vouloir-saisir → je reconnais parfois cette passion en moi au calme dans lequel j'accueille le spectacle des "vouloir-saisir", des dogmatismes. Mais ceci est discontinue, erratique, comme l'est toujours le désir: il ne s'agit pas d'une sagesse, mais d'un désir'.

86 During the session of 25 February 1978, Barthes says that 'sceptical silence is a silence not of the mouth [...] but of "thought", of "reason"' ('le silence sceptique est un silence, non de la bouche [...], mais de la "pensée", de la "raison"'), and that scepticism objects to 'systematic (dogmatic) speech' ('la parole systématique (dogmatique)' (*Le Neutre*, p. 54)). The Sceptic speaks, in other words, but does not remain dogmatically fixed upon a single truth. For a discussion of the role of scepticism and self-doubt in Proust's work, see Christopher Prendergast, *Mirages and Mad Beliefs: Proust the Skeptic* (Princeton: Princeton University Press, 2013).

87 See *Le Neutre*, p. 83: 'le neutre, c'est la moire: ce qui change finement d'aspect, peut-être de sens, selon l'inclinaison du regard du sujet'.

88 'Or le camaïeu (le Neutre) substitue à la notion d'opposition celle de différence légère, de début, d'effort de différence, autrement dit de nuance: la nuance devient un principe d'organisation totale (qui couvre tout l'espace, comme pour le paysage du triptyque) qui en quelque sorte saute par-dessus le paradigme: cet espace totalement et comme exhaustivement nuancé, c'est la moire'.

89 Claude Coste, '"J'ai toujours eu envie d'*argumenter* mes humeurs": savoir et subjectivité dans *La Chambre claire* et *Sur Racine*', *What's So Great About Roland Barthes?*, ed. Thomas Baldwin, Katja Haustein and Lucy O'Meara, *L'Esprit Créateur* (Special Issue), 55/4 (Winter 2015), p. 91.

90 Barthes discusses affective 'blackmail' on several occasions in *Le*

Discours amoureux. Séminaire à l'École pratique des hautes études 1974–1976,
suivi de Fragments d'un discours amoureux: inédits, ed. Claude Coste (Paris:
Seuil, 2007). See, for example, the fragment on 'Cacher' (pp. 106–08), which
is also the name of the figure on which he focuses in 'Les Lunettes noires', and
'Ascèse' (p. 98), in which he refers to the wearing of dark glasses as a form of
guilty self-mutilation on the part of the lover.

91   Coste, '"J'ai toujours eu envie d'*argumenter* mes humeurs"', p. 91.

92   'D'un côté, je me dis: et si l'autre, par quelque disposition de sa propre
structure, avait besoin de ma demande? Ne serais-je pas justifié, alors, de
m'abandonner à l'expression littérale, au dire lyrique de ma "passion"? L'excès,
la folie, ne sont-ils pas ma vérité, ma force? Et si cette vérité, cette force,
finissaient par impressionner? Mais, d'un autre côté, je me dis: les signes de
cette passion risquent d'étouffer l'autre. Ne faut-il pas alors, *précisément parce*
que je l'aime, lui cacher combien je l'aime? Je vois l'autre d'un double regard:
tantôt je le vois comme objet, tantôt comme sujet; j'hésite entre la tyrannie et
l'oblation. Je me prends ainsi moi-même dans un chantage: si j'aime l'autre, je
suis tenu de vouloir son bien; mais je ne puis alors que me faire mal: piège: je
suis condamné à être un saint ou un monstre: saint ne puis, monstre ne veux:
donc, je tergiverse: je montre *un peu* ma passion'.

93   See, for example, pp. 86–89 (on 'la demande') and pp. 218–20 (on
'oblation'). For Lacan, 'la demande' is a subject's demand for love. It is not the
same thing as need. In *Lacan*, Malcolm Bowie describes it as follows: '[t]he
divided subject, haunted by absence and lack, looks to the other not simply to
supply his needs but to pay him the compliment of an unconditional *yes*. [...]
But the paradox and the perversity to be found in any recourse to persons is that
the other to whom the appeal [the demand] is addressed is never in a position to
answer it unconditionally' (Malcolm Bowie, *Lacan* (Cambridge, MA: Harvard
University Press, 1991), pp. 135–36). For a discussion of 'la demande' in Lacan's
own work, see, for example, 'La Signification du phallus/*Die Bedeutung des*
Phallus', in *Écrits* (Paris: Seuil, 1966), pp. 685–95. 'Oblation', Barthes suggests,
is not the same thing as 'oblativity' in the psychoanalytical sense, even if it is
related to it. It is 'the precise figure through which the amorous subject makes
a gift to the loved object of the *mourning* into which he or she will be plunged
in deciding to leave him or her' ('la figure précise par laquelle le sujet amoureux
fait don à l'objet aimé du *deuil* dans lequel il va être plongé en décidant de le
quitter' (*Le Discours amoureux*, p. 219)). In 'Les Lunettes noires', Barthes uses
the term as a synonym for selflessness or self-sacrifice (it refers to dissemblance
and is the opposite of tyranny and sadism). According to Dylan Evans's *An*
Introductory Dictionary of Lacanian Psychoanalysis (London: Routledge,
2006), 'oblativity' is 'a term used by some psychoanalysts to designate a mature
form of love in which one loves the other person for what he is rather than for
what he can give', and its 'formula', which Lacan repudiates as 'a fantasy of the
obsessional neurotic', is 'everything for the other' (p. 75).

94 As indicated in the previous chapter, Barthes's teaching notes from this year form part of the 'Fonds Roland Barthes' held at the Bibliothèque nationale de France, Paris. They are contained within folder BRT2. A3. 03 'Rabat (1969–70)'.

95 Among other things, Barthes is interested in the use of quotation marks in this passage – in the linguistic study ('étude de langages') that it provides.

96 'souvent obligé pour que ma grand'mère permît qu'on m'en donnât, de ne pas dissimuler, de faire presque montre de mon état de suffocation'.

97 'D'ailleurs, dès que je le sentais s'approcher, toujours incertain des proportions qu'il prendrait, j'en étais inquiet à cause de la tristesse de ma grand'mère que je craignais beaucoup plus que ma souffrance. Mais en même temps mon corps [...] me donnait le besoin d'avertir ma grand'mère de mes malaises avec une exactitude où je finissais par mettre une sorte de scrupule physiologique. Apercevais-je en moi un symptôme fâcheux que je n'avais pas encore discerné, mon corps était en détresse tant que je ne l'avais pas communiqué à ma grand'mère. Feignait-elle de n'y prêter aucune attention, il me demandait d'insister. Parfois j'allais trop loin; et le visage aimé qui n'était plus toujours aussi maître de ses émotions qu'autrefois, laissait paraître une expression de pitié, une contraction douloureuse. Alors mon cœur était torturé par la vue de la peine qu'elle avait; comme si mes baisers eussent dû effacer cette peine, comme si ma tendresse eût pu donner à ma grand'mère autant de joie que mon bonheur, je me jetais dans ses bras. Et les scrupules étant d'autre part apaisés par la certitude qu'elle connaissait le malaise ressenti, mon corps ne faisait pas opposition à ce que je la rassurasse. Je protestais que ce malaise n'avait rien de pénible, que je n'étais nullement à plaindre, qu'elle pouvait être certaine que j'étais heureux; mon corps avait voulu obtenir exactement ce qu'il méritait de pitié [...]. Un soir que ma grand'mère m'avait laissé assez bien, elle rentra dans ma chambre très tard dans la soirée, et s'apercevant que la respiration me manquait: "Oh! mon Dieu, comme tu souffres", s'écria-t-elle, les traits bouleversés. Elle me quitta aussitôt, j'entendis la porte cochère, et elle rentra un peu plus tard avec du cognac qu'elle était allée acheter parce qu'il n'y en avait pas à la maison. Bientôt je commençai à me sentir heureux. Ma grand'mère, un peu rouge, avait l'air gêné, et ses yeux une expression de lassitude et de découragement. "J'aime mieux te laisser et que tu profites un peu de ce mieux", me dit-elle, en me quittant brusquement. Je l'embrassai pourtant et je sentis sur ses joues fraîches quelque chose de mouillé dont je ne sus pas si c'était l'humidité de l'air nocturne qu'elle venait de traverser. Le lendemain, elle ne vint que le soir dans ma chambre parce qu'elle avait eu, me dit-on, à sortir. Je trouvai que c'était montrer bien de l'indifférence pour moi, et je me retins pour ne pas la lui reprocher'.

98 See 'Les Lunettes noires', V, 72: 'I advance pointing to my mask: I set a mask upon my passion, but with a discreet (and wily) finger I designate this mask' ('je m'avance en montrant mon masque du doigt: je mets un masque sur ma passion, mais d'un doigt discret (et retors) je désigne ce masque').

99 See Marty, 'Marcel Proust dans la "chambre claire"', pp. 131–32.

100 'la finalité du chantage (obtenir) est dépassée au profit de la demande (au sens lacanien)'.

101 Bowie, *Lacan*, p. 135.

102 Bowie, *Lacan*, p. 136.

103 'annule[r] [...] la particularité de tout ce qui peut être accordé en le transmuant en preuve d'amour' (Lacan, *Écrits*, p. 691).

104 'la bonne réponse à la demande, ce n'est pas la satisfaction [...], mais le message de la présence: le signe de la présence de l'autre en vient à dominer les satisfactions qu'apporte cette présence' (*Le Discours amoureux*, p. 87).

105 Bowie, *Lacan*, p. 135.

106 'c'est le regard qui compte; ou plutôt, c'est le spectacle en tant qu'il révèle un observateur particulier dont on suit la cohérence de livre en livre' (Coste, '"J'ai toujours eu envie d'*argumenter* mes humeurs"', p. 91).

Afterword

Insect Life

The title of Georges Didi-Huberman's *Survivance des lucioles* (2009) is a nod in the direction of two texts: first, Pier Paolo Pasolini's controversial opinion piece 'L'articolo delle lucciole', which appeared in *Scritti corsari* in 1975; and second, Denis Roche's *La Disparition des lucioles (réflexions sur l'acte photographique)* (1982), which contains, among other things, a gently critical letter to Barthes on the relationship between *La Chambre claire* and the disappearance (or extinction) of fireflies.[1]

For Didi-Huberman, Pasolini's essay is a lamentation on 'the moment when the fireflies disappeared in Italy – when these gentle, humane signals of innocence were annihilated by the night (or by the "ferocious", projected light) of a triumphant fascism'.[2] With considerable justification, Pasolini views the disappearance of the fireflies' modest, intermittent glow from the Italian countryside as a direct consequence of an ecological crisis produced by the advance of industrialization. Its loss also serves as a metaphor in his work for the decline in Italy during the 1970s of resistance to a resurgent fascism's 'blinding clarity' ('aveuglante clarté').[3] In his letter to Barthes, Roche recycles Pasolini's metaphor as he reproaches his addressee for having omitted from *La Chambre claire* 'all that photography is able to bring to bear on questions of "style", "freedom" and "intermittence"'.[4] According to Roche, in focusing predominantly upon 'the frontal mourning of the "that-has-been"' ('l'endeuillement frontal du "ça-a-été"')[5] and upon what he describes as a near-tautological relationship between the photographic image and its referent,[6] Barthes fails to take the intermittent illumination ('*éclairage intermittent*')[7] of the photographer-firefly, of the 'Operator', into account. For Roche, as Didi-Huberman notes, photographers are 'little flickers of light [...] accompanied by a motor that transforms an attentive gaze into a luminous chant',[8] and Barthes's fascination with the unrelenting referential light of a photographic what-has-been puts an end to any awareness or appreciation of the flickering rhythm, the 'lumière-extinction',[9] of the photographer's style. Thus, in the culture of Pasolini's Italy and in Barthes's conception of the photographic image as described by Roche, what we might term *luciolity* has been extinguished by a certain kind of lucidity (and in the case of Pasolini's Italy, by a particularly ferocious and frightening form thereof): the small and fragile light of the firefly (Pasolini's *lucciola*) has been overcome by *luce*, 'la grande lumière'.[10]

In *Survivance des lucioles*, Didi-Huberman rejects Pasolini's and Roche's pessimism concerning the fate of the fireflies' glow (echoes of which Didi-Huberman also hears in Giorgio Agamben's writing on the apocalyptic destruction of experience).[11] He identifies 'l'image', understood in broadly Benjaminian terms,[12] as a prime locus of *luciolic* operations: the image, he contends, is characterized by 'its intermittence, its fragility, the rhythm of its unending appearances, disappearances, reappearances, and re-disappearances'.[13] In addition to Pasolini's oeuvre generally, Didi-Huberman singles out the work of Bataille, Samuel Beckett, René Char, Henri Michaux and 'manuscripts written by members of the *Sonderkommando* and hidden beneath the ashes of Auschwitz'[14] as places from which 'la grande lumière' does not emerge triumphant – from which the fireflies' glimmer has not been entirely removed.

While, as Roche complains, the modest intermittence of the fireflies' light – its style or 'liberté' – may be given little or no attention in Barthes's work on photography, it is a light that shines on – or rather in – his encounters with Proust's novel. These encounters also suggest that what might usefully be called the 'image of Proust' (in which we hear an echo of the title of a well-known essay by Walter Benjamin) would be a worthy addition to Didi-Huberman's eclectic list.[15] For Barthes, as we saw in the Introduction, *À la recherche* emits the shifting lambency of a cloud of fireflies rather than the steady beam of a projector: it is intermittent, as if controlled by the variable current of a resistor. We might be tempted to read Barthes's observations here as related in one way or another to the intermittences of the heart of which Proust's narrator speaks,[16] or to the epiphanic operations of involuntary memory, but Barthes's writing on Proust (and on various other things) across the larger part of his oeuvre suggests something quite different: in its liminal treatment of objects, its erotic *signifiance*, its theme-less variations (its 'variety'), its musical force of difference, its intensive shimmers, its myriad diffractions and vacillations, its semantic decentrings and its rhapsodic neutrality, for example, Proust's novel is an unmistakably lampyridaean creature. As such, *À la recherche* corresponds to the 'dream' text described by Barthes in *Roland Barthes par Roland Barthes* as 'neither a text of vanity, nor a text of lucidity, but a text with uncertain quotation marks, with floating parentheses (never to close the parenthesis is very specifically: to drift)'.[17] Proust's novel is no text of lucidity: it is the 'crucial empowerment', as Bowie puts it, precisely because it is the drifting, *luciolic* stuff of which (Barthes's) fantasies are made. Its light possesses what Barthes, in a letter to Philippe Sollers written in September 1967, calls an 'illuminating clarity [...] that changes the landscape with each of its sudden flashes'.[18]

For Didi-Huberman, Agamben's reduction – via Carl Schmitt and Guy Debord – of images to mediatized consumer spectacles (to commodity fetishes by virtue of which a passive identification with the spectacle supplants genuine activity and hinders critical thought) is too peremptory: there is no room in his analysis for an understanding of the image as *lucciola* – as an alternative to the *luce*.[19] The image, for Agamben, is a ruthless, unethical servant of the kingdom and its glory, a pure function of power that is 'incapable of the slightest force of opposition, of the slightest insurrection, of the slightest counter-glory',[20] and this, Didi Huberman suggests, is what he sees as its final, appalling truth. While Didi-Huberman is critical of the apocalyptic tone, he also acknowledges that Agamben's diagnosis may not be entirely false: it corresponds, he says, to the 'sensations of suffocation and anguish that take hold of us as we confront the calculated proliferation of images used as vehicles of propaganda and commodification'.[21] Indeed, the 'afterlives' of Proust's novel suggest that it has been unable to resist the bright lights of a society of the spectacle, even in its *survivances*. As we saw in the Introduction, Proust's name has a definite currency (it circulates in the creative economy and in the cultural imagination), and André Benhaïm has argued that '"Proust" (the work, the man, their joint image) has been so much read (that is, been so well assimilated), that it has transcended the canonical library and has been adopted into the culture at large'.[22] Athough Benhaïm elides processes of reading and domestication, it is unclear precisely what models of reading, if any, are embodied and fostered by the assimilations of Proust into the batteries and enclosures of mainstream culture. Moreover, while there is certainly something refreshing and compelling about Margaret E. Gray's claim that 'the encounter with popular culture, far from signalling the demise of Proust, renews the Proustian aura', or that 'popular culture's episodic, scattered and idiosyncratic appropriations reveal in its popularized Proust an activity of cultural resistance',[23] it is also difficult to ignore the possibility that such appropriations, manipulations and other mechanical reproductions, as informative and entertaining as they may be (and in spite of their capacity, like *À la recherche* itself, to transform art into the everyday, to make the 'matter of everyday life itself into the art of literature',[24] or even to teach us to value 'the formal and material vibrancy of inestimably ordinary things'),[25] might also serve to turn up the light of Proust's novel to the incapacitating lucidity of a cultural fetish. The fetishization of Proust's work is in danger of substituting for and simultaneously screening out a reading encounter with the novel itself. We might say, then, that the burgeoning field of Proustiana risks pinning Proust's firefly to a board, and that this activity is similar in its effects to photographs – as they are described by Barthes – in which there is no *punctum*, no 'champ aveugle':

> confronting thousands of photographs, including those which have a good *studium*, I sense no blind field: everything that happens within the frame dies absolutely once this frame is passed beyond. When we define the Photograph as a motionless image, this does not mean only that the figures it represents do not move; it means that they do not emerge, do not leave: they are anaesthetized and fastened down, like butterflies. Yet once there is a *punctum*, a blind field is created (is divined) [...]. The presence (the dynamics) of this blind field is, I believe, what distinguishes the erotic photograph from the pornographic photograph. Pornography ordinarily represents the sexual organs, making them into a motionless object (a fetish), flattered like an idol that does not leave its niche; for me, there is no *punctum* in the pornographic image [...]. The erotic photograph, on the contrary (and this is its very condition), does not make the sexual organs into a central object; it may very well not show them at all; it takes the spectator outside its frame, and it is there that I animate this photograph and that it animates me. The *punctum*, then, is a kind of subtle beyond – as if the image launched desire beyond what it permits us to see. (*La Chambre claire*, V, 834)[26]

This passage tells us as much about the singularity and subtle movement of Barthes's writing, in fact, as it does about the fate of the Proustian *luciole* (or *papillon*) in an age of unrestrained commodity fetishism (it also reveals that the intermittence of the photograph – its eroticism – is located by Barthes in the affective responses it provokes). While Barthes may fetishize Proust's novel in the sense that he conceives of it as *mathesis* and *mandala* and loves it to bits, his work on *À la recherche* is undeniably more erotic, more productive of blind fields, than it is overlit or pornographic. It reflects the mutual animations of a desiring subject and a desired object: its erotic *papillotage*[27] is liable to propel our own desires and expectations as readers of his work for another nuance, another critical flutter, just as the non-developmental mobility of Proust's text compels Barthes to operate variations upon it and, more generally or intransitively, simply to write.

Bowie suggests that the following entomological metaphor, taken from Benjamin's 'The Image of Proust', might point us in the direction of a 'useful general principle for readers of *À la recherche du temps perdu*, a guideline on how to read the novel':[28]

> Proust's most accurate, most convincing insights fasten on their objects as insects fasten on leaves, blossoms, branches, betraying nothing of their existence until a leap, a beating of wings, a vault [...], show the startled observer that some incalculable individual life has imperceptibly crept into an alien world.[29]

For Bowie, critics of Proust's work have failed to acknowledge and to do justice to the startling phasmatic illuminations it provides. Confronted by its 'copiousness, its polyphonic and polysemantic richness', he argues, civic-minded Proustians rarely try 'to catch the shimmer of the text on the wing, to allow it to be multifarious, iridescent, and flighty'.[30] Instead, they deploy 'muscular themes, heavy-duty motifs and ponderous patterns of recurrent imagery', and in so doing, they 'settle for a serenely flat tone, and begin to lose contact – even as observers – with his [Proust's] audacity at the level of syntax, lexis, plotting, and metaphor-making'.[31] Barthes's entomological criticism does not settle in this way: its erratic dogmatism, affective *moire*, diachronic neutrality and unstable variation allow it to remain in touch with what Bowie calls the 'time-bound signifying process of Proust's novel, its murmuring and echoings, its long-range insect life'.[32] Indeed, Barthes rewrites *À la recherche* not by replicating (or even interpreting) its content or the convolutions of its serpentine sentences (Barthes does not write 'like' Proust in this sense), or by reproducing its narrative 'with a notable, formal surplus, and an ideological, revisionary difference to boot',[33] but by producing a form of what Stephen Benson and Claire Connors call 'creative criticism': Barthes's writing 'feels like a record of something being made rather than of a made something: the finding rather than the found, or rather the finding within the found'.[34] It is a mobile and inconsistent body of writing – we could certainly call it a body without organs[35] – that integrates, covers, nuances and deforms as it moves to the intermittent rhythm that, for Barthes, is the productive principle, the motor and motto, of Proust's novel. Moreover, several of the metaphors Barthes uses to describe *À la recherche* can be understood as rewritings of (as images that do not lose contact with) figures that appear in Proust's work. First, as we have already seen, what Proust calls a unity that is vital and not logical (insofar as it is inhabited by 'variety' rather than a systematic thematic development) is close to what Barthes identifies as rhapsody and variations without a theme. Second, as is well known, Proust viewed the writing of pastiches as creative exercises in which he could replicate aspects of style and technique characteristic of the voice – the musical 'chant'[36] – of other authors in order to purge himself of a 'natural vice of idolatry and imitation' ('vice naturel d'idolâtrie et d'imitation').[37] Furthermore, in a letter to Robert Dreyfus in 1908, Proust describes these exercises as 'la critique littéraire "en action"'.[38] The pastiches themselves might thus be understood as Proustian circulations of the currency of Flaubert or Balzac, for example, and, more importantly perhaps, as 'critique' rather than 'lecture' – as one of the first examples of a productive and actively intrusive (potentially ruinous) form of criticism and rewriting (of covering) that seeks neither to interpret, nor to instrumentalize, nor to make a thematic programme out of the work of these authors, but to conduct experiments and operate variations upon them.[39] Finally, as far as 'opérer des variations' and Proust's infinitely explorable 'galaxie' are concerned, these metaphors have counterparts – and are conjoined – in *La Prisonnière*, where Albertine plays Vinteuil's music on the pianola:

> She chose pieces which were quite new or which she had played to me only once or twice, for, as she began to know me better, she had learned that I liked to fix my thoughts only upon what was still obscure to me, glad to be able, in the course of these successive renderings, to join together, thanks to the increasing but, alas, distorting and alien light of my intellect, the fragmentary and interrupted lines of the structure which at first had been almost hidden in the fog. She knew and, I think, understood, the joy that my mind derived, at these first hearings, from this task of modelling a still shapeless nebula. (*ALR*, III, 874)[40]

As Bowie puts it in *Proust among the Stars*, the 'Proustian imaginist leads a nomadic life. He is at home inside his comet-tail of images'.[41] In Marcel's and in Barthes's hands, the punctured, loss-ridden contours of the musical work – the nebula – are not simply identified and interpreted. They are there to be modelled, composed (and not merely played or executed), shaped into formations and deformations: bits of light.

Notes

1 Pasolini's article on fireflies first appeared in *Il corriere della sera* on 1 February 1975 under the title 'Il vuoto di potere in Italia' ('The Void of Power in Italy'). The title of Roche's text pays homage to the Italian poet and film-maker, who was murdered in 1975. For the letter to Barthes, see Denis Roche, 'Lettre à Roland Barthes sur la disparition des lucioles', in *La Disparition des lucioles (réflexions sur l'acte photographique)* (Paris: Éditions de l'étoile, 1982), pp. 153–66.

2 'le moment où, en Italie, disprarurent des lucioles, ces signaux humains de l'innocence anéantis par la nuit – ou par la lumière "féroce" des projecteurs – du fascisme triomphant' (Georges Didi-Huberman, *Survivance des lucioles* (Paris: Minuit, 2009), p. 21).

3 Didi-Huberman, *Survivance*, p. 26.

4 'tout ce que la photographie se montre capable de mettre en œuvre sur le plan du "style", de la "liberté" et [...] de l'"intermittence"' (Didi-Huberman, *Survivance*, pp. 37–38).

5 Didi-Huberman, *Survivance*, p. 39.

6 Barthes says that 'a photo is always invisible: it is not it that we see' ('une photo est toujours invisible: ce n'est pas elle qu'on voit') and that 'the referent adheres' ('le référent adhère') (V, 793).

7 Didi-Huberman, *Survivance*, p. 39.

8 'occupées à leur éclairage intermittent [...], petits éclairages brefs [...] avec l'adjonction d'un moteur qui fera du regard attentif une psalmodie de lumière' (Roche, 'Lettre à Roland Barthes', pp. 149–50; cited by Didi-Huberman in *Survivance*, pp. 39–40).

9 Roche, 'Lettre à Roland Barthes', p. 166.

10 Didi-Huberman, *Survivance*, p. 9. Didi-Huberman observes that in Dante's *Inferno*, the light of Paradise is *luce*, 'la grande lumière', and that the *lucciola*, 'la petite lumière' of glow-worms and fireflies, is condemned to a 'discreet but significant fate' ('sort discret mais significatif' (p. 9)). As Didi-Huberman suggests, Pasolini's understanding of the distinction between the firefly's gentle glow and the bright lights of fascism thus represents an inversion of the relationship between *luce* and *lucciole* in Dante's work (see Didi-Huberman, *Survivance*, p. 13).

11 See Giorgio Agamben, *Infancy and History: On the Destruction of Experience* (London and New York: Verso, 2007). For Agamben, 'the most peremptory objection against the modern concept of experience has been raised in the work of Proust', since 'the object of the *Recherche* is not a lived experience but, quite the contrary, something which has been neither lived nor experienced' (p. 48).

12 Historical experience is understood by Walter Benjamin as the discharge of an explosive force that blasts open the continuum of history. The dialectical

image is one that 'emerges suddenly, in a flash' (Walter Benjamin, *The Arcades Project*, trans. Howard Eiland and Kevin McLaughlin (Cambridge, MA and London: Belknap Press, 1999), p. 473).

13 'son intermittence, sa fragilité, son battement d'apparitions, de disparitions, de réapparitions et de redisparitions incessantes' (Didi-Huberman, *Survivance*, p. 74).

14 'les manuscrits des membres du *Sonderkommando* cachés sous les cendres d'Auschwitz' (Didi-Huberman, *Survivance*, p. 112). Didi-Huberman refers to Beckett on p. 109 of *Survivance des lucioles*.

15 See Walter Benjamin, 'The Image of Proust', in *Illuminations*, ed. Hannah Arendt and trans. Harry Zohn (London: Fontana Press, 1992), pp. 197–210.

16 See *ALR*, II, 148. As is well known, this is also a title Proust considered giving to his novel.

17 'Le rêve serait donc: ni un texte de vanité, ni un texte de lucidité, mais un texte aux guillemets incertains, aux parenthèses flottantes (ne jamais fermer la parenthèse, c'est très exactement *dériver*)' (II, 682).

18 'la clarté éclairante [...] qui, à coups d'éclairs, change à chaque fois le paysage' (Roland Barthes, letter to Philippe Sollers (11 September 1967), in Philippe Sollers, *L'Amitié de Roland Barthes* (Paris: Seuil, 2015), p. 77). Barthes also observes that there are other kinds of clarity: 'd'autres clartés' (p. 77).

19 See Didi-Huberman, *Survivance*, p. 87.

20 'incapable du moindre contre-pouvoir, de la moindre insurrection, de la moindre contre-gloire' (Didi-Huberman, *Survivance*, p. 87).

21 'sensations d'étouffement et d'angoisse qui nous prennent devant la prolifération calculée des images utilisées tout à la fois comme véhicules de la propagande et de la marchandise' (Didi-Huberman, *Survivance*, p. 87).

22 André Benhaïm, 'Preamble', p. 5.

23 Margaret E. Gray, 'Adaptations/Afterlives', in *Marcel Proust in Context*, ed. Adam Watt (Cambridge: Cambridge University Press, 2013), p. 221.

24 Gray, 'Adaptations/Afterlives', p. 228.

25 Hannah Freed-Thall, *Spoiled Distinctions: Aesthetics and the Ordinary in French Modernism* (Oxford: Oxford University Press, 2015), p. 3.

26 'devant des milliers de photos, y compris celles qui possèdent un bon *studium*, je ne sens aucun champ aveugle: tout ce qui se passe à l'intérieur du cadre meurt absolument, ce cadre franchi. Lorsqu'on définit la photo comme une image immobile, cela ne veut pas dire seulement que les personnages qu'elle représente ne bougent pas; cela veut dire qu'ils ne *sortent* pas: ils sont anesthésiés et fichés, comme des papillons. Cependant, dès qu'il y a *punctum*, un champ aveugle se crée (se devine) [...]. La présence (la dynamique) de ce champ aveugle, c'est, je crois, ce qui distingue la photo érotique de la photo pornographique. La pornographie représente ordinairement le sexe, elle en fait

un objet immobile (un fétiche), encensé comme un dieu qui ne sort pas de sa niche; pour moi, pas de *punctum* dans l'image pornographique [...]. La photo érotique, au contraire (c'en est la condition même), ne fait pas du sexe un objet central; elle peut très bien ne pas le montrer; elle entraîne le spectateur hors de son cadre, et c'est en cela que cette photo, je l'anime et elle m'anime. Le *punctum* est alors une sorte de hors-champ subtil, comme si l'image lançait le désir au-delà de ce qu'elle donne à voir'.

27 'Papillotage' is defined in the *Trésor de la langue française informatisé* as an 'impression produced by a scattering of luminous points, a multiplication of levels and a confusion of details that are detrimental to the unity of the whole' ('impression produite par un éparpillement des points lumineux, par une multiplication des plans, une confusion des détails, qui nuisent à l'unité d'ensemble').

28 Bowie, 'Reading Proust between the Lines', p. 125.

29 Walter Benjamin, cited by Bowie in 'Reading Proust between the Lines', p. 125. For the passage quoted by Bowie, see Benjamin, 'The Image of Proust', p. 204.

30 Bowie, 'Reading Proust between the Lines', p. 125.

31 Bowie, 'Reading Proust between the Lines', p. 125.

32 Bowie, 'Reading Proust between the Lines', p. 126.

33 Christian Moraru, *Rewriting: Postmodern Narrative and Cultural Critique in the Age of Cloning* (Albany: State University of New York Press, 2001), p. 7.

34 Stephen Benson and Clare Connors, 'Introduction', in *Creative Criticism: An Anthology and Guide*, ed. Stephen Benson and Clare Connors (Edinburgh: Edinburgh University Press, 2014), pp. 1–47 (p. 36).

35 In *Francis Bacon*, Deleuze describes the 'corps sans organes' not as an organ-free, amorphous blob, but as an intensive body traversed by an oscillating wave of variable intensity, whose organs are only ever temporary and provisional (see p. 50, for example).

36 Marcel Proust, 'À propos du "style" de Flaubert', in *Contre Sainte-Beuve, précédé de Pastiches et mélanges et suivi de Essais et articles*, ed. Pierre Clarac and Yves Sandre (Paris: Gallimard, Bibliothèque de la Pléiade, 1971), pp. 586–600 (p. 594).

37 Marcel Proust, letter to Ramon Fernandez (1919), cited in *Contre Sainte-Beuve*, p. 690.

38 Marcel Proust, letter to Robert Dreyfus, in *Correspondance de Marcel Proust*, ed. Philip Kolb, 21 vols (Paris: Plon, 1970–93), VIII, p. 61. For a detailed analysis of Proust's pastiches, see, for example, Jean Milly's *Les Pastiches de Proust* (Paris: Colin, 1970), Annick Bouillaguet's *Proust lecteur de Balzac et de Flaubert: l'imitation cryptée* (Paris: Honoré Champion, 2000) and James Austin's *Proust, Pastiche, and the Postmodern, or Why Style Matters* (Lewisburg: Bucknell University Press, 2013).

39 In the final paragraph of *Critique et vérité*, Barthes refers to Proust's pastiches as he distinguishes between reading and criticism. The former, he says, 'is to desire the work, to want to be the work, to refuse to echo the work using any discourse other than that of the work: the only commentary which a pure reader could produce, if he were to remain purely a reader, would be a pastiche (as the example of Proust, lover of reading and of pastiches, shows)' ('c'est désirer l'œuvre, c'est vouloir être l'œuvre, c'est refuser de doubler l'œuvre en dehors de toute autre parole que la parole même de l'œuvre: le seul commentaire que pourrait produire un pur lecteur, et qui le resterait, c'est le pastiche (comme l'indiquerait l'exemple de Proust, amateur de lectures et de pastiches)'). To shift from reading to criticism, he argues, 'is to change desires, it is no longer to desire the work but to desire one's own language' ('changer de désir, c'est désirer non plus l'œuvre, mais son propre langage' (II, 801)).

40 'Elle choisissait des morceaux ou tout nouveaux ou qu'elle ne m'avait encore joués qu'une fois ou deux, car, commençant à me connaître, elle savait que je n'aimais proposer à mon attention que ce qui m'était encore obscur, heureux de pouvoir, au cours de ces exécutions successives, rejoindre les unes aux autres, grâce à la lumière croissante, mais hélas! dénaturante et étrangère de mon intelligence, les lignes fragmentaires et interrompues de la construction, d'abord presque ensevelie dans la brume. Elle savait, et, je crois, comprenait, la joie que donnait, les premières fois, à mon esprit, ce travail de modelage d'une nébuleuse encore informe'.

41 Malcolm Bowie, *Proust among the Stars* (London: Harper Collins, 1998), p. 2.

Bibliography

Works by Roland Barthes

Comment vivre ensemble: simulations romanesques de quelques espaces quotidiens. Cours et séminaires au Collège de France 1976–1977, ed. Claude Coste (Paris: Seuil/IMEC, 2002).

Le Discours amoureux. Séminaire à l'École pratique des hautes études 1974–1976, suivi de Fragments d'un discours amoureux: inédits, ed. Claude Coste (Paris: Seuil, 2007).

Journal de deuil: 26 octobre 1977–15 septembre 1979, ed. Nathalie Léger (Paris: Seuil/IMEC, 2009).

Le Lexique de l'auteur. Séminaire à l'École pratique des hautes études 1973–1974, ed. Anne Herschberg Pierrot (Paris: Seuil, 2010).

Le Neutre. Notes de cours au Collège de France 1977–1978, ed. Thomas Clerc (Paris: Seuil/IMEC, 2002).

Œuvres complètes, ed. Éric Marty, 5 vols (Paris: Seuil, 2002).

La Préparation du roman I et II. Cours et séminaires au Collège de France 1978–1979 et 1979–1980, ed. Nathalie Léger (Paris: Seuil/IMEC, 2003).

'Sarrasine' de Balzac. Séminaires à l'École pratique des hautes études 1967–1968 et 1968–1969, ed. Claude Coste and Andy Stafford (Paris: Seuil, 2011).

'Les Sorties du texte', in *Bataille*, ed. Philippe Sollers (Paris: Union générale d'éditions, 1973), pp. 49–62.

'Table ronde sur Proust' (with Gilles Deleuze, Serge Doubrovsky, Gérard Genette, Jean Ricardou and Jean-Pierre Richard), in Gilles Deleuze, *Deux régimes de fous: textes et entretiens 1975–1995*, ed. David Lapoujade (Paris: Minuit, 2003), pp. 29–55.

'Un homme, une ville: Marcel Proust à Paris avec Roland Barthes' (with Jean Montalbetti), *Cassettes Radio France*, 3 episodes (Paris: Radio France, 1978).

Folder BRT2. A3. 01 'Freud (1969–70)', 'Fonds Roland Barthes', Bibliothèque nationale de France, Paris.

Folder BRT2. A3. 03 'Rabat (1969–70)', 'Fonds Roland Barthes', Bibliothèque nationale de France, Paris.

Translations

Below are listed translations of Barthes's work that have been cited in this book. Essays collected in longer texts have not been listed separately; details and page extents for these can be found in the notes.

A Lover's Discourse: Fragments, trans. Richard Howard (New York: Hill and Wang, 1978).

'An Introduction to the Structural Analysis of Narrative', trans. Lionel Duisit, *New Literary History*, 6/2 (Winter 1975), pp. 237–72.

Camera Lucida: Reflections on Photography, trans. Richard Howard (New York: Hill and Wang, 1981).

Critical Essays, trans. Richard Howard (Evanston, IL: Northwestern University Press, 1972).

How to Live Together: Novelistic Simulations of Some Everyday Spaces. Notes for a Lecture Course and Seminar at the Collège de France (1976–1977), trans. Kate Briggs (New York: Columbia University Press, 2013).

Michelet, trans. Richard Howard (Berkeley and Los Angeles, CA: University of California Press, 1987).

The Neutral. Lecture Course at the Collège de France (1977–1978), trans. Rosalind E. Kraus and Denis Hollier (New York: Columbia University Press, 2005).

The Pleasure of the Text, trans. Richard Miller (New York: Hill and Wang, 1975).

The Preparation of the Novel. Lecture Courses and Seminars at the Collège de France (1978–1979 and 1979–1980), trans. Kate Briggs (New York: Columbia University Press, 2011).

The Responsibility of Forms: Critical Essays on Music, Art and Representation, trans. Richard Howard (Oxford: Blackwell, 1986).

The Rustle of Language, trans. Richard Howard (Berkeley and Los Angeles, CA: University of California Press, 1989).

Writing Degree Zero, trans. Annette Lavers and Colin Smith (London: Jonathan Cape, 1967).

Works by Marcel Proust

À la recherche du temps perdu, ed. Jean-Yves Tadié, 4 vols (Paris: Gallimard, Bibliothèque de la Pléiade, 1987–89).

Choix de lettres, ed. Philip Kolb (Paris: Plon, 1965).

Contre Sainte-Beuve, précédé de Pastiches et mélanges et suivi de Essais et articles, ed. Pierre Clarac and Yves Sandre (Paris: Gallimard, Bibliothèque de la Pléiade, 1971).

Correspondance de Marcel Proust, ed. Philip Kolb, 21 vols (Paris: Plon, 1970–93).

In Search of Lost Time, trans. C. K. Scott Moncrieff (except for *Time Regained*, trans. Andreas Mayor and Terence Kilmartin), revised by Terence Kilmartin and D. J. Enright (London: Vintage, 2000–02).

Other References

Acquisto, Joseph, *Proust, Music, and Meaning: Theories and Practices of Listening in the Recherche* (London: Palgrave Macmillan, 2017).

Agamben, Giorgio, *Infancy and History: On the Destruction of Experience* (London and New York: Verso, 2007).

Alpers, Svetlana, *The Art of Describing: Dutch Art in the Seventeenth Century* (Chicago: University of Chicago Press, 1983).

Aristotle, *Rhetoric*, ed. Jenny Bak and trans. W. Rhys Roberts (New York: Dover Publications, 2004).

Attridge, Derek, 'Roland Barthes's Obtuse, Sharp Meaning', in *Writing the Image After Roland Barthes*, ed. Jean-Michel Rabaté (Philadelphia: University of Pennsylvania Press, 1997), pp. 77–89.

Austin, James, *Proust, Pastiche, and the Postmodern, or Why Style Matters* (Lewisburg: Bucknell University Press, 2013).

Baldwin, Thomas, *The Picture as Spectre in Diderot, Proust and Deleuze* (Oxford: Legenda, 2011).

—— 'Félix Guattari's *Swann*', *Swann at 100/Swann à 100 ans*, ed. Adam Watt, *Marcel Proust Aujourd-hui*, 12 (October 2015), pp. 35–49.

Bataille, Georges, 'La Notion de dépense', in *La Part maudite* (Paris: Minuit, 1967), pp. 25–45.

Bayard, Pierre, *Le Hors-sujet: Proust et la digression* (Paris: Minuit, 1996).

Benhaïm, André, 'Preamble', in *The Strange M. Proust*, ed. André Benhaïm (Oxford: Legenda, 2009), pp. 1–11.

Benjamin, Walter, 'The Image of Proust', in *Illuminations*, ed. Hannah Arendt and trans. Harry Zohn (London: Fontana Press, 1992), pp. 197–210.

—— *The Arcades Project*, trans. Howard Eiland and Kevin McLaughlin (Cambridge, MA and London: Belknap Press, 1999).

Benson, Stephen, and Clare Connors, 'Introduction', in *Creative Criticism: An Anthology and Guide*, ed. Stephen Benson and Clare Connors (Edinburgh: Edinburgh University Press, 2014), pp. 1–47.

Bersani, Leo, *Homos* (Cambridge, MA: Harvard University Press, 1995).

Blanchot, 'L'Expérience de Proust', in *Le Livre à venir* (Paris: Gallimard, 1986), pp. 19–37.

Borrel, Anne, Alain Senderens and Jean-Bernard Naudin, *Proust, la cuisine retrouvée* (Paris: Éditions du chêne, 1991).

Boucourechliev, André, *Beethoven* (Paris: Seuil, 1963).

Bouillaguet, Annick, *Proust lecteur de Balzac et de Flaubert: l'imitation cryptée* (Paris: Honoré Champion, 2000).

Bowie, Malcolm, *Lacan* (Cambridge, MA: Harvard University Press, 1991).

—— *Proust among the Stars* (London: Harper Collins, 1998).

—— 'Barthes on Proust', *The Yale Journal of Criticism*, 14/2 (2001), pp. 513–18.

—— 'Reading Proust between the Lines', in *The Strange M. Proust*, ed. André Benhaïm (Oxford: Legenda, 2009), pp. 125–34.

Briggs, Kate, *Exercise in Pathetic Criticism* (York: information as material, 2011).

Butor, Michel, *Dialogue avec 33 variations de Ludwig van Beethoven sur une valse de Diabelli* (Paris: Gallimard, 1971).

—— *Mobile*, trans. Richard Howard (Champaign: Dalkey Archive Press, 2004).

Compagnon, Antoine, *Proust entre deux siècles* (Paris: Seuil, 1989).

—— 'Proust et moi', <http://www.college-de-france.fr/site/antoine-compagnon/articles_en_ligne.htm> [accessed 1 June 2019].

Connors, Clare, *Force from Nietzsche to Derrida* (Oxford: Legenda, 2010).

Coste, Claude, 'Notes de cours pour le Maroc', in *Roland Barthes au Maroc*, ed. Ridha Boulaâbi, Claude Coste and Mohamed Lehdahda (Meknès: Publications de l'Université Moulay Ismaïl, 2013), pp. 9–22.

—— '"J'ai toujours eu envie d'*argumenter* mes humeurs": savoir et subjectivité dans *La Chambre claire* et *Sur Racine*', *What's So Great About Roland Barthes?*, ed. Thomas Baldwin, Katja Haustein and Lucy O'Meara, *L'Esprit Créateur* (Special Issue), 55/4 (Winter 2015), pp. 86–100.

Culler, Jonathan, 'Preparing the Novel: Spiralling Back', *Roland Barthes Retroactively: Reading the Collège de France Lectures*, ed. Jürgen Pieters and Kris Pint, *Paragraph* (Special Issue), 31/1 (2008), pp. 109–20.

De Botton, Alain, *How Proust Can Change Your Life* (London: Picador, 1997).

Deleuze, Gilles, *Nietzsche et la philosophie* (Paris: PUF, 1962).

—— *Proust et les signes* (Paris: PUF, 1996).

—— *Francis Bacon: logique de la sensation* (Paris: Seuil, 2002).

Deleuze, Gilles, and Félix Guattari, *Capitalisme et schizophrénie I. L'Anti-Œdipe* (Paris: Minuit, 1972–73).

—— *Capitalisme et schizophrénie II. Mille plateaux* (Paris: Minuit, 1980).

De Man, 'Reading (Proust)', in *Allegories of Reading: Figural Language in Rousseau, Nietzsche, Rilke and Proust* (New Haven and London: Yale University Press, 1979), pp. 57–78.

—— *Blindness and Insight: Essays in the Rhetoric of Contemporary Criticism* (London: Routledge, 1983).

Derrida, Jacques, 'Force et signification', in *L'Écriture et la différence* (Paris: Seuil, 1967), pp. 9–49.

—— 'Violence et métaphysique', in *L'Écriture et la différence* (Paris: Seuil, 1967), pp. 117–228.

—— 'Les Morts de Roland Barthes', in *Psyché: inventions de l'autre* (Paris: Galilée, 1987), pp. 273–304.

—— *La Bête et le souverain, volume I (2001–2002)* (Paris: Galilée, 2008).

Didi-Huberman, Georges, *Survivance des lucioles* (Paris: Minuit, 2009).

Dosse, François, *Histoire du structuralisme*, 2 vols (Paris: Éditions la découverte, 1992).

—— *Gilles Deleuze et Félix Guattari: biographie croisée* (Paris: Éditions la découverte, 2007).

Evans, Dylan, *An Introductory Dictionary of Lacanian Psychoanalysis* (London: Routledge, 2006).

ffrench, Patrick, 'Barthes and the Voice: The Acousmatic and Beyond', *What's So Great About Roland Barthes?*, ed. Thomas Baldwin, Katja Haustein and Lucy O'Meara, *L'Esprit Créateur* (Special Issue), 55/4 (Winter 2015), pp. 56–69.

Foucault, Michel, 'Nietzsche, Freud, Marx', in *Nietzsche*, ed. Gilles Deleuze (Paris: Minuit, 1964), pp. 183–92.

Fraisse, Luc, *Le Processus de la création chez Marcel Proust: le fragment expérimental* (Paris: Corti, 1988).

—— *L'Œuvre cathédrale: Proust et l'architecture médiévale* (Paris: Corti, 1990).

Freed-Thall, Hannah, *Spoiled Distinctions: Aesthetics and the Ordinary in French Modernism* (Oxford: Oxford University Press, 2015).

Gil, Marie, *Roland Barthes: au lieu de la vie* (Paris: Flammarion, 2012).

Gray, Margaret E., 'Adaptations/Afterlives', in *Marcel Proust in Context*, ed. Adam Watt (Cambridge: Cambridge University Press, 2013), pp. 221–29.

Guattari, Félix, 'Les Ritournelles du temps perdu', in *L'Inconscient machinique: essais de schizo-analyse* (Paris: Éditions recherches, 1979), pp. 257–364.

Hämäläinen, Nora, *Literature and Moral Theory* (London and New York: Bloomsbury Academic, 2016).

Haustein, Katja, *Regarding Lost Time: Photography, Identity and Affect in Proust, Benjamin and Barthes* (Oxford: Legenda, 2012).

Hill, Leslie, 'Roland Barthes', in *Radical Indecision: Barthes, Blanchot, Derrida and the Future of Criticism* (Notre Dame: University of Notre Dame Press, 2010), pp. 71–153.

Johnson, Barbara, 'The Critical Difference', in *Critical Essays on Roland Barthes*, ed. Diana Knight (New York: G. K. Hall & Co., 2000), pp. 174–82.

Johnson, Jr., J. Theodore, 'La Lanterne Magique: Proust's Metaphorical Toy', *L'Esprit Créateur*, 11/1 (Spring 1971), pp. 17–31.

Kinderman, William, *Beethoven's Diabelli Variations* (Oxford: Oxford University Press, 1989).

Knight, Diana, 'Roland Barthes, or The Woman Without a Shadow', in *Writing the Image after Roland Barthes*, ed. Jean-Michel Rabaté (Philadelphia: University of Pennsylvania Press, 1997), pp. 132–43.

—— *Balzac and the Model of Painting: Artist Stories in 'La Comédie humaine'* (Oxford: Legenda, 2007).

—— 'What Turns the Writer into a Great Writer? The Conversion Narrative of Barthes's *Vita nova*', *What's So Great About Roland Barthes?*, ed. Thomas Baldwin, Katja Haustein and Lucy O'Meara, *L'Esprit Créateur* (Special Issue), 55/4 (Winter 2015), pp. 165–80.

Lacan, Jacques, *Écrits* (Paris: Seuil, 1966).

Landy, Joshua, *Philosophy as Fiction: Self, Deception, and Knowledge in Proust* (Oxford: Oxford University Press, 2004).

Large, Duncan, *Nietzsche and Proust* (Oxford: Oxford University Press, 2001).

Larkin, Áine, *Proust Writing Photography: Fixing the Fugitive in 'À la recherche du temps perdu'* (Oxford: Legenda, 2011).

Leblanc, Cécile, *Proust écrivain de la musique: l'allégresse du compositeur* (Turnhout: Brepols, 2017).

Lehrer, Jonah, *Proust Was a Neuroscientist* (Edinburgh and London: Cannongate, 2007).

Lorent, Fanny, *Barthes et Robbe-Grillet: un dialogue critique* (Brussels: Les Impressions nouvelles, 2015).

Lyotard, Jean-François, *Discours, figure* (Paris: Klincksieck, 1971).

Macé, Marielle, 'Barthes romanesque', in *Barthes, au lieu du roman*, ed. Marielle Macé and Alexandre Gefen (Paris: Éditions Desjonquères/Nota Bene, 2002), pp. 173–88.

Malt, Johanna, 'The Blob and the Magic Lantern: On Subjectivity, Faciality and Projection', *Paragraph*, 36/3 (2013), pp. 305–23.

Marty, Éric, 'Marcel Proust dans "la chambre claire"', *Proust en devenir*, ed. Luc Fraisse, *L'Esprit Créateur* (Special Issue), 46/4 (2006), pp. 125–33.

—— *Roland Barthes, le métier d'écrire* (Paris: Seuil, 2006).

—— 'Barthes et la musique, avec et contre Proust', <https://vimeo.com/129974841> [accessed 1 June 2019].

Milly, Jean, *Les Pastiches de Proust* (Paris: Colin, 1970).

Moraru, Christian, *Rewriting: Postmodern Narrative and Cultural Critique in the Age of Cloning* (Albany: State University of New York Press, 2001).

Nietzsche, Friedrich, *Twilight of the Idols*, trans. Duncan Large (Oxford: Oxford University Press, 1998).

O'Meara, Lucy, 'Atonality and Tonality: Musical Analogies in Roland Barthes's Lectures at the Collège de France', *Paragraph*, 31/1 (2008), pp. 9–22.

—— *Roland Barthes at the Collège de France* (Liverpool: Liverpool University Press, 2012).

Painter, George D., *Marcel Proust 1871–1922*, 2 vols (Paris: Mercure de France, 1966).

Pasolini, Pier Paolo, *Scritti corsari* (Milan: Garzanti, 1975).

Plotnitsky, Arkady, 'Un-Scriptible', in *Writing the Image After Roland Barthes*, ed. Jean-Michel Rabaté (Philadelphia: University of Pennsylvania Press, 1997), pp. 243–58.

Prendergast, Christopher, *Mirages and Mad Beliefs: Proust the Skeptic* (Princeton: Princeton University Press, 2013).

Richard, Jean-Pierre, *Proust et le monde sensible* (Paris: Seuil, 1974).

Robbe-Grillet, Alain, *Pourquoi j'aime Barthes* (Paris: Christian Bourgois, 2001).

Roche, Denis, 'Lettre à Roland Barthes sur la disparition des lucioles', in *La Disparition des lucioles (réflexions sur l'acte photographique)* (Paris: Éditions de l'étoile, 1982), pp. 153–66.

Sartre, Jean-Paul, *L'Être et le néant* (Paris: Gallimard, 1943).

Scherer, Jacques, *Le 'Livre' de Mallarmé: premières recherches sur des documents inédits* (Paris: Gallimard, 1954).

Sheringham, Michael, 'Everyday Rhythms, Everyday Writing', in *Rhythms: Essays in French Literature, Thought, and Culture*, ed. Elizabeth Lindley and Laura McMahon (Bern and Oxford: Peter Lang, 2008), pp. 147–58.

Simon, Anne, *Trafics de Proust: Merleau-Ponty, Sartre, Deleuze, Barthes* (Paris: Hermann, 2016).

Sollers, Philippe, *L'Amitié de Roland Barthes* (Paris: Seuil, 2015).

Sonneck, Oscar George, 'Beethoven to Diabelli: A Letter and a Protest', *The Musical Quarterly*, 13/2 (April 1927), pp. 294–316.

Spitzer, Leo, *Études de style* (Paris: Gallimard, 1970).

Stafford, Andy, '*Classé, Surclasser, Déclassé*, or, Roland Barthes, Classification without Class', *What's So Great About Roland Barthes?*, ed. Thomas Baldwin, Katja Haustein and Lucy O'Meara, *L'Esprit Créateur* (Special Issue), 55/4 (Winter 2015), pp. 148–64.

Tanner, Tony, 'Introduction', in Herman Melville, *Moby Dick* (Oxford: Oxford University Press, 1988), pp. vii–xxvi.

Tovey, Donald Francis, *Essays in Musical Analysis: Chamber Music* (Oxford: Oxford University Press, 1972).

Ungar, Steven, 'Circular Memories', in *Roland Barthes: The Professor of Desire* (Lincoln, NE and London: University of Nebraska Press, 1983), pp. 135–51.

Watt, Adam, *The Cambridge Introduction to Marcel Proust* (Cambridge: Cambridge University Press, 2011).

—— 'Reading Proust in Barthes's *Journal de deuil*', *Writing, Reading, Grieving: Essays in Memory of Suzanne Dow*, ed. Ruth Cruickshank and Adam Watt, *Nottingham French Studies* (Special Issue), 53/1 (Spring 2014), pp. 102–12.

Yacavone, Kathrin, 'Barthes et Proust: *La Recherche* comme aventure photographique', *L'Écrivain préféré, Fabula LHT (Littérature, histoire, théorie)*, 4 (March 2008), <http://www.fabula.org/lht/4/Yacavone.html> [accessed 1 June 2019].

—— 'Reading through Photography: Roland Barthes's Last Seminar "Proust et la photographie"', *French Forum*, 34/1 (2009), pp. 97–112.

—— 'The "Scattered" Proust: On Barthes's Reading of the *Recherche*', in *'When familiar meanings dissolve …': Essays in French Studies in Memory of Malcolm Bowie*, ed. Naomi Segal and Gill Rye (Bern and Oxford: Peter Lang, 2011), pp. 219–31.

Index